IMPROVING VOCABULARY SKILLS

Sherrie L. Nist
UNIVERSITY OF GEORGIA

Carole Mohr

TOWNSEND PRESS Marlton, NJ 08053

The Seven Books in the Townsend Press Vocabulary Series:

GROUNDWORK FOR A BETTER VOCABULARY
BUILDING VOCABULARY SKILLS
IMPROVING VOCABULARY SKILLS
ADVANCING VOCABULARY SKILLS
BUILDING VOCABULARY SKILLS, SHORT VERSION
IMPROVING VOCABULARY SKILLS, SHORT VERSION
ADVANCING VOCABULARY SKILLS, SHORT VERSION

Supplements Available for Each Book:

Instructor's Manual and Test Bank
Set of Computer Disks

For information on any of these books or supplements, or other books on the Townsend Press reading list, write to the address shown below.

Printed in the United States of America
ISBN 0-944210-81-3

Townsend Press, Inc.
Pavilions at Greentree—408
Marlton, New Jersey 08053
609-772-6410

LIBRARY OF CONGRESS
Library of Congress Cataloging-in-Publication Data
Nist, Sherrie L.
Improving vocabulary skills / Sherrie L. Nist, Carole Mohr
p. cm.
Includes index.
ISBN 0-944210-81-3
1. Vocabulary. I. Mohr, Carole. II. Title.
PE1449.N5 1990 90-10932
428.1 CIP

Contents

Note: For ease of reference, the title of the passage that concludes each chapter appears in parentheses.

UNIT FOUR

UNIT FIVE

Appendixes

Preface

The problem is all too familiar: *students just don't know enough words.* Reading, writing, and content teachers agree that many students' vocabularies are inadequate to the demands of courses. Weak vocabularies limit students' understanding of what they read and the clarity and depth of what they write.

The purpose of the Townsend Press vocabulary series is to provide a solid, workable answer to the vocabulary problem. The series consists of three books, each of which *teaches* 300 important words or word parts. Within each book are 30 chapters, with 10 words or word parts in each chapter. Here are the distinctive features of IMPROVING VOCABULARY SKILLS and the other books in the series.

1 An intensive words-in-context approach. Studies show that students learn words best by seeing them repeatedly in different contexts, not through rote memorization. IMPROVING VOCABULARY SKILLS gives students an intensive in-context experience by presenting each word in seven different contexts. Each chapter takes students through a productive sequence of steps:

- Students first see a word in a preview.
- They then infer the meaning of the word by considering two sentences in which it appears.
- Based on their inferences, students select and confirm each word's meaning in a matching test. They are then in a solid position to further deepen their knowledge of a word.
- Finally, they strengthen their understanding of a word by applying it three times: in two sentence practices and in a passage practice.

Each encounter with a word brings it closer to becoming part of the student's permanent word bank.

2 Abundant practice. In addition to the extensive practice in each chapter, there are *four unit tests* at the end of each six-chapter unit. These tests reinforce students' knowledge of every word in every chapter. Further, there are added tests in the *Test Bank* and the *computer disks* that accompany the book. All this practice means that students learn in the surest possible way: by working closely and repeatedly with each word.

3 Controlled feedback. Students receive feedback on two of the practices in each vocabulary chapter. A limited answer key at the back of the book lets them see how they did with the opening preview of words. The key also provides answers for the first sentence check in the chapter. The key enables students to take an active role in their own learning. And they are likely to use the answer key in an honest and positive way if they know they may be tested on the many activities and selections for which answers are not provided. (Answers not in the book are in the Instructor's Edition.They can, of course, be copied and passed out at the teacher's discretion.)

4 Focus on essential words. A good deal of time and research went into selecting the 300 words and word parts featured in the book. Word frequency lists were consulted, along with lists in a wide number of vocabulary books. In addition, the authors and editors each prepared their own lists. A computer was used to help in the consolidation of the many word lists. A long process of group discussion then led to final decisions about the words and word parts that would be more helpful for students on a basic reading level.

5 Appealing content. Dull practice materials work against learning. On the other hand, meaningful, lively, and at times even funny sentences and passages can spark students' attention and thus encourage their grasp of the material. For this reason, a great deal of effort was put into creating sentences and passages with both widespread appeal *and* solid context support. We have tried throughout to make the practice materials truly enjoyable for teachers and students alike. Look, for example, at the passage on page 8 that closes the first chapter of this book.

6 Clarity of format. The book has been designed so that its very format contributes to the learning process. All ten words of a chapter appear on a single page, and each practice begins and ends on one page. In particular, each chapter has a two-page spread (turn, for example, to pages 6-7) so that students can refer to the ten words in context on one side while working on the matching test and sentence check on the other side. And a second color has been used within the book to help make the content as visually appealing as possible.

7 Supplementary materials.

a A combined *Instructor's Manual and Test Bank* is available at no charge to instructors using the book. It can be obtained by writing to the Reading Editor, Townsend Press, Pavilions at Greentree—408, Marlton, NJ 08053. This booklet contains pre- and post-tests for all five units in the text as well as teaching suggestions, a model syllabus, an answer key, and a set of mastery tests for each chapter.

b A *comprehensive series of computer disks* also accompanies the book. These disks provide up to four tests for each vocabulary chapter in the book. The disks are self-booting and contain a number of other user- and instructor-friendly features, including brief explanations of answers, a sound option, frequent mention of the user's first name, a running score at the bottom of the screen, and a record-keeping file.

Probably in no other area of reading instruction is the computer more useful than in reinforcing vocabulary. This vocabulary program takes full advantage of the computer's unique capabilities and motivational appeal. Here's how the program works:

- Students are tested on the ten words in a chapter, with each word in a sentence context different from any in the book itself.
- After students answer each question, they receive immediate feedback: The computer tells if a student is right or wrong and *why*, frequently using the student's first name and providing a running score.
- When the test is over, the computer supplies a test score and—this especially is what is unique about this program—a chance to retest on the specific words the student got wrong. For example, if a student misses four items on a test, the retest provides *four different sentences* that test just those four words. Students then receive a score for this special retest. What is so valuable about this, of course, is that the computer gives students added practice in the words they most need to review.
- In addition, the computer offers a *second*, more challenging test in which students must identify the meanings of the chapter words without benefit of context. This test is a final check that students have really learned the words. And, again, there is the option of a retest, tailor-made to recheck only those words missed on the first definition test.

By the end of this program, students' knowledge of each word in the chapter will have been carefully reinforced. And this reinforcement will be the more effective for having occurred in an electronic medium that especially engages today's students.

A demo disk will be sent to any teacher requesting it. The full set of disks, with unlimited copying privileges, will be available at no charge to departments that have adopted the book.

8 Realistic pricing. We wanted a book that would offer the highest possible quality at the best possible price. We are delighted that Townsend Press has committed to sell this book to students at a price under ten dollars. While the book is comprehensive enough to serve as a primary text, its modest price also makes it an inexpensive supplement.

9 One in a sequence of three books. IMPROVING VOCABULARY SKILLS is one of seven books in the Townsend Press Vocabulary Series. GROUNDWORK FOR A BETTER VOCABULARY is the basic book in the series. It is followed by the three main books in the series: BUILDING VOCABULARY SKILLS (also a basic text), IMPROVING VOCABULARY SKILLS (an intermediate text), and ADVANCING VOCABULARY SKILLS (a more advanced text); there are also short versions of these three books. Suggested grade levels for the three main books are included in the *Instructor's Manual.* Together, the books will help create a vocabulary foundation that will make any student a better reader, writer, and thinker.

Acknowledgments

Our thanks go to the talented group of writers and editors at Townsend Press who have worked closely with us on the book: John Langan, Joan Dunayer, Jane Mackay, and Beth Johnson Ruth. We also acknowledge the extraordinary computer programming efforts of Terry Hutchison. Inspiration for the cover came from an idea by Janet M. Goldstein, and the cover itself owes thanks to the artistry of Larry Didona. Finally, we are grateful for the design, editing, and proofreading skills of Janet M. Goldstein.

Sherrie L. Nist *Carole Mohr*

Introduction

WHY VOCABULARY DEVELOPMENT COUNTS

You have probably often heard it said, "Building vocabulary is important." Maybe you've politely nodded in agreement and then forgotten the matter. But it would be fair for you to ask, "Why *is* vocabulary development important? Provide some evidence." Here are four compelling kinds of evidence.

1 Common sense tells you what many research studies have shown as well: vocabulary is a basic part of reading comprehension. Simply put, if you don't know enough words, you are going to have trouble understanding what you read. An occasional word may not stop you, but if there are too many words you don't know, comprehension will suffer. The *content* of textbooks is often challenge enough; you don't want to work as well on understanding the *words* that make up that content.

2 Vocabulary is a major part of almost every standardized test, including reading achievement tests, college entrance exams, and armed forces and vocational placement tests. Test authors know that vocabulary is a key measure of both one's learning and one's ability to learn. So they have a separate vocabulary section as well as a reading comprehension section. The more words you know, then, the better you are likely to do on such important tests.

3 Studies have made clear that students with strong vocabularies are more successful in school. And one widely known study found that a good vocabulary, more than any other factor, was common to people enjoying successful careers in life. Words are in fact the tools not just of better reading, but of writing, speaking, listening, and thinking as well. The more words you have at your command, the more effective your communication can be, and the more influence you can have on the people around you.

4 In the world of the 1990s, a good vocabulary will count more than ever. Far fewer people will work on farms or in factories. Far more will be in jobs that provide services or process information. More than ever, words will be the tools of our trade: words we use in reading, writing, listening, and speaking. Furthermore, experts say that workers of the 90s will be called on to change jobs and learn new skills at an ever-increasing pace. The keys to survival and success will thus be the abilities to communicate skillfully and learn quickly. A solid vccabulary is essential for both of these skills.

The evidence is overwhelming, then, that building vocabulary is crucial. The question thus becomes, "What is the best way of going about it?"

WORDS IN CONTEXT: THE KEY TO VOCABULARY DEVELOPMENT

Memorizing lists of words is a traditional method of vocabulary development. But a person is likely to forget such memorized lists quickly. Studies show that to master a word (or a word part), you must see and use it in various contexts. By working actively and repeatedly with a word, you greatly increase the chance of really learning it.

The following activity will make clear how the book is organized and how it uses a words-in-context approach. Answer the questions or fill in the missing words in the spaces provided.

Contents

Turn to the table of contents on pages iii-iv.

- How many chapters are in the book? ________
- Most chapters present vocabulary words. How many chapters present word parts? _______
- Three short sections follow the chapters. The first provides a limited answer key; the second gives helpful information on using ______________________; and the third is an index of the 300 words and word parts in the book.

Vocabulary Chapters

Turn to Chapter 1 on pages 5-8. This chapter, like all the others, consists of six parts:

- The ***first part***, on page 5, is titled ____

This preview introduces you to the ten words covered in the chapter. After you try filling in the blanks, you are asked to check the ______________ at the back and to fill in any empty blanks.

- The ***second part*** of the chapter, on page 6, is titled ____________________________

The left-hand column lists the ten words. Under each word is its ____________________ (in parentheses) and its part of speech (*noun, verb,* or *adjective*). For example, we are told that *acknowledge,* the first word on page 6, is a verb.

Using the pronunciation guide requires only a bit of information: Short vowels have no special mark, while long vowels are indicated with a line above the vowel. (Note that long vowels have the sound of their own name.) What is the first word in the list with a long vowel? ___________________ . Symbols that sound like "uh"—like the "uh" a speaker makes when hesitating—are symbolized by the schwa (ə), which looks like an upside down *e*. What is the first word in the list with a schwa? ___________________. Finally, an accent mark (′) tells which syllable to emphasize when pronouncing a word. What is the first word in the list with an accent on the second syllable? __________________ A brief guide to the dictionary on page 167 gives further information on pronouncing words.

To the right of each word are two sentences that help you understand its meaning. In each sentence, the *context* —the words surrounding the boldfaced word—provides clues you can use to figure out the definition. For example, look at the first sentence for the word *absolve.*

> Some people get rich by cheating others and then think a large donation to a charity will **absolve** them of guilt.

Based on the context, what is the meaning of *absolve*?

a. accuse   b. surprise   c. free from blame   d. send to prison

A second sentence also helps you pin down the meaning:

> The mayor, accused of taking bribes, told reporters, "In the end, I'll clear my name and be **absolved** of any wrongdoing."

By looking closely at each pair of sentences, you can decide on the meaning of a word. (In the example above, *absolve* clearly means *free from blame.)* As you figure out each meaning, you are working actively with the word. You are creating the groundwork you need to understand *and* to remember the word. Getting involved with the word and developing a feel for it, based upon its use in context, is the key to word mastery.

It is with good reason, then, that the directions at the top of page 6 tell you to look ________________ and ________________at the context. Doing so deepens your sense of the word and prepares you for the next activity.

• The ***third part*** of the chapter, on page 7, is titled ______________________________.

According to research, it is not enough to see a word in context. At a certain point, it is important as well to see the meaning of a word. The matching test provides that meaning, but it also makes you look for and think about that meaning. In other words, it continues the active learning that is your surest route to learning and remembering a word.

Note the caution that follows the test. Do not proceed any further until you are sure that you know the correct meaning of each word.

• The ***fourth part*** of the chapter (also on page 7) is titled ________________________.

Here are ten sentences that give you an opportunity to apply your understanding of the ten words. After inserting the words, check your answers in the limited key at the back of the book. Be sure to use the answer key as a learning tool only. Doing so will help you to master the words and to prepare for the last two activities and the unit tests, for which answers are not provided.

• The ***fifth part*** of the chapter, on page 8, is titled ________________________, and the ***sixth part*** is titled ________________________.

Both practices test you on all ten words, giving you a chance to deepen your mastery. In the second activity, you have the context of an entire passage in which you can practice and apply the words.

At the bottom of the last page of this chapter is a box where you can enter your score for the final two checks. These scores should also be entered into the vocabulary performance chart located on the inside back page of the book. To get your score, take 10% off for each item wrong, as shown in the following chart:

0 wrong = 100%
1 wrong = 90%
2 wrong = 80%
3 wrong = 70%
4 wrong = 60%
5 wrong = 50%
and so on.

Word Parts Chapters

In all, there are 260 words in the chapters and 40 word parts. *Word parts*, also known as *prefixes, suffixes,* and *roots,* are building blocks used in many common English words. Learning word parts can help you to spell and pronounce words, to unlock the meanings of unfamiliar words, and to remember new words.

Each of the four word parts chapters follows the same sequence as the vocabulary chapters do. Keep the following guideline in mind as well. To find the meaning of a word part, you should do two things.

1 First decide on the meaning of each boldfaced word in "Ten Word Parts in Context." If you don't know a meaning, use context clues to find it. For example, consider the two sentences for the word part *-ward*:

> Everyone at the fair looked **skyward** in horror as the colorful hot-air balloon exploded.
>
> The children tried walking to school **backward** but gave up before even reaching the end of their block.

You can conclude that *skyward* means "in the direction of the sky." You can also determine that *backward* means "in the direction of the back."

2 Then decide on the meaning each pair of boldfaced words has in common. This will also be the meaning of the word part they share. In the case of the two sentences above, both words include the idea of doing something in the direction of something else. Thus *-ward* must mean "in the direction of."

You now know, in a nutshell, how to proceed with the words in each chapter. Make sure that you do each page very carefully. *Remember, as you work through the activities, you are learning the words.*

How many times in all will you use each word? If you look, you'll see that each chapter gives you the opportunity to work with each word seven times. Each "impression" adds to the likelihood that the word will become part of your active vocabulary. You will have further opportunities to use the word in the four unit tests that follow each chapter and on the computer disks that are available with the book.

Information on the computer disks and the other two books in the Townsend Press vocabulary series can be obtained by writing to the address on the back cover.

FINAL THOUGHTS

The facts are in. A strong vocabulary is a source of power. Words can make you a better reader, writer, speaker, thinker, and learner. They can dramatically increase your chances of success in school and in your job.

But words will not come automatically. They must be learned in a program of regular study. If you commit yourself to learning words, and you work actively and honestly with the chapters in this book, you will not only enrich your vocabulary—you will enrich your life as well.

Unit One

CHAPTER

1

Previewing the Words

Find out how many of the ten words in this chapter you already know. Try to complete each sentence with the most suitable word from the list below. Use each word once.

Leave a sentence blank rather than guessing at an answer. Your purpose here is just to get a sense of the ten words and what you may know about them.

absolve	adamant	amiable	amoral	animosity
antagonist	eccentric	encounter	epitome	malign

1. The wrestler caught his __________________ by the hair and then pulled him to the mat.
2. The __________________ of refreshment is drinking an ice-cold lemonade on a sizzling hot day.
3. Some criminals are __________________—they truly don't care whether or not their actions are evil.
4. June is very __________________. She always greets me with a warm smile and a pleasant, "Hi! How are you?"
5. The book so __________________(e)d the actress that she sued the author for extreme damage to her public image.
6. I was surprised to __________________ Matt in a supermarket in Los Angeles, since I thought he still lived in Chicago.
7. Willy hoped the new witness would __________________ him of guilt by testifying that he had been bowling the night of the murder.
8. My little sister was __________________ in her refusal to go to Aunt Eva's house. She held on to the knob of her bedroom door as my mother tried to yank her loose.
9. You might think family businesses have the advantage of friendly relationships, but there is often great __________________ between relatives who work together.
10. Florence Nightingale, the famous nursing reformer, had the __________________ habit of carrying around a pet owl in one of her pockets.

Now check your answers by turning to page 163. Fix any mistakes and fill in any blank spaces by writing in the correct answers. By doing so, you will complete this introduction to the ten words.

You're now ready to strengthen your knowledge of the words you already know and to master the words you're only half sure of, or don't know at all. Turn to the next page.

Ten Words in Context

Figure out the meanings of the following ten words by looking *closely and carefully* at the context in which the words appear. Doing so will prepare you for the matching test and practices on the two pages that follow.

1 **absolve** (ab-zolv') *-verb*

a. Some people get rich by cheating others and then think a large donation to a charity will **absolve** them of guilt.

b. The mayor, accused of taking bribes, told reporters, "In the end, I'll clear my name and be **absolved** of any wrongdoing."

2 **adamant** (ad'-ə-mənt) *-adjective*

a. Ron is **adamant** about not changing plans. He insists we still camp out even though the weather report now says it will be cold and rainy.

b. **Adamant** in his support of gun control, Senator Keen won't give in to pressure from the powerful people who tried to silence him.

3 **amiable** (ā'-mē-ə-bəl) *-adjective*

a. My **amiable** dog greets both strangers and old friends with a friendly yip and energetic tail-wagging.

b. At first, our history teacher doesn't seem very friendly, but once you get to know her, she shows her **amiable** side.

4 **amoral** (ə-mor'-əl) *-adjective*

a. Jerry is almost totally **amoral**. He cares only about making money and having fun and couldn't care less about right or wrong.

b. A former president of Uganda, Idi Amin, was truly **amoral.** Lacking ethical principles, he jailed, tortured and killed innocent opponents.

5 **animosity** (an'-ə-mos'-ə-tē) *-noun*

a. I was shocked when Sandy said she hated Lionel. I'd never realized she felt such **animosity** toward him.

b. Ill will between the two families went back so many generations that nobody remembers what originally caused the **animosity**.

6 **antagonist** (an-tag'-ə-nist) *-noun*

a. At the divorce hearing, the husband and wife were such bitter **antagonists** that it was hard to believe they once loved each other.

b. In the ring, the two boxers were **antagonists**, but in their private lives they were good friends.

7 **eccentric** (ik-sen'-trik) *-adjective*

a. Bruce is quite **eccentric**. For example, he lives in a circular house and drives to work on a motorcycle, in a three-piece suit.

b. Perhaps more of us would be **eccentric** in ways if we didn't worry so much about being considered odd.

8 **encounter** (en-koun'-tər) *-verb*

a. Some people claim to have **encountered** space aliens, but there is no convincing evidence of such meetings.

b. I dislike returning to my small hometown, where I am likely to **encounter** people who knew me as a troubled kid.

9 **epitome** (i-pit'-ə-mē) *-noun*

a. To many, the **epitome** of cuteness is a furry round-eyed puppy.

b. The great ballplayer and civil rights leader Jackie Robinson was the **epitome** of both physical and moral strength.

10 **malign** (mə-līn') *-verb*

a. Stacy continually **maligns** her ex-husband. The way she describes him, you'd think he was a cross between a mass murderer and a blockhead.

b. Those who say the female crocodile eats her young **malign** her. She simply takes them into a protective pouch inside her mouth.

Matching Words and Definitions

Check your understanding of the ten words by matching each word with its definition. Look back at the sentences in "Ten Words in Context" as needed to decide on the meaning of each word.

_____	1. **absolve**	a.	firm in opinion or purpose; stubborn
_____	2. **adamant**	b.	without principles; uncaring about right and wrong
_____	3. **amiable**	c.	odd; out of the ordinary
_____	4. **amoral**	d.	to clear of guilt or blame
_____	5. **animosity**	e.	to meet unexpectedly; come upon
_____	6. **antagonist**	f.	a perfect or typical example of a general quality or type
_____	7. **eccentric**	g.	an opponent; one who opposes or competes
_____	8. **encounter**	h.	a strong dislike; hatred; ill will
_____	9. **epitome**	i.	to make false statements that harm a reputation; speak evil of
_____	10. **malign**	j.	good-natured; friendly and pleasant

CAUTION: Do not go any further until you are sure the above answers are correct. If you have studied the "Ten Words in Context," you will know how to match each word. Then you can use the matches to help you in the following practices. Your goal is to reach a point where you don't need to check definitions at all.

➢Sentence Check 1

Complete each sentence below with the most suitable word from the box. Use each word once.

absolve	**adamant**	**amiable**	**amoral**	**animosity**
antagonist	**eccentric**	**encounter**	**epitome**	**malign**

1. Lilly was ___________________ in her belief that Sam was faithful. Even lipstick on his cheek didn't weaken her faith in him.
2. My brothers had planned to meet in the department store, but they ___________________(e)d each other in the parking lot.
3. I'm tired of hearing the two candidates for mayor ___________________ each other with stupid insults.
4. Mac remains polite and ___________________ even when he's annoyed with a customer because he doesn't want to lose a sale.
5. The congressman is so ___________________ that he'll make promises to get elected and then break them whenever it suits him.
6. To many foreigners who watch Hollywood westerns, the cowboy is the ___________________ of the American male—rough, tough, and fast-moving.
7. Lena often says cruel things and then apologizes afterwards, but a mere "I'm sorry" doesn't remove the hurt or ___________________ her of guilt.
8. The owners of the department store were always competing with each other. They acted more like ___________________s than partners.
9. I avoid serious discussions with my sister because she shows great ___________________ toward me if I don't share her opinion.
10. When my mother attended high school, female students who took wood shop were considered______________. Now, however, it's not odd for women to learn carpentry.

Now check your answers to these questions by turning to page 163. Going over the answers carefully will help you prepare for the next two checks, for which answers are not given.

➣Sentence Check 2

Complete each sentence below with two words from the box. Use each word once.

absolve	**adamant**	**amiable**	**amoral**	**animosity**
antagonist	**eccentric**	**encounter**	**epitome**	**malign**

1-2. The ________________ millionaire dressed so shabbily that anyone who ________________(e)d him thought he was poor.

3-4. Her brother feels such ________________ toward Carol that he never says a single kind thing about her; he only ________________s her.

5-6. The congresswoman was ________________ in her opposition to the nuclear power plant. She didn't back down even when facing the toughest ________________.

7-8. Wayne is so ________________ that he doesn't even have the desire to be ________________(e)d of guilt for all the times he has lied, cheated, and stolen.

9-10. With his friendly air, good-natured laugh and generosity, Santa Claus is the ________________ of the ________________ grandfather.

➤*Final Check:* Joseph Palmer

Here is a final opportunity for you to strengthen your knowledge of the ten words. First read the following passage carefully. Then fill in each blank with a word from the box at the top of this page. (Context clues will help you figure out which word goes in which blank.) Use each word once.

In 1830, a Massachusetts farmer named Joseph Palmer moved to the city, only to find that people continually reacted to him with anger and hatred. Why? Palmer certainly wasn't a(n) (1) ________________ man. No, he had a strong sense of right and wrong, and he was a friendly and (2) ________________ person. And on the whole, Palmer was the (3) ________________ of a normal citizen, living a typical life with his family. Yet his neighbors crossed to the other side of the street when they (4) ________________(e)d him. Children insulted Palmer and sometimes threw stones at him. Grown men hurled rocks through the windows of his house. Even the local minister (5) ________________(e)d Palmer, telling the congregation that Palmer admired only himself.

One day, four men carrying scissors and a razor attacked Palmer and threw him to the ground. Pulling out a pocketknife, Palmer fought back, slashing at their legs. His (6) ________________s fled. Afterward, Palmer was the one arrested and jailed. While in jail he was attacked two more times. Both times, he fought his way free. After a year—although his accusers still wouldn't (7) ________________ him of guilt—he was released.

Palmer had won. The cause of all the (8) ________________ and abuse had been his long, flowing beard. Palmer, (9) ________________ to the end, had refused to shave.

By thirty years after Palmer's difficulties, it was no longer (10) ________________ to wear whiskers. Among the many who wore beards then was the President of the United States, Abraham Lincoln.

SCORES: Sentence Check 2 ________%	Final Check ________%

Enter your scores above and in the vocabulary performance chart on the inside back cover of the book.

CHAPTER

2

Previewing the Words

Find out how many of the ten words in this chapter you already know. Try to complete each sentence with the most suitable word from the list below. Use each word once.

Leave a sentence blank rather than guessing at an answer. Your purpose here is just to get a sense of the ten words and what you may know about them.

curt	**demoralize**	**dilemma**	**inclination**	**irate**
retort	**sabotage**	**subsequent**	**wary**	**zeal**

1. I choked back a(n) ___________________ to laugh when Barbara showed me her new purple and green coat.
2. Although failure ___________________s some people, it encourages others to try harder.
3. It's wise to be ___________________ when walking through an unfamiliar neighborhood at night.
4. The first time I drove on a highway, I was terrified. But each ___________________ time, I felt more and more relaxed.
5. Frank tried to start a conversation with Stella, but she dismissed him with a calm but ___________________ "Buzz off."
6. My father always became ___________________ when any of us kids came home after curfew. One time he began yelling at me even before my date had left.
7. I'm facing a(n) ___________________. Do I tell the truth and risk losing Lori's friendship, or do I conceal the fact that her boyfriend has been asking me out?
8. One neighbor decided to ___________________ the local drug trade by burning down an empty house used for drug sales.
9. Ever since it was announced that fiber is healthy, people have been eating it with great ___________________ in their cereals, soups, and even potato chips and cookies.
10. When my brother said my hairdo was "yuk," I ___________________(e)d, "If you don't like it, then I feel I've accomplished something."

Now check your answers by turning to page 163. Fix any mistakes and fill in any blank spaces by writing in the correct answers. By doing so, you will complete this introduction to the ten words.

You're now ready to strengthen your knowledge of the words you already know and to master the words you're only half sure of, or don't know at all. Turn to the next page.

Ten Words in Context

Figure out the meanings of the following ten words by looking *closely and carefully* at the context in which the words appear. Doing so will prepare you for the matching test and practices on the two pages that follow.

1 **curt**
(kûrt)
-adjective

a. The fast-food manager trained workers to give polite, full answers to customers, not **curt** responses.

b. Betsy doesn't mean to be **curt**. She seems rudely brief with people because she's so shy.

2 **demoralize**
(di-môr'-ə-līz')
-verb

a. Nan's refusal to date my brother **demoralized** him to the point that he lacked the confidence to ask another woman out for months.

b. When Bonita gained a pound during her diet, it so **demoralized** her that she ate a banana split.

3 **dilemma**
(di-lem'-ə)
-noun

a. The store manager faced the **dilemma** of either having an elderly, needy man arrested or ignoring store rules about shoplifters.

b. In old romantic movies, the heroine's **dilemma** often involves choosing between a rich boyfriend and the poor man she really loves.

4 **inclination**
(in-klə-nā'-shən)
-noun

a. My **inclination** is to major in nursing, but I'm going to speak to a few nurses before I make my final decision.

b. Our two-year-old has some irritating tendencies, such as her **inclination** to say "no" to any request at all.

5 **irate**
(ī-rāt')
-adjective

a. If Kate got angry only occasionally, I could take her more seriously, but she's always **irate** about something or other.

b. I get cross when my wife misplaces the TV's remote control, and she becomes **irate** when I write a check and forget to record it in the checkbook.

6 **retort**
(ri-tôrt')
-verb

a. When the wisecracking waiter said, "That hat looks ridiculous, lady," the woman stated, "I didn't come here to be insulted." "That's what you think!" **retorted** the waiter.

b. "What do you want?" the young woman asked Dracula. "Only to drink in your charms," he **retorted**.

7 **sabotage**
(sab'-ə-tozh')
-verb

a. Terrorist groups train their members to **sabotage** airplanes and other public places.

b. A fired computer operator **sabotaged** the company's computer system by planting a "virus" in it.

8 **subsequent**
(sub'-si-kwənt')
-adjective

a. "I was hired as a stockboy," said the company president. "My **subsequent** jobs took me steadily up the company ladder."

b. My first date with Angie was terrible. The car broke down, and it took all night to fix it. We felt the **subsequent** date was really our first.

9 **wary**
(wâr'-ē)
-adjective

a. Whoever said "There's no such thing as a free lunch" was telling us to be **wary** about promises of something for nothing.

b. I'm a little **wary** of people who, when they first meet me, treat me as if I'm their best friend.

10 **zeal**
(zēl)
-noun

a. Flo attacked her food with such **zeal** that I thought she hadn't eaten for a week!

b. My neighbor has so much **zeal** about keeping our neighborhood clean that he spends weekends sweeping our sidewalks if we don't do it ourselves.

Matching Words and Definitions

Check your understanding of the ten words by matching each word with its definition. Look back at the sentences in "Ten Words in Context" as needed to decide on the meaning of each word.

_____ 1. **curt** a. a tendency or bias

_____ 2. **demoralize** b. rudely brief

_____ 3. **dilemma** c. cautious; on one's guard; careful

_____ 4. **inclination** d. to reply, especially in a quick, sharp, or witty way

_____ 5. **irate** e. to lower the spirits of; weaken the confidence or cheerfulness of

_____ 6. **retort** f. a situation requiring a choice between two alternatives; a situation in which a difficult choice must be made

_____ 7. **sabotage** g. following, in order or time

_____ 8. **subsequent** h. enthusiastic devotion; intense enthusiasm

_____ 9. **wary** i. to deliberately destroy or damage

_____ 10. **zeal** j. very angry

CAUTION: Do not go any further until you are sure the above answers are correct. If you have studied the "Ten Words in Context," you will know how to match each word. Then you can use the matches to help you in the following practices. Your goal is to reach a point where you don't need to check definitions at all.

➢Sentence Check 1

Complete each sentence below with the most suitable word from the box. Use each word once.

curt	**demoralize**	**dilemma**	**inclination**	**irate**
retort	**sabotage**	**subsequent**	**wary**	**zeal**

1. Rob's ________________ was whether to stay home and lose a day's pay or go to work feeling sick.
2. Be ________________ when something sounds too good to be true—it probably is.
3. I have to watch my budget because I have a(n) ________________ to overspend.
4. The Broadway director cut off most of the auditioning singers with a ________________ "Thank you. That will be all."
5. The striking miners planned to ________________ one of the mines by blowing up the main entrance.
6. Breaking up with Phil ________________(e)d me so much that I didn't think my spirits could be lower—until I got fired.
7. The team played miserably in the first game of the season, but they managed to win all ________________ games.
8. I expected Manny to be angry when his car wouldn't start, but not so ________________ that he'd throw his books out the window.
9. If adolescents could apply to studying just a bit of the ________________ they feel for music and partying, their grades would skyrocket.
10. When I told my parents I'd wash the supper dishes the next morning, my father ________________(e)d, "Maybe we should serve you dinner in the mornings, too."

Now check your answers to these questions by turning to page 163. Going over the answers carefully will help you prepare for the next two checks, for which answers are not given.

➢*Sentence Check 2*

Complete each sentence below with two words from the box. Use each word once.

curt	**demoralize**	**dilemma**	**inclination**	**irate**
retort	**sabotage**	**subsequent**	**wary**	**zeal**

1-2. Already angry, the customer became even more __________ when he received only this __________ response: "No returns."

3-4. When I answer my phone and hear someone demand, "Who is this?" my __________ is to __________, "I'm the person whose phone was ringing. Who is this?"

5-6. Because of terrorist attempts to __________ flights, airline security workers are __________ of even the most innocent-looking passengers.

7-8. I began the semester with great __________ for my chemistry class, but the realization that I didn't have the necessary background quickly __________(e)d me.

9-10. Margo intended to take the job as a salad chef, but a(n) __________ offer for an office job has presented her with a(n) __________: Should she take the interesting restaurant job, which pays poorly, or the higher-paying job that may not interest her much?

➢*Final Check:* Telephone Salespeople

Here is a final opportunity for you to strengthen your knowledge of the ten words. First read the following passage carefully. Then fill in each blank with a word from the box at the top of this page. (Context clues will help you figure out which word goes in which blank.) Use each word once.

If my carpets need cleaning or I want a freezer, I will do some comparison shopping. I am not likely to suddenly buy anything over the dinner hour just because a complete stranger has phoned to sell it. For this and other reasons, I have always been (1)__________ of telephone salespeople. I don't like their perky voices and their forward suggestions as to how I might easily pay for whatever it is they are selling. My (2)__________ is to get off the phone as soon as possible.

My husband, however, creates a(n) (3)__________ for me when he takes these calls. He doesn't want what is being sold either, but he feels sorry for the salespeople. He doesn't want to (4)__________ them with a (5)__________ "No." When they begin their sales pitch, he is overcome by their (6)__________ for their product and therefore listens politely. Then he (7)__________s my efforts to discourage (8)__________ calls by suggesting that the salespeople call back later to talk to his wife! I don't know who gets more (9)__________ when that happens—me or the salespeople, disappointed when they realize we never intended to buy a thing. More than once, when I've finally said "No sale" for the last time, a salesperson has (10)__________(e)d, "Well, thanks for wasting my time."

SCORES:	Sentence Check 2 ______%	Final Check ______%

Enter your scores above and in the vocabulary performance chart on the inside back cover of the book.

CHAPTER 3

Previewing the Words

Find out how many of the ten words in this chapter you already know. Try to complete each sentence with the most suitable word from the list below. Use each word once.

Leave a sentence blank rather than guessing at an answer. Your purpose here is just to get a sense of the ten words and what you may know about them.

acclaim	**adjacent**	**elicit**	**engross**	**escalate**
exploit	**methodical**	**obsolete**	**tangible**	**terminate**

1. Kim is so ________________ that she even shelves her spices in alphabetical order.

2. The invention of electricity soon made gaslight ________________.

3. A wedding ring is a(n) ________________ expression of a couple's commitment to each other.

4. Sometimes an article I'm reading on the bus will ________________ me so much that I pass my stop.

5. Peter's jokes are in such bad taste that they ________________ looks of disgust instead of laughter.

6. It's best for a dining room to be ________________ to a kitchen, so that food can more easily be served.

7. "We need to ________________ our fund-raising efforts," the theater manager said. "Otherwise, the company won't survive."

8. Dustin Hoffman's performance in *Rain Man* won him an Oscar and the ________________ of admiring critics.

9. When Luke was caught stealing money from the company, his employment was ________________(e)d, and he was brought up on criminal charges.

10. At the turn of the century, factory owners ________________(e)d children by making them work in terrible conditions for as many as 18 hours a day.

Now check your answers by turning to page 163. Fix any mistakes and fill in any blank spaces by writing in the correct answers. By doing so, you will complete this introduction to the ten words.

You're now ready to strengthen your knowledge of the words you already know and to master the words you're only half sure of, or don't know at all. Turn to the next page.

Ten Words in Context

Figure out the meanings of the following ten words by looking *closely and carefully* at the context in which the words appear. Doing so will prepare you for the matching test and practices on the two pages that follow.

1 **acclaim**
(ə-klām')
-noun

a. Any subway system that is clean, quiet, and safe deserves **acclaim**.

b. Although Vincent Van Gogh is now considered a genius, the artist received little **acclaim** in his lifetime.

2 **adjacent**
(ə-jā'-sənt)
-adjective

a. Because their desks are **adjacent**, Jeff and Kellie often exchange looks and comments.

b. If you keep your dishes in a cupboard that's **adjacent** to the dishwasher, you won't have to walk when putting away the clean dishes.

3 **elicit**
(i-lis'-it)
-verb

a. Elizabeth Taylor's violet eyes always **elicit** admiration and wonder.

b. Wes is such a troublemaker in Mrs. Turner's class that his late arrival one day **elicited** this sharp comment from her: "In your case, Wes, never is better than late."

4 **engross**
(en-grōs')
-verb

a. The TV movie so **engrossed** Bryan that he didn't even budge when he was called to dinner.

b. The fascinating single-file march of black ants along the sidewalk **engrossed** me for several minutes.

5 **escalate**
(es'-kə-lāt')
-verb

a. The fight between the two hockey players **escalated** into an all-out battle among members of both teams.

b. Male turkeys challenge each other by strutting with tails spread like fans. As the contest **escalates** and they get more excited, their naked heads turn blue.

6 **exploit**
(eks-ploit')
-verb

a. Some wealthy people obtained their money when they **exploited** individuals less fortunate than themselves.

b. Ricky **exploited** the fact that his parents were out of town for two days by having a wild, two-day party at home.

7 **methodical**
(mə-thod'-i-kəl)
-adjective

a. With a **methodical** filing system, you can find a single piece of paper in minutes, even if thousands of papers are filed.

b. Joan is so **methodical** about her diet that she classifies the foods in each meal into different nutrition categories.

8 **obsolete**
(ob'-sə-lēt')
-adjective

a. Word processors have made typewriters almost **obsolete**.

b. In the United States, the automobile quickly made travel by horse and carriage **obsolete**.

9 **tangible**
(tan'-jə-bəl)
-adjective

a. The sculptor loved making her ideas **tangible** by giving them form in metal and stone.

b. Corn-chip crumbs, empty soda bottles, and dirty napkins were **tangible** evidence that a party had taken place the night before.

10 **terminate**
(tûr'-mə-nāt')
-verb

a. The students waited patiently for the bell to **terminate** Mr. Leeman's boring lecture.

b. The referee should have **terminated** the boxing match when he first saw the weaker fighter losing the ability to defend himself.

Matching Words and Definitions

Check your understanding of the ten words by matching each word with its definition. Look back at the sentences in "Ten Words in Context" as needed to decide on the meaning of each word.

_____	1. **acclaim**	a. to draw forth
_____	2. **adjacent**	b. to stop; bring to an end
_____	3. **elicit**	c. orderly; systematic
_____	4. **engross**	d. near or next to
_____	5. **escalate**	e. able to be touched; having form and matter
_____	6. **exploit**	f. no longer in use or practice; out-of-date
_____	7. **methodical**	g. to increase or intensify
_____	8. **obsolete**	h. enthusiastic praise or applause; great approval
_____	9. **tangible**	i. to hold the full attention of
_____	10. **terminate**	j. to use selfishly or unethically; take unfair advantage of

CAUTION: Do not go any further until you are sure the above answers are correct. If you have studied the "Ten Words in Context," you will know how to match each word. Then you can use the matches to help you in the following practices. Your goal is to reach a point where you don't need to check definitions at all.

➢*Sentence Check 1*

Complete each sentence below with the most suitable word from the box. Use each word once.

acclaim	**adjacent**	**elicit**	**engross**	**escalate**
exploit	**methodical**	**obsolete**	**tangible**	**terminate**

1. The perfect crime leaves no ____________________ clues.
2. If solar energy becomes as cheap and plentiful as sunshine, nuclear energy may become __________________.
3. Only Hank's essay received the teacher's ____________________; all others received negative comments.
4. Our house is __________________ to one with a tall wooden fence, so our view on that side is completely blocked.
5. The shouting match between Rose and her brother __________________(c)d until it was so loud that the neighbors complained.
6. I never read a novel in bed at night because it may __________________ me so much that I'll stay up half the night trying to finish it.
7. When teachers feel ____________________(e)d, they often go on strike for larger salaries and better working conditions.
8. Diana is very ___________________ about letter writing. She keeps her writing materials in one spot, makes a list of the people she owes letters to, and writes letters once a week.
9. Sometimes the only way to ___________________ a faulty computer program is by shutting off the machine. Otherwise, the program may keep repeating itself endlessly.
10. In one disturbing survey, the question "Which do you like better, Daddy or TV?" ___________________(e)d this response from a number of children: "TV."

Now check your answers to these questions by turning to page 163. Going over the answers carefully will help you prepare for the next two checks, for which answers are not given.

➢Sentence Check 2

Complete each sentence below with two words from the box. Use each word once.

acclaim	adjacent	elicit	engross	escalate
exploit	methodical	obsolete	tangible	terminate

1-2. The gifted ice skater's routine ________________(e)d the audience. At the end, he ________________(e)d a burst of applause with a long, rapid spin.

3-4. Although hand-crafted furniture is almost ____________, mass production hasn't yet______________(e)d all demand for it.

5-6. Workers want such __________________ rewards as money and a pension, but they also welcome less concrete benefits, such as _________________ for a job well done.

7-8. The more the British _________________(e)d the American colonies by taxing them unfairly, the more the anti-British sentiment __________________(e)d among the colonists.

9-10. Patty's __________________ baking technique includes arranging all ingredients in a row, with each one __________________ to the one it is used after.

➢*Final Check:* A Cruel Sport

Here is a final opportunity for you to strengthen your knowledge of the ten words. First read the following passage carefully. Then fill in each blank with a word from the box at the top of this page. (Context clues will help you figure out which word goes in which blank.) Use each word once.

The room lights dimmed, and a spotlight revealed a short, fat man holding a heavy chain. He tugged the chain and a muzzled bear appeared. The man, the animal's owner, announced that the bear's name was Sally. He would give a hundred dollars, he said, to anyone who wrestled Sally to the floor. Alex, sitting in the nightclub audience, was shocked. He had thought bear wrestling was (1)_________________, given up long ago as a cruel sport.

The offer (2)______________(e)d an eager response. "I'll do it!" one man called. The audience showed its (3)______________ for the event by cheering him on. He went up and started to swing at Sally. She tried to back away. The match greatly (4)_______________(e)d most members of the audience, who watched every move. A stranger sitting (5)________________ to Alex became so excited that he accidentally knocked over Alex's drink.

"Knock her on her rear!" the owner shouted. When Sally finally raised her arm to defend herself, her owner jerked her back with a sharp tug. Sally's opponent then saw that she had no claws. He thus felt more confident, so his attack (6)_________________(e)d. When the man fighting the bear seemed likely to pin Sally, her owner allowed the bear to throw him off. At that, the owner (7)_________________(e)d the match, calling out "Next!"

Another man then sprang to his feet. And soon another. The same type of match took place six more times—with the same results. It was clear to Alex that this show always followed the same (8)______________ routine.

Finally, the owner led Sally away. Her drooped head and labored walk were (9)_______________ expressions of the animal's misery. Alex was more certain than ever that bear-wrestling (10)_________________(e)d the animal for human entertainment. As Sally passed his table, Alex heard her soft moans. He then saw that the bear was old, and completely blind.

SCORES: Sentence Check 2 ________% Final Check ________%

Enter your scores above and in the vocabulary performance chart on the inside back cover of the book.

CHAPTER

4

Previewing the Words

Find out how many of the ten words in this chapter you already know. Try to complete each sentence with the most suitable word from the list below. Use each word once.

Leave a sentence blank rather than guessing at an answer. Your purpose here is just to get a sense of the ten words and what you may know about them.

deter	**implication**	**inequity**	**infirmity**	**infringe**
innovation	**revitalize**	**sparse**	**subjective**	**succinct**

1. To ___________________ burglars, my father put a sign on our lawn that says, "Beware of German shepherd."
2. The African violets in my kitchen aren't doing well. Do you think some fertilizer would ___________________ them?
3. Blasting a radio on a street or beach ___________________s on others' right to a comfortable environment.
4. When the boss said company profits were down, the ___________________ was that nobody would be getting a raise.
5. The messages on traffic signs must be ___________________ so that all the important information can be read quickly.
6. Mahatma Gandhi experienced racial ___________________ in South Africa, where he was thrown off a "whites only" train.
7. Not so long ago, parents believed left-handedness to be a(n) ___________________. They thus forced left-handed children to use their right hands.
8. Most New Hampshire residents live in the southern and central part of the state. Further north, the population becomes quite ___________________.
9. Movie reviews are always ___________________ as they represent the personal opinions of critics, no matter how knowledgeable the critics may be.
10. The high cost of college has led to such financial ___________________s as paying for children's education while they're as young as infants.

Now check your answers by turning to page 163. Fix any mistakes and fill in any blank spaces by writing in the correct answers. By doing so, you will complete this introduction to the ten words.

You're now ready to strengthen your knowledge of the words you already know and to master the words you're only half sure of, or don't know at all. Turn to the next page.

Ten Words in Context

Figure out the meanings of the following ten words by looking *closely and carefully* at the context in which the words appear. Doing so will prepare you for the matching test and practices on the two pages that follow.

1 **deter**
(di-tûr')
-verb

a. Opponents of the death penalty say it does not actually **deter** anyone from committing murder.

b. If the dangers of skydiving don't **deter** Ben, maybe the cost will.

2 **implication**
(im-pli-kā'-shən)
-noun

a. The possible **implications** of a child doing poorly in elementary school range from poor vision to problems at home.

b. Carla didn't actually say she was quitting her job, but when her plans include a three-month trip and a move to Baltimore, that's a clear **implication**.

3 **inequity**
(in-ek'-wit-ē)
-noun

a. Young people complain when life is unfair. Unfortunately, they will learn that **inequity** is a natural part of life.

b. Most Americans consider it an **inequity** that some millionaires pay less in taxes than ordinary citizens do.

4 **infirmity**
(in-fûr'-mə-tē)
-noun

a. Rick is confined to a wheelchair, but he doesn't let his **infirmity** keep him from traveling.

b. Certain **infirmities**, such as arthritis and diabetes, are more likely to affect the elderly.

5 **infringe**
(in-frinj')
-verb

a. The protesters may picket the nuclear power plant as long as they don't **infringe** on other people's right to enter and exit freely.

b. When my mother is doing her homework, no one is allowed to **infringe** on her quiet.

6 **innovation**
(in'-ə-vā'-shən)
-noun

a. When commercial bakers first offered sliced bread, it was considered an exciting **innovation**.

b. An interesting **innovation** in food packaging is a bottle from which salad dressing is squirted, rather than poured.

7 **revitalize**
(rē-vīt'-əl-īz')
-verb

a. If Dwight is tired after work, he finds a brief nap will **revitalize** him for a night on the town with friends.

b. The City Council hopes to **revitalize** the currently lifeless shopping district by offering tax breaks for new businesses.

8 **sparse**
(spars)
-adjective

a. There are thick pine forests at the foot of the mountain, but higher up, the trees become **sparse**.

b. The turnout for the team pep rally was **sparse**; organizers hope to have a bigger crowd on the day before the game.

9 **subjective**
(səb-jek'-tiv)
-adjective

a. Mary, a highly **subjective** judge of her son's abilities, feels he's brilliant in every respect. The boy's father, however, has a more detached view of him.

b. The reporter refused to write about his friend's trial. He knew any story he wrote would be too **subjective** to be published as an unbiased article.

10 **succinct**
(sək-singkt')
-adjective

a. Your telegram should be **succinct** so that you get your message across clearly without paying for more words than necessary.

b. "What's new?" is a **succinct** way of asking, "Has anything of interest happened to you lately, my friend?"

Matching Words and Definitions

Check your understanding of the ten words by matching each word with its definition. Look back at the sentences in "Ten Words in Context" as needed to decide on the meaning of each word.

_____	1. **deter**	a. injustice; unfairness; an instance of injustice
_____	2. **implication**	b. a new custom, method, or invention; something newly introduced
_____	3. **inequity**	c. based on personal opinions, feelings, and attitudes; biased; not objective
_____	4. **infirmity**	d. to prevent or discourage from doing something
_____	5. **infringe (on** or **upon)**	e. expressed clearly in a few words; concise; brief and clear
_____	6. **innovation**	f. to renew strength and energy of; restore to a vigorous, active condition
_____	7. **revitalize**	g. a physical weakness or defect; ailment
_____	8. **sparse**	h. spread out thinly; not thickly settled or grown; not crowded
_____	9. **subjective**	i. to intrude or trespass on; break in on
_____	10. **succinct**	j. an idea that is suggested or hinted at; something indicated indirectly

CAUTION: Do not go any further until you are sure the above answers are correct. If you have studied the "Ten Words in Context," you will know how to match each word. Then you can use the matches to help you in the following practices. Your goal is to reach a point where you don't need to check definitions at all.

➢*Sentence Check 1*

Complete each sentence below with the most suitable word from the box. Use each word once.

deter	**implication**	**inequity**	**infirmity**	**infringe**
innovation	**revitalize**	**sparse**	**subjective**	**succinct**

1. Although Marie joked about her broken leg, the __________________ kept her from work for a month.
2. When a restaurant's tables have ashtrays, the __________________ is that smoking is permitted.
3. "Now" is a __________________ way of saying "At this particular point in time."
4. Our democratic rights do not include the freedom to __________________ on other people's rights.
5. Our grass is __________________ along a path at the corner of the lot, where kids take a shortcut through our yard.
6. A medical __________________ called a PET scan can show which parts of a person's brain are most active at a given time.
7. The company's in-service day __________________(e)d my interest in my job by giving me new skills and suggesting new goals.
8. *The Diary of Anne Frank* is a __________________ view of events during World War II, from the point of view of a young Jewish girl in hiding.
9. The company was accused of the __________________ of hiring women for less pay than was given to men doing the same work.
10. The fact that Beethoven was totally deaf by age 50 did not __________________ him from composing one of his most loved works, his *Ninth Symphony*, at the age of 53.

Now check your answers to these questions by turning to page 163. Going over the answers carefully will help you prepare for the next two checks, for which answers are not given.

➢Sentence Check 2

Complete each sentence below with two words from the box. Use each word once.

deter	implication	inequity	infirmity	infringe
innovation	revitalize	sparse	subjective	succinct

1-2. When the candidate for mayor saw the ________________ turnout for his speech, he knew he had to do something to ________________ his campaign.

3-4. Future ________________s in technology may make it more difficult for computer thieves to ________________ on other people's computer files.

5-6. Although arthritis can be a painful ________________, Aunt Fern doesn't let it ________________ her from attending her weekly square-dance meetings.

7-8. All editorials are ________________—they represent someone's opinions. In an editorial, for example, writers are free to argue against the ________________ of police brutality, instead of just reporting on it.

9-10. A sign may be brief and still have several ________________s. For example, the ________________ sign "Dangerous Curve" suggests that drivers should slow down, that the curve ahead is sharp, and that bad accidents have happened there before.

➤*Final Check:* Bald Is Beautiful

Here is a final opportunity for you to strengthen your knowledge of the ten words. First read the following passage carefully. Then fill in each blank with a word from the box at the top of this page. (Context clues will help you figure out which word goes in which blank.) Use each word once.

Looking through a hair-care magazine, I noticed many ads for toupees and hair thickeners. The (1)________________ seemed to be that a man's baldness is a major (2)________________. Well, I'm not going to let anyone (3)________________ on the right of a man to be bald. Listen, all you baldies. You may feel it's a great (4)________________ that some heads have only (5)________________ hair while others are thickly covered, but I think bald men are terrifically attractive. Sure, that's just my (6)________________ opinion, but I'm not alone. I know another woman whose boyfriend went so far as to shave his head in order to (7)________________ their tired romance. My thick-haired boyfriend hasn't offered to go quite that far, but I wouldn't (8)________________ him from going bald if he wanted to. I know drug companies are working on medications to produce hair on bald heads, but that's one (9)________________ I hope is never introduced. I'd hate to see all those beautiful, shiny bald heads covered up. Or, to be more (10)________________, bald is beautiful.

SCORES: Sentence Check 2 ________% Final Check ________%

Enter your scores above and in the vocabulary performance chart on the inside back cover of the book.

CHAPTER

5

Previewing the Words

Find out how many of the ten words in this chapter you already know. Try to complete each sentence with the most suitable word from the list below. Use each word once.

Leave a sentence blank rather than guessing at an answer. Your purpose here is just to get a sense of the ten words and what you may know about them.

allusion	**altruistic**	**appease**	**arbitrary**	**assail**
banal	**euphemism**	**mercenary**	**syndrome**	**taint**

1. The two candidates continuously __________________(e)d each other with accusations of fraud.
2. Jet lag is a(n) __________________ resulting from flying that often includes exhaustion, headache, and loss of appetite.
3. "Gail isn't the only athlete in the family," Clarence said, making a(n) __________________ to Gail's father, a bowling champion.
4. The government scandal __________________(e)d the reputation of everyone involved.
5. My mother will never say directly that someone has "died"; instead, she always uses the __________________ "passed away."
6. A(n) __________________ person might prefer a low-paying job with a charitable organization over a high-paying corporate job.
7. The boss's decision to fire Nora was not at all __________________. Company rules clearly state that her behavior was unacceptable.
8. The question "How are you doing?" is so overused that it's even hard to ask it sincerely without sounding __________________.
9. My cousin has always been openly __________________. At the age of ten, he answered "What do you want to be when you grow up?" with a single word: "Rich."
10. When the customer returned, angry at having bought a broken clock, the salesman quickly __________________(e)d her by giving her a full refund.

Now check your answers by turning to page 163. Fix any mistakes and fill in any blank spaces by writing in the correct answers. By doing so, you will complete this introduction to the ten words.

You're now ready to strengthen your knowledge of the words you already know and to master the words you're only half sure of, or don't know at all. Turn to the next page.

Ten Words in Context

Figure out the meanings of the following ten words by looking *closely and carefully* at the context in which the words appear. Doing so will prepare you for the matching test and practices on the two pages that follow.

1 **allusion**
(ə-lo͞o'-zhən)
-noun

a. After I suggested that Monty have fruit for dessert instead of chocolate cake, he responded, "Is that an **allusion** to my weight?"

b. Ray didn't have the courage to come right out and ask Lucy to marry him. Instead, he only made an **allusion** to marriage by asking, "Wouldn't it be easier if we had to fill out just one tax form?"

2 **altruistic**
(al'-tro͞o-is'-tik)
-adjective

a. "I'm not often **altruistic**," Brett admitted. "I usually put my own welfare first."

b. When an enemy approaches, ground squirrels show **altruistic** behavior. They risk their own lives to give alarm calls to nearby relatives.

3 **appease**
(ə-pēz')
-verb

a. My sister was so outraged when I accidentally scratched her favorite old Beatles record that nothing I could say or do would **appease** her.

b. Roger was furious when he saw me out with another guy, but I quickly **appeased** him by explaining that the "date" was my cousin.

4 **arbitrary**
(ar'-bi-trer'-ē)
-adjective

a. Professor Miller's students were angry that he graded essays in an **arbitrary** way, rather than using precise standards.

b. Parents should not impose and enforce rules according to their moods. Such **arbitrary** discipline only confuses and angers children.

5 **assail**
(ə-sāl')
-verb

a. The storm **assailed** us with hail and heavy rains.

b. The press **assailed** the company responsible for the oil spill until it increased its efforts to clean up the mess.

6 **banal**
(bā'-nəl)
-adjective

a. The film, with its overused expressions and commonplace plot, was the most **banal** I had ever seen.

b. "Nice to see you" may be a **banal** comment, but what it lacks in originality it makes up for in friendliness.

7 **euphemism**
(yo͞o'-fə-miz'-əm)
-noun

a. Common **euphemisms** include "final resting place" (for *grave*), "intoxicated" (for *drunk*), and "powder room" and "comfort station" (for *toilet*).

b. The Central Intelligence Agency is on record as having referred to assassination with the **euphemism** "change of health."

8 **mercenary**
(mûr'-sə-ner'-ē)
-adjective

a. Ed is totally **mercenary**. His philosophy is, "Pay me enough, and I'll do anything."

b. The con man pretended to love the wealthy widow, but he actually married her for **mercenary** reasons.

9 **syndrome**
(sin'-drōm)
-noun

a. Headaches are usually harmless, but as part of a **syndrome** including fever and neck stiffness, they may be a sign of a serious illness.

b. For many gardeners, spring fever is a **syndrome** of contradictory symptoms—extreme laziness and a desire to slave over a patch of earth.

10 **taint**
(tānt)
-verb

a. The involvement of organized crime has **tainted** many sports, including boxing and horse racing.

b. The Pulitzer Prize became **tainted** when a newspaper reporter won it for a story that turned out to be a fake.

Matching Words and Definitions

Check your understanding of the ten words by matching each word with its definition. Look back at the sentences in "Ten Words in Context" as needed to decide on the meaning of each word.

_____	1. **allusion**	a. determined by personal judgment, not rule or reason; based on impulse
_____	2. **altruistic**	b. motivated only by financial gain; greedy
_____	3. **appease**	c. an indirect reference
_____	4. **arbitrary**	d. a group of symptoms typical of a particular disease or other abnormal condition
_____	5. **assail**	e. a substitute for a direct word or phrase considered offensive
_____	6. **banal**	f. to bring to a state of calm or peace, especially by providing what is demanded
_____	7. **euphemism**	g. lacking originality; overused; commonplace
_____	8. **mercenary**	h. to stain the honor of a person or thing
_____	9. **syndrome**	i. to attack physically or verbally
_____	10. **taint**	j. unselfishly concerned for the welfare of others; unselfish

CAUTION: Do not go any further until you are sure the above answers are correct. If you have studied the "Ten Words in Context," you will know how to match each word. Then you can use the matches to help you in the following practices. Your goal is to reach a point where you don't need to check definitions at all.

➢*Sentence Check 1*

Complete each sentence below with the most suitable word from the box. Use each word once.

allusion	**altruistic**	**appease**	**arbitrary**	**assail**
banal	**euphemism**	**mercenary**	**syndrome**	**taint**

1. There have been people __________________ enough to sell their own children for the right price.
2. "Someone hasn't shown me his report card," my mother said, making a(n) __________________ to my brother.
3. It takes a(n) __________________ person to adopt a handicapped child.
4. Madge is a tough debater who __________________s the opposing side with sharp questions and arguments.
5. The local undertaker insists on using a(n) __________________ for the chapel of his funeral parlor. He calls it "the slumber room."
6. The report that the team's halfback was addicted to drugs greatly __________________(e)d the team's image.
7. The only thing that would __________________ the dead boy's parents was imprisonment of the drunk driver who had killed him.
8. Abraham Lincoln is thought to have had Marfan's __________________, a group of symptoms which includes unusually long bones and abnormal blood circulation.
9. The judge's sentence was __________________. Rather than being based on past similar cases or on the seriousness of the crime, it was based on the judge's opinion of the defendant.
10. "You're special" probably appears on thousands of greeting cards, but when someone says it to you and means it, it never seems __________________.

Now check your answers to these questions by turning to page 163. Going over the answers carefully will help you prepare for the next two checks, for which answers are not given.

➢Sentence Check 2

Complete each sentence below with two words from the box. Use each word once.

allusion	altruistic	appease	arbitrary	assail
banal	euphemism	mercenary	syndrome	taint

1-2. ________________ people tend to place the public's welfare above their own self-interest. In contrast, ________________ people will sell even harmful products to make a profit.

3-4. The parents of a girl who had been suspended ________________(e)d the principal with charges of incompetence. The principal finally ________________(e)d them by showing them the teacher's report of the girl's behavior.

5-6. My boss judges performance in a(n) ________________ manner, praising and scolding according to his moods. And if he wants me to work late for an hour or so, he uses this ________________: "Please stay a few minutes longer today."

7-8. The ________________ of a certain rare disease includes a very odd symptom—an uncontrollable urge to use obscene language. Because some acquaintances won't understand the reason for the foul language, the illness can ________________ the reputations of its victims.

9-10. Instead of writing a(n) ________________ comment such as "That ballerina is light on her feet," the critic made this interesting ______________ to the dancer's movements: "She was never heavier than moonlight."

➢*Final Check:* No Luck with Women

Here is a final opportunity for you to strengthen your knowledge of the ten words. First read the following passage carefully. Then fill in each blank with a word from the box at the top of this page. (Context clues will help you figure out which word goes in which blank.) Use each word once.

I don't have much luck with women. The other night at a singles dance, I asked an attractive lady, "Excuse me, do you have the time?" (I admit the question is a bit (1)________________, but I couldn't think of anything more clever.) She answered, "Isn't that kind of personal?" Another woman got really upset just because I asked, "Haven't we met before, at Weight Watchers?" Okay, so I was wrong. I didn't mean to make a(n) (2)________________ to her size. Still, after that, nothing I said would (3)________________ her.

Women don't appreciate how nice I am. First of all, I'm not particularly (4)________________. For instance, I've never considered a woman's wealth the most important thing about her. It's the second most important thing. And I would never (5)________________ a woman's reputation by letting her be seen with me in a decent place. I'm so (6)________________ that I once took care of a guy who was drunk by sending him home in a cab. Instead of being grateful, his attractive date (who had been in the ladies' room) (7)________________(e)d me with all sorts of accusations. How was I supposed to know she was his wife?

When I ask women out, they often answer me with (8)________________s such as "I'm busy" or "I already have plans." What they really mean is, "I'm busy making plans to avoid you." You'd think I suffer from some horrible, infectious (9)________________.

Women's behavior is totally (10)________________. At least, I can't see any reason to it. Last night, for example, a woman I was nice enough to treat to a Coke threw it in my face. Thank goodness, she didn't get any on my day-glo Mickey Mouse tie.

SCORES: Sentence Check 2 ________% Final Check ________%

Enter your scores above and in the vocabulary performance chart on the inside back cover of the book.

CHAPTER

6

Previewing the Word Parts

Common word parts—also known as *prefixes, suffixes,* and *roots*—are used in forming many words in English. This page will introduce you to ten common word parts.

Try to match each word part on the left with its definition on the right. Use the words in parentheses as hints to help you guess the meanings. If you can't decide on an answer, leave the space blank. Your purpose here is just to get a sense of the ten word parts and what you may know about them. (You'll have another chance to try this exercise after considering the word parts in context.)

	Word Parts	Definitions
_____	1. **ann, enn** (annual, bicentennial)	a. four, fourth
_____	2. **audi, audio-** (audible, audiovisual)	b. feeling, suffering
_____	3. **cycl, cyclo-** (tricycle, cyclone)	c. in a certain manner
_____	4. **-hood** (statehood, manhood)	d. hear, listen
_____	5. **hyper-** (hypersensitive, hyperactive)	e. to hang
_____	6. **-ly** (easily, helplessly)	f. state, condition
_____	7. **non-** (nonstop, nonessential)	g. year
_____	8. **path, -pathy** (pathetic, sympathy)	h. more than normal; overly
_____	9. **pend** (suspended, pendulum)	i. circle
_____	10. **quart, quadr-** (quarters, quadruplets)	j. not; the opposite of

Now go on to "Ten Word Parts in Context" on the next page. Working through this chapter will help you to strengthen your knowledge of the word parts you already know and to master the word parts you're only half sure of, or don't know at all.

Keep in mind that learning word parts can pay several dividends. Word parts can help with the spelling and pronunciation of many words. They can also help you to unlock the meanings of unfamiliar words.

Ten Word Parts in Context

Figure out the meanings of the following ten word parts by looking *closely and carefully* at the context in which they appear. Doing so will prepare you for the matching test and practices on the two pages that follow.

1 **ann, enn**

a. This year's **annual** family reunion will be held, as always, at Christmastime.

b. Our town is having a big **bicentennial** parade exactly 200 years after the day the town was founded.

2 **audi, audio-**

a. The bride's softly spoken wedding vows were not **audible** to those at the back of the church.

b. The sound system in the new **auditorium** is so good that music can be heard clearly even in the upper balconies.

3 **cycl, cyclo-**

a. When Bob asked his parents if he could buy a new "two-wheeler," they didn't realize he meant a **motorcycle**.

b. A **cyclone** travels in a circular motion.

4 **-hood**

a. When children reach **adulthood**, how much help should their parents give them?

b. Alaska and Hawaii were both granted **statehood** in 1959, becoming the country's 49th and 50th states.

5 **hyper-**

a. Nancy is **hypersensitive** to conflict. When people disagree with her, she thinks they are rejecting her personally.

b. The **hypermarket**, a combination of department store and supermarket, is relatively new in the United States, but it's been popular in Europe for some time.

6 **-ly**

a. One cannot **easily** drown in Utah's Great Salt Lake because the lake's high percentage of salt helps people float.

b. During the American Revolution, many brides **proudly** wore red instead of white, as a symbol of rebellion.

7 **non-**

a. The paints used in elementary schools are **nontoxic** so that any child who might swallow some won't be poisoned.

b. The story about the aliens was supposed to be **nonfiction**, but it sure sounded made-up to me.

8 **path, -pathy**

a. Andrea and her mother claim to have powers of **telepathy**. They say that they know each other's feelings and thoughts without being told.

b. When Rich's marriage fell apart, Ben felt great **empathy** because he has also been rejected by a loved one.

9 **pend**

a. The children's swing is an old tire that's **suspended** from a strong oak branch.

b. I can't sit and watch the swinging **pendulum** of a grandfather clock without starting to feel sleepy.

10 **quart, quadr-**

a. Let's cut the apple into **quarters** so all four of us can have a piece.

b. The ad said I would **quadruple** my money in two months. But instead of making four times as much money, I lost what I invested.

Matching Word Parts and Definitions

Check your understanding of the ten word parts by matching each with its definition. See also the suggestions on page 4.

_____	1. **ann, enn**	a. four, fourth
_____	2. **audi, audio-**	b. feeling, suffering
_____	3. **cycl, cyclo-**	c. in a certain manner
_____	4. **-hood**	d. hearing, sound
_____	5. **hyper-**	e. to hang
_____	6. **-ly**	f. state, condition
_____	7. **non-**	g. year
_____	8. **path, -pathy**	h. more than normal; overly
_____	9. **pend**	i. circle
_____	10. **quart, quadr-**	j. not; the opposite of

CAUTION: Do not go any further until you are sure the above answers are correct. If you have studied the "Ten Word Parts in Context," you will know how to match each word part. Then you can use the matches to help you in the following practices. Your goal is to reach a point where you don't need to check definitions at all.

➢Sentence Check 1

Complete each partial word in the following sentences with a word part from the box. Use each word part only once. You may want to check off each word part as you use it.

ann	**audi**	**cyclo-**	**-hood**	**hyper-**
-ly	**non-**	**path**	**pend**	**quart**

1. Peter loves playing the piano, especially when he has a(n) (. . . *ence*) ________________.
2. It's hard for me to be (*sym. . .etic*) ________________ when my sister complains because she causes so many of her problems herself.
3. Because of therapy, Grace is a well-adjusted adult, but her (*child. . .*) ________________ years were unhappy and troublesome.
4. When I lost one of my diamond earrings, I had the other made into a (. . . *ant*) ________________ to hang around my neck.
5. The children's odd (. . . *et*) ________________ consisted of a toy-drum player, a building-block clapper, a piano player, and a bell ringer.
6. We were told to bring only necessary equipment on our camping trip, so I was surprised to see how much (. . . *essential*) ________________ gear others brought.
7. Mrs. Baker said she and her husband have been (*happi. . .*) ________________ married for 47 years. But Mr. Baker, correcting her, said 1952 wasn't so great.
8. In Gettysburg, Pennsylvania, we went to a (. . . *rama*) ________________, a round theater in which pictures of Civil War battles were shown all around us.
9. Our boss said we would be evaluated (. . . *ually*) ________________ for possible promotions. So if we don't get a promotion one year, we might get one the next.
10. Alan thought he would become extra healthy if he took a lot of vitamins, but he took too many and ended up with an abnormal condition called (. . . *vitaminosis*) ________________.

Now check your answers to these questions by turning to page 163. Going over the answers carefully will help you prepare for the next two checks, for which answers are not given.

➢Sentence Check 2

Complete each partial word in the sentences below with a word part from the box. Use each word part once. If there are two forms of a word part, use the *first* one for this practice.

ann	audio-, audi	cycl	-hood	hyper-
-ly	non-	path, -pathy	pend	quart, quadr-

1-2. Some males act as if their (*man. . .*) ________________ (*de. . . ed*) ________________ on how many women they go out with, rather than on maturity and strength of character.

3-4. The (*. . . ist*) ________________ stood there (*helpless. . .*) ________________ staring at the tire he had chained to the tree. The rest of the bike had been stolen.

5-6. Stan, a (*. . .drinker*) ________________, is (*. . . critical*) ________________ of anyone who touches alcohol. He says even a single drink shows a self-destructive personality.

7-8. My nursing class watched an (*. . . visual*) ________________ show about the horrible conditions in a 1950's mental institution. The patients looked (*. . .etic*) ________________; clearly, they were suffering.

9-10. For my research report, I used two magazines—one (*. . .erly*) ________________, published in March, June, September, and December; and an (*. . . ual*) ________________ that appears only every January.

➤*Final Check:* A Taste of Parenthood

Here is a final opportunity for you to strengthen your knowledge of the ten word parts. First read the following passage carefully. Then complete each partial word in the parentheses below with a word part from the box at the top of this page. If there are two forms of a word part, use the *second* one in this practice. Context clues will help you figure out which word part goes in which blank. Use each word part once.

I have a lot of (*sym. . .*) (1)________________ for parents of twins, triplets, and (*. . .uplets*) (2)________________. I just spent the weekend babysitting for my four nieces and nephews.

First, I offered to watch my brother's two children so that he and his wife could go away for their sixth wedding (*. . .iversary*) (3)________________. Then my sister called and said that her husband, an actor, had a chance to (*. . . tion*) (4)________________ for a big part in a TV drama. He had to fly to California for the weekend. She said she'd love to go along if I could watch their children, aged two and three. I (*willing. . .*) (5)________________ agreed.

What a time I had! The children's activity was (*. . . stop*) (6)________________. It seemed as if they never sat down. They went from peddling their tiny (*tri . . . es*) (7)________________ to building with their blocks to banging their toy drums. They "washed" the dishes, let the dog loose, and made mudpies in the tomato garden. By Sunday, I was convinced they were all (*. . . active*) (8)________________.

Besides all the activity. I had to cope with the knowledge that four little ones were entirely (*de. . .ent*) (9)________________ on me for their needs. So I kept worrying about making mistakes. What if one got hurt? What if they got sick? Fortunately, we survived without a disaster.

I can't imagine what it must be like for parents with two or more children. I guess I'm not ready to have kids yet—not even one. At least I could give these children back to their parents on Sunday night. But (*parent. . .*) (10)________________ is for keeps. I think I'll wait.

SCORES: Sentence Check 2 ________%	Final Check ________%

Enter your scores above and in the vocabulary performance chart on the inside back cover of the book.

UNIT ONE: Test 1

PART A

Choose the word that best completes each sentence and write it in the space provided.

1. **syndrome** **dilemma** **euphemism** **zeal** — A common __________________ for *corpse* is "remains."

2. **elicits** **appeases** **escalates** **absolves** — In the winter, the price of tomatoes __________________ while their quality goes down.

3. **mercenary** **amiable** **curt** **wary** — The taxi driver was so __________________ that he charged his own mother for rides.

4. **allusion** **inclination** **inequity** **acclaim** — Do you consider it an __________________ that only one percent of Americans own a third of the nation's wealth?

5. **methodical** **sparse** **amoral** **subjective** — The plants look __________________ now, but within a year or two they'll multiply and fill in the empty spaces.

6. **adamant** **curt** **tangible** **obsolete** — You probably thought that mail delivery by mule was __________________, but it still exists in the Grand Canyon.

7. **succinct** **adamant** **tangible** **eccentric** — You can make your essays more __________________ by going through them carefully to remove all unnecessary words.

8. **taint** **epitome** **animosity** **innovation** — Fruitcake may be the __________________ of Christmas gifts, but a survey indicates that it's the nation's least wanted one.

9. **Wary** **Altruistic** **Amoral** **Curt** — __________________ enough to refuse to take money from the public for his discovery of X-rays, Wilhelm Roentgen died poor.

10. **deter** **elicit** **assail** **engross** — To __________________ employees from stealing, the Los Angeles Rapid Transit Authority has workers wear uniforms without pockets.

11. **animosity**
sabotage
innovation
acclaim

Although Marilyn Monroe received great praise from fans and critics, she never received the _______________ of an Academy Award.

12. **assailed**
demoralized
taint
absolved

The model realized if she wanted to be _______________ of the charges, she'd better hire a detective to find the real murderer.

13. **animosity**
infirmity
inclination
syndrome

You might have a stronger _______________ to work for high grades if you were a student in any Cleveland public high school, where each A earns $40 toward college tuition.

PART B

Circle **C** if the italicized word is used **correctly**. Circle **I** if the word is used **incorrectly**.

C I 14. Compact disks are already so popular that it's easy to forget how recent an *innovation* they are.

C I 15. Ants have the *infirmity* of being able to survive under water for up to two weeks.

C I 16. Students often *exploit* the presence of a substitute teacher by using fake names.

C I 17. We had to trim the oak tree *adjacent* to our home so that its branches wouldn't reach into the porch.

C I 18. If you worry about the environment, you're *eccentric.* According to a poll, over three-fourths of Americans do.

C I 19. Our *amiable* neighbor scares our children so much that they refuse to knock on his door even on Halloween.

C I 20. The symptoms of fetal alcohol *syndrome* include deformed limbs and mental retardation.

C I 21. I'm *wary* of any food product labeled "light" because there are no rules governing the use of the word.

C I 22. The passerby showed his *animosity* by entering the burning house and pulling the child to safety.

C I 23. In 1876, Wild Bill Hickok was in a poker game that was *terminated* by a bullet entering the back of his head.

C I 24. It's much harder to define the words for *tangible* things such as love and intelligence than it is to define terms for physical objects such as chairs and cars.

C I 25. Many taxpayers become *irate* when they learn that in a single year, the U.S. Air Force spent over $5 million on imported goat-skin jackets.

SCORE: (Number correct) ________ x 4 = ________ %

Enter your scores above and in the vocabulary performance chart on the inside back cover of the book.

UNIT ONE: Test 2

PART A

Complete each sentence with a word from the box. Use each word once.

adamant	**allusion**	**amoral**	**antagonist**
appease	**demoralized**	**elicit**	**infringe**
retorted	**revitalize**	**sabotaged**	**subsequent**
zeal			

1. A competitor ________________ a batch of the company's shampoo by throwing some blue dye in it.
2. Do you think supermarket tabloids ________________ on celebrities' privacy?
3. Despite all the wars that have taken place, England and Portugal have never faced each other as wartime ________________s.
4. Most Americans show little ________________ for "The Great Outdoors," spending only about 2 percent of their time there.
5. Apparently, the chance to be President wouldn't ________________ much enthusiasm from most Americans—89 percent say they wouldn't want the job.
6. A permanent involves the contradictory steps of burning hair to a lifeless state and then smearing on conditioners to ________________ it.
7. It's often said that Nature is ________________, but humans are part of Nature, and most of them *do* care about right and wrong.
8. Our congressional representative, ________________ in her opposition to pesticides, often reminds voters that pesticides kill about 14,000 people each year.
9. When a woman told Winston Churchill, "If you were my husband, I'd put poison in your tea," he ________________, "If I were your husband, I'd drink it."
10. Although Thomas Edison's teachers thought he'd be a failure and his father called him a "dunce," the strong encouragement of Edison's mother kept him from being totally ________________.
11. Manny did poorly on his first biology test because he had trouble memorizing diagrams. Then he learned a memorization method and did much better on ________________ tests.
12. In a(n) ________________ to the city's varied population, our professor mentioned that more than half of the city's daily newspapers are in languages other than English.
13. When Kathleen stood up Evan for the prom, an apology did not ________________ him. He's suing her for the cost of his rented tux and the prom tickets.

PART B

Circle **C** if the italicized word is used **correctly**. Circle **I** if the word is used **incorrectly**.

C I 14. Cory was so *engrossed* in the film that he fell asleep.

C I 15. When, during our drive, we *encountered* an unexpected hailstorm, we felt as if we were inside a metal can being pelted with stones.

C I 16. Upon his retirement from the law, the judge was praised for his consistently *subjective* verdicts.

C I 17. My interview with the *curt* personnel officer was the friendliest and most comfortable I've ever experienced.

C I 18. Phyllis is very *methodical* in her efforts to be the life of any party. She keeps a file cabinet of jokes, indexed by occasion.

C I 19. The critic *maligned* the folk singer by saying her voice has both richness and sparkle, like velvet trimmed with gold.

C I 20. Eager to *taint* his opponent's reputation, the candidate spent thousands of dollars on research aimed at uncovering some scandal.

C I 21. In 1971, three dolphins *assailed* a drowning woman by keeping her afloat and protecting her from sharks across 200 miles of ocean.

C I 22. When the evidence in a case is unclear, a jury's decision may be *arbitrary,* based only on the jurors' "gut feeling."

C I 23. Alice Walker's novel *The Color Purple* won both the Pulitzer Prize and the National Book Award because critics found the novel so *banal.*

C I 24. Parents of young children often face the *dilemma* of whether both parents should work or one should put a career on hold and stay home for a few years.

C I 25. When we say something moves "at a snail's pace," the *implication* is that it's moving slowly.

SCORE: (Number correct) ________ x 4 = ________ %

Enter your scores above and in the vocabulary performance chart on the inside back cover of the book.

UNIT ONE: Test 3

PART A

Complete each sentence in a way that clearly shows you understand the meaning of the boldfaced word. Take a minute to plan your answer before you write.

Example: It would **deter** me from attending classes one day if ___*four feet of snow were on the ground.*___

1. One day typewriters will become **obsolete** because ______________________________

____

2. If I were looking for a job, I would be **demoralized** by ______________________________

____

3. One **tangible** indication of affection is ______________________________

____

4. One behavior that makes me **irate** is ______________________________

____

5. I think that ______________________________

______________________________ **infringes** on other people's rights.

6. The **eccentric** teacher has a habit of ______________________________

____

7. This year I face the **dilemma** of ______________________________

____

8. The most **altruistic** thing I ever saw anyone do was to ______________________________

____

9. The actor received this **acclaim** for his performance: ______________________________

____

10. I'm **wary** of driving at night, so I ______________________________

____

PART B

After each boldfaced word are a *synonym* (a word that means the same as the boldfaced word), an *antonym* (a word that means the opposite of the boldfaced word), and a word that is neither. Mark the antonym with an *A*.

Example: **irate**	_____ angry	__*A*__ calm	_____ well-informed
11. **terminate**	_____ end	_____ begin	_____ grow
12 **amoral**	_____ ethical	_____ costly	_____ unprincipled
13. **amiable**	_____ friendly	_____ natural	_____ unfriendly
14. **assail**	_____ flow	_____ attack	_____ defend
15. **subsequent**	_____ previous	_____ hidden	_____ following

PART C

Use five of the following ten words in sentences. Make it clear that you know the meaning of the word you use. Feel free to use the past tense or plural form of a word.

absolve	**adjacent**	**animosity**	**appease**	**curt**
deter	**epitome**	**innovation**	**methodical**	**zeal**

16. ____

____

17. ____

____

18. ____

____

19. ____

____

20. ____

SCORE: (Number correct) _______ x 5 = _______ %

Enter your scores above and in the vocabulary performance chart on the inside back cover of the book.

UNIT ONE: Test 4 (Word Parts)

PART A

Listed in the left-hand column below are ten common word parts, along with words in which the parts are used. In each blank, write in the letter of the correct definition on the right.

Word Parts		**Definitions**
____ 1. **ann, enn**	annual, centennial	a. in a certain manner
____ 2. **audi, audio-**	inaudible, audiovisual	b. feeling, suffering
____ 3. **cycl, cyclo-**	bicycle, cyclone	c. circle
____ 4. **-hood**	womanhood, parenthood	d. to hang
____ 5. **hyper-**	hypertension, hyperactivity	e. year
____ 6. **-ly**	carelessly, energetically	f. four, fourth
____ 7. **non-**	nonsense, nonprofit	g. state, condition
____ 8. **path, -pathy**	pathetic, sympathy	h. not; the opposite of
____ 9. **pend**	suspend, pendulum	i. hearing, sound
____10. **quart, quadr-**	quartet, quadruplets	j. more than normal

PART B

Find the word part that correctly completes each word. Then write the full word in the blank space. Not every word part will be used.

ann	**audi-**	**cycl-**	**-hood**	**hyper-**
-ly	**non-**	**-pathy**	**pend**	**quadr-**

11. Mickey Mouse had no (*boy . . .*) ________________ —he was "born" as an adult.

12. I enjoy riding an exercise bike because I don't have to (*. . . e*) ________________ uphill.

13. My dog didn't know why I was crying, but I could tell that she felt (*sym . . .*) ________________ for me.

14. The spider, (*sus . . . ed*) ________________ from the ceiling on its own silken thread, dangled above a bowl of popcorn.

15. Children's rhymes include such (*. . . sense*) ________________ words as "Hickory, dickory, dock."

PART C

Use your knowledge of word parts to determine the meaning of the boldfaced words. Circle the letter of each meaning.

16. Noel **secretly** slipped a note under Anna's plate.

a. in a secret manner b. at a secret time c. without being secret

17. Should I buy a **quart** or a gallon of chocolate milk?

a. a third of a gallon b. a fourth of a gallon c. a half of a gallon

18. The public library's **biennial** hobby show will take place next month.

a. happening every two weeks b. happening every two months c. happening every two years

19. Mrs. Bush was troubled by **hyperthyroidism**.

a. too little activity of the thyroid gland b. too much activity of the thyroid gland c. a missing thyroid gland

20. There's a problem at the television station. Only the **audio** portion of the show is coming through.

a. sound b. picture c. top

SCORE: (Number correct) ________ x 5 = ________ %

Enter your scores above and in the vocabulary performance chart on the inside back cover of the book.

Unit Two

CHAPTER

7

Previewing the Words

Find out how many of the ten words in this chapter you already know. Try to complete each sentence with the most suitable word from the list below. Use each word once.

Leave a sentence blank rather than guessing at an answer. Your purpose here is just to get a sense of the ten words and what you may know about them.

calamity	**comprehensive**	**conventional**	**flagrant**	**fluctuate**
persevere	**ponder**	**rehabilitate**	**turmoil**	**venture**

1. Michelle's flirting is so ___________________ that I feel embarrassed for her.
2. If you ___________________ in your good study habits, you will be able to pass chemistry.
3. At tomorrow's staff meeting, I will ___________________ saying what I really think and cross my fingers that I don't get fired.
4. Peter's moods ___________________ wildly. One minute he feels totally happy; the next, he wishes he had never been born.
5. If the ___________________ method of opening a jar doesn't work, try again after wrapping a rubber band around the lid.
6. Most prisons make little effort to___________________ inmates so that they can lead productive, wholesome lives upon release.
7. Hurricane Camille was a ___________________—along the coasts of Louisiana, Mississippi, and Alabama, 241 people died.
8. Ricardo asked the librarian for a ___________________ tour of the library so that he would learn how to locate any materials he might need in the future.
9. In ___________________ over the absence of a teacher, the sixth-grade class quickly came to order when the principal entered the room.
10. At age 16, I would sit on our backyard swing and ___________________ life and death and whether Bobby Giordano liked me or not.

Now check your answers by turning to page 164. Fix any mistakes and fill in any blank spaces by writing in the correct answers. By doing so, you will complete this introduction to the ten words.

You're now ready to strengthen your knowledge of the words you already know and to master the words you're only half sure of, or don't know at all. Turn to the next page.

Ten Words in Context

Figure out the meanings of the following ten words by looking *closely and carefully* at the context in which the words appear. Doing so will prepare you for the matching test and practices on the two pages that follow.

1 **calamity**
(kə-lam'-i-tē)
-noun

a. The earthquake survivors slowly rebuilt their homes and lives after the **calamity**.

b. Our neighbor's house burned down one night in May. Ever since that **calamity**, the children have been afraid to go to bed at night.

2 **comprehensive**
(kom'-prē-hen'-siv)
-adjective

a. That article on sightseeing in New Orleans was not **comprehensive**. It failed to mention many points of interest in that wonderful city.

b. The company's **comprehensive** medical insurance plan covers most health services, including hospitals, doctors, and dentists.

3 **conventional**
(kən-ven'-shə-nəl)
-adjective

a. Barb's work is hardly **conventional**—she owns and operates a day-care center for pets.

b. Dad had wanted to propose to my mother in the **conventional** manner, so in the middle of a restaurant, he got down on his knees.

4 **flagrant**
(flā'-grənt)
-adjective

a. The congressman's use of campaign funds for his private business was a **flagrant** violation of the law.

b. When Charlene lost her job because she spoke up for a fellow employee, it was a **flagrant** violation of her union rights.

5 **fluctuate**
(fluk'-cho͞o-āt')
-verb

a. My weight used to **fluctuate** between 150 and 190 pounds. Now it's steady, at 170 pounds.

b. Desert temperatures can **fluctuate** between the day and the night by as much as 50 degrees.

6 **persevere**
(pûr'-sə-vîr')
-verb

a. "I know you're tired," Jack said, "but we've got to **persevere** and get to the camp before the storm hits."

b. It was not easy to attend English classes while working two jobs, but Nina **persevered** until she could speak English well.

7 **ponder**
(pon'-dər)
-verb

a. Too often we don't take time to **ponder** the possible consequences of our actions.

b. Over the years, Mr. Madigan rarely took time to **ponder** life. Since his heart attack, however, he's thought a lot about what is important to him.

8 **rehabilitate**
(rē'-hə-bil'-ə-tāt')
-verb

a. To **rehabilitate** people who have lost the ability to work, it is necessary to stress good work habits as well as job skills.

b. My grandfather learned to walk, write, and speak again in a program that **rehabilitates** stroke victims.

9 **turmoil**
(tûr'-moil)
-noun

a. There was much **turmoil** among the passengers when a sudden blizzard shut down all flights coming to and leaving the airport.

b. After the **turmoil** of crying babies, active children, and trying to feed 120 people, I'm glad when our family reunions end.

10 **venture**
(ven'-chər)
-verb

a. "I'll **venture** any ride in this amusement park except the Twister," said Nick. "I'll risk getting sick to my stomach, but I won't risk my life."

b. Sue has decided to **venture** her security by giving up her job and starting her own business.

Matching Words and Definitions

Check your understanding of the ten words by matching each word with its definition. Look back at the sentences in "Ten Words in Context" as needed to decide on the meaning of each word.

_____	1. **calamity**	a.	shockingly obvious; outrageous
_____	2. **comprehensive**	b.	to risk; take the risks of
_____	3. **conventional**	c.	including much; taking much or everything into account
_____	4. **flagrant**	d.	to restore to a normal life through therapy and/or education
_____	5. **fluctuate**	e.	to continue with an effort or plan despite difficulties
_____	6. **persevere**	f.	complete confusion; uproar
_____	7. **ponder**	g.	a disaster; an event of great loss and misery
_____	8. **rehabilitate**	h.	to vary irregularly
_____	9. **turmoil**	i.	to consider carefully; think deeply about
_____	10. **venture**	j.	customary; ordinary

CAUTION: Do not go any further until you are sure the above answers are correct. If you have studied the "Ten Words in Context," you will know how to match each word. Then you can use the matches to help you in the following practices. Your goal is to reach a point where you don't need to check definitions at all.

➣*Sentence Check 1*

Complete each sentence below with the most suitable word from the box. Use each word once.

calamity	**comprehensive**	**conventional**	**flagrant**	**fluctuate**
persevere	**ponder**	**rehabilitate**	**turmoil**	**venture**

1. Iris is so vain that she considers it a ________________ if a pimple appears anywhere on her face.
2. Too many people have a child without taking time to ________________ parenthood. They give less thought to having a baby than to buying a sofa.
3. In ________________ disregard of his parents' wishes, Art wore a T-shirt and jeans to the dinner party.
4. Our psychology exam will be ________________; it will cover everything we've studied since September.
5. Nobody in Doug's family has a ________________ job. His mother is a drummer, his father is a magician, and his uncle is a wine taster.
6. Learning the computer program was difficult, but when Maria realized how useful it would be in her work, she was glad she had ________________(e)d.
7. It took many months to ________________ my aunt after she lost her sight, but now she can get around her home and neighborhood on her own.
8. The day we moved, the apartment was in ________________. Boxes and people seemed to be constantly on the move, and the baby wouldn't stop crying.
9. The way my dog's appetite ________________(e)d this week worries me. One day she hardly ate anything, and the next she gulped down everything I gave her.
10. Instead of hiring a lawyer, the defendant will ________________ pleading her own case in court.

Now check your answers to these questions by turning to page 164. Going over the answers carefully will help you prepare for the next two checks, for which answers are not given.

➢ *Sentence Check 2*

Complete each sentence below with two words from the box. Use each word once.

calamity	**comprehensive**	**conventional**	**flagrant**	**fluctuate**
persevere	**ponder**	**rehabilitate**	**turmoil**	**venture**

1-2. The one time my cousin __________________(e)d skydiving, the result was a __________________. Her parachute didn't open, and she was injured so badly in the fall that she almost died.

3-4. The drug-treatment center can __________________ most addicts. Among the failures are addicts who don't __________________ with the treatment and leave the center early.

5-6. When driving alone, Marshall is very __________________, obeying all the traffic rules. But when his friends are with him, he shows off with a __________________ violation of the speed limits.

7-8. "We need to ______________ all we might do to help families in trouble," said the social worker to her staff. "We must plan a __________________ program, not just a narrow plan dealing with one part of their lives."

9-10. Our boss's moods and orders __________________ so wildly at times that they throw the office into __________________.

➢ *Final Check:* Accident and Recovery

Here is a final opportunity for you to strengthen your knowledge of the ten words. First read the following passage carefully. Then fill in each blank with a word from the box at the top of this page. (Context clues will help you figure out which word goes in which blank.) Use each word once.

Anna's (1)__________________ disregard for our warnings led to a (2)__________________ that would change her life forever. Before we could stop her, she dove off a rock into a river none of us was sure was deep enough. When she hit the bottom, she broke her back.

I visited Anna at the hospital every day for the next few weeks. I saw her mood (3)__________________ between anger and quiet depression. Her whole life seemed in (4)__________________; she was too confused and troubled to think reasonably about her future.

Within about a month, however, I began to see a change in Anna. She had moved to Henner House to participate in a (5)__________________ program, designed to meet all the needs of patients like Anna. The program (6)__________________s accident victims so that they can return to fulfilling lives. Anna gained hope once she saw she could learn to do such everyday tasks as cooking, cleaning, and bathing. After learning how to get around indoors, she (7)__________________(e)d traveling around the city in her wheelchair. The more she did, the better she felt. The staff also helped Anna plan for her future. They urged her to (8)__________________ her goals and how she might meet them. At times, it was difficult for her to (9)__________________ with the program, but she didn't quit.

Now, ten months later, Anna is able to live a somewhat (10)__________________ life. She is able to do many of the ordinary things she used to do—work, drive, and live in an apartment with a friend. Yes, her life has changed forever. But Anna is once again glad to be alive.

SCORES: Sentence Check 2 ________%	Final Check ________%

Enter your scores above and in the vocabulary performance chart on the inside back cover of the book.

CHAPTER 8

Previewing the Words

Find out how many of the ten words in this chapter you already know. Try to complete each sentence with the most suitable word from the list below. Use each word once.

Leave a sentence blank rather than guessing at an answer. Your purpose here is just to get a sense of the ten words and what you may know about them.

attest	**attribute**	**discern**	**dispatch**	**enhance**
enigma	**exemplify**	**mobile**	**nocturnal**	**orient**

1. My nephew's favorite toys are the ____________ ones, those that can walk, jump, or travel on wheels.
2. When my china clown broke, I glued it back together so carefully that no one could ____________ the crack.
3. The positions of the stars help sailors ____________ themselves on the open seas.
4. Because its climate is too cold for most germs, Antarctica has the ____________ of being nearly germ-free.
5. Parents, serving as role models, usually ____________ adulthood to their children.
6. How the thief entered our house was a(n) ____________ until we remembered that the cellar door had been left unlocked.
7. Good communication skills will ____________ a career in any field.
8. I know when my brother has enjoyed one of his ____________ feasts because I find a stack of dishes in the sink in the morning.
9. My mother used to ____________ me to the store for milk or some missing cooking ingredient as often as twice a day.
10. Witnesses ____________ to the fact that rainfall makes the ground of Death Valley so slippery that boulders slide across it.

Now check your answers by turning to page 164. Fix any mistakes and fill in any blank spaces by writing in the correct answers. By doing so, you will complete this introduction to the ten words.

You're now ready to strengthen your knowledge of the words you already know and to master the words you're only half sure of, or don't know at all. Turn to the next page.

Ten Words in Context

Figure out the meanings of the following ten words by looking *closely and carefully* at the context in which the words appear. Doing so will prepare you for the matching test and practices on the two pages that follow.

1 **attest** (ə-test') *-verb*

a. Anyone who has seen the Golden Gate Bridge in the rose-gold light of sunset can **attest** to its beauty.

b. My uncle, a New York City policeman, can **attest** to the existence of bullet-proof clipboards.

2 **attribute** (at'-rə-byōōt') *-noun*

a. A 300-page novel written in 1939 has the odd **attribute** of containing no *e*, the most common letter in English.

b. In Japan, some cars have such computerized **attributes** as windshield wipers that automatically turn on when it rains.

3 **discern** (di-zûrn') *-verb*

a. An experienced jeweler can **discern** almost immediately whether a diamond is genuine or fake.

b. People who are red-green colorblind can **discern** the colors of traffic lights by recognizing shades of gray.

4 **dispatch** (di-spach') *-verb*

a. On his job, Harold is treated like an errand boy. His boss often **dispatches** him to the deli for sandwiches or donuts.

b. My sister got in trouble when she **dispatched** a message to another student in class by way of a paper airplane.

5 **enhance** (en-hans') *-verb*

a. Our gym teacher **enhanced** her appearance with a more attractive hairstyle.

b. The college catalogue stated that the writing course would "**enhance** all students' writing skills" by improving their grammar and style.

6 **enigma** (i-nig'-mə) *-noun*

a. Many fairy tales involve the challenge of an **enigma**. The hero must solve some puzzle or die.

b. The "singing sands" of Scotland remained an **enigma** until scientists learned that footsteps caused the round grains of sand and the surrounding air pockets to make musical vibrations.

7 **exemplify** (ig-zem'-plə-fī') *-verb*

a. The many IRS employees who give citizens inaccurate information **exemplify** government incompetence.

b. Mr. Pell, who emphasizes original thinking and freedom of expression, **exemplifies** the best in teaching.

8 **mobile** (mō'-bəl) *-adjective*

a. My parents own a **mobile** home, which can be moved from place to place on a long truck.

b. When I was a bedridden hospital patient, the highlight of my days was the **mobile** library that a volunteer wheeled into my room each morning.

9 **nocturnal** (nok-tûr'-nəl) *-adjective*

a. The painting was of a restful **nocturnal** scene. Lamplit houses were set against a night sky.

b. Being **nocturnal**, owls are rarely seen during the day.

10 **orient** (ôr'-ē-ent) *-verb*

a. When coming up from the subway, I often need to look at a street sign to **orient** myself.

b. Drivers of the future may **orient** themselves in unfamiliar places with the help of an electronic map that shows the car's location.

Matching Words and Definitions

Check your understanding of the ten words by matching each word with its definition. Look back at the sentences in "Ten Words in Context" as needed to decide on the meaning of each word.

_____	1. **attest**	a.	a mystery or puzzle
_____	2. **attribute**	b.	to send to a specific place or on specific business
_____	3. **discern**	c.	of, about, or happening in the night; active at night
_____	4. **dispatch**	d.	to give evidence; bear witness; testify
_____	5. **enhance**	e.	to determine the location or direction of
_____	6. **enigma**	f.	to recognize; make out clearly
_____	7. **exemplify**	g.	to improve
_____	8. **mobile**	h.	moving or able to move from place to place
_____	9. **nocturnal**	i.	a quality or feature of a person or thing
_____	10. **orient**	j.	to be an example of; represent; be typical of

CAUTION: Do not go any further until you are sure the above answers are correct. If you have studied the "Ten Words in Context," you will know how to match each word. Then you can use the matches to help you in the following practices. Your goal is to reach a point where you don't need to check definitions at all.

➢Sentence Check 1

Complete each sentence below with the most suitable word from the box. Use each word once.

attest	attribute	discern	dispatch	enhance
enigma	exemplify	mobile	nocturnal	orient

1. Fresh garlic may not ____________________ the breath, but it certainly improves spaghetti sauce.
2. A witness ____________________(e)d to the truth of the defendant's claim that she had loved the murdered man.
3. I wanted to ____________________ the package as quickly as possible, so I sent it by Federal Express.
4. The lives of such reformers as Susan B. Anthony, Gandhi, and Martin Luther King ____________________ greatness.
5. How the crime had been committed was a(n) ____________________ until Perry Mason solved the mystery.
6. The convicts decided on a(n) ____________________ escape. The darkness would hide them as they fled through the forest.
7. Sue's hairpiece is so natural looking that it's impossible to ____________________ where the hairpiece ends and her own hair begins.
8. Birds use the angle of the sun and stars to help them ____________________ themselves during their long migrations.
9. My mother is unable to walk, but with her wheelchair she is ____________________ enough to get around her one-story home, move along a sidewalk, and even shop at a mall.
10. Giant kelp, a form of seaweed, has some amazing ____________________s. Not only is it the world's fastest-growing vegetable, but the more it is cut, the faster it grows.

Now check your answers to these questions by turning to page 164. Going over the answers carefully will help you prepare for the next two checks, for which answers are not given.

➢Sentence Check 2

Complete each sentence below with two words from the following list. Use each word once.

attest	attribute	discern	dispatch	enhance
enigma	exemplify	mobile	nocturnal	orient

1-2. Because Helen Keller could not hear or see, the senses she did have were ____________________(e)d by keen use. It is said that she could ________________ who was in a room simply by smell.

3-4. A ________________ robot that collects and delivers mails throughout our office building________________s itself with electric eyes.

5-6. In fables, animals often illustrate human ____________________s. In the story of the tortoise and the hare, the slow tortoise is meant to ____________________ the human quality of being slow but steady.

7-8. The reason the boss likes to ____________________ Oliver on lengthy errands is no ________________. Everyone knows that the office functions better with Oliver out of the way.

9-10. Anyone who has ever gone to college can ____________________ to the fact that, during finals, many students become ____________________ animals, staying up all night before an exam and then sleeping during the day after taking it.

➢*Final Check:* Animal Senses

Here is a final opportunity for you to strengthen your knowledge of the ten words. First read the following passage carefully. Then fill in each blank with a word from the box at the top of this page. (Context clues will help you figure out which word goes in which blank.) Use each word once.

Animals possess sensory powers that humans lack. Homing pigeons fly with great speed and accuracy when (1)____________________(e)d with messages to faraway places. How do pigeons (2)____________________ themselves in unfamiliar regions? This remains something of a(n) (3)____________________. The mystery, however, is partly explained by a pigeon's ability to see ultraviolet light, which reveals the sun's position even through clouds. In addition, pigeons can hear sound waves that have traveled hundreds of miles. These waves (4)____________________ a pigeon's sense of direction by indicating distant mountains and seas. Pigeons even appear to (5)____________________ changes in the earth's magnetic field.

Bats have (6)____________________s no less impressive. As (7)____________________ animals, they search for food in complete darkness. They do so by screeching in tones higher than any human can hear and then locating prey by the returning echoes.

Scorpions also (8)____________________ the night hunter. Tiny leg hairs enable them to feel vibrations in the sand made by a (9)____________________ insect as far as two feet away.

People with knowledge of the pigeon, bat and scorpion can (10)____________________ to the fact that such "inventions" as the magnetic compass, radar, and the motion detector are nothing new.

SCORES: Sentence Check 2 ________% Final Check ________%

Enter your scores above and in the vocabulary performance chart on the inside back cover of the book.

CHAPTER

9

Previewing the Words

Find out how many of the ten words in this chapter you already know. Try to complete each sentence with the most suitable word from the list below. Use each word once.

Leave a sentence blank rather than guessing at an answer. Your purpose here is just to get a sense of the ten words and what you may know about them.

concurrent	**confiscate**	**constitute**	**decipher**	**default**
hypothetical	**nominal**	**predominant**	**prerequisite**	**recession**

1. My kids think that pizza, peanut butter, hot dogs, and soda __________________ the four basic food groups.
2. Some nightclubs charge only a __________________ entrance fee but a fortune for each drink.
3. Knowing basic math skills is a __________________ for learning the more advanced concepts of algebra.
4. Do doctors take a course to learn how to write prescriptions which nobody but the pharmacist can __________________?
5. While seashore businesses suffer a __________________ in the winter, they do very well from spring to fall.
6. Diana had a chance of winning the swim marathon, but she __________________(e)d by not signing up in time.
7. Law schools hold pretend court sessions with __________________ cases so that students can practice their skills.
8. Anger and frustration were the __________________ emotions among students when they heard that tuition would be raised again.
9. Because their classes are __________________, Brad and Rene can conveniently take turns driving each other to campus.
10. The police officer would __________________ illegal fireworks from teenagers and then set them off at his own home on July 4.

Now check your answers by turning to page 164. Fix any mistakes and fill in any blank spaces by writing in the correct answers. By doing so, you will complete this introduction to the ten words.

You're now ready to strengthen your knowledge of the words you already know and to master the words you're only half sure of, or don't know at all. Turn to the next page.

Ten Words in Context

Figure out the meanings of the following ten words by looking *closely and carefully* at the context in which the words appear.Doing so will prepare you for the matching test and practices on the two pages that follow.

1 **concurrent**
(kən-kûr'-ənt)
-adjective

a. Having mistakenly registered for two **concurrent** classes, Joe had to change one class to a different time.

b. Just when the town's steel mill closed, a new toy factory opened. If the two events had not been **concurrent,** half the town would be unemployed.

2 **confiscate**
(kon'-fis-kāt')
-verb

a. Not only did the teacher **confiscate** the note I passed to my boyfriend, but she also read it out loud to the entire class.

b. Chinese drug agents once **confiscated** $2 million worth of heroin wrapped in plastic and inserted into live goldfish. The agents took possession of the drugs as they were being sent out of the country.

3 **constitute**
(kon'-sti-to͞ot')
-verb

a. A good movie, a pizza, and animated conversation **constitute** my idea of a perfect night out.

b. Twelve business and professional people **constitute** the board of directors of the local women's shelter.

4 **decipher)**
(di-sī'-fər)
-verb

a. Why do contracts have to use language that's so difficult to **decipher**?

b. On one of Holly's essays, her English teacher wrote, "Please type your papers. I can't **decipher** your handwriting."

5 **default**
(di-fôlt')
-verb

a. We won our case against the appliance repairman because he **defaulted** by failing to appear in court.

b. Jay's mother said, "I'll co-sign on your car loan, but you have to make every payment. If you **default,** it will hurt my credit rating."

6 **hypothetical**
(hī'-pō-thet'-i-kəl)
-adjective

a. Imagine the **hypothetical** situation of going to live alone on an island. Which books and music tapes would you take along?

b. My husband didn't actually ask me to marry him. Instead, he asked a **hypothetical** question: "What would you say *if* I asked you to marry me?"

7 **nominal**
(nom'-ə-nəl)
-adjective

a. Apart from a **nominal** registration fee, the camp for needy children is entirely free.

b. Professor Banks gave only **nominal** extra credit for participating in psychology experiments. She wanted our course grade to be based primarily on our test scores.

8 **predominant**
(pri-dom'-ə-nənt)
-adjective

a. Rock is the **predominant** music in our dorm, but country music is also popular.

b. Though the **predominant** type of car in New York City in 1900 used gasoline, a third of the cars ran on electricity.

9 **prerequisite**
(prē-rek'-wi-zit)
-noun

a. You can't take Spanish Literature I unless you've taken the **prerequisite,** Spanish III.

b. Do you think it was right for Kathy to tell Joel that his quitting smoking was a **prerequisite** for their marriage?

10 **recession**
(ri-sesh'-ən)
-noun

a. Some restaurants offer special discounts during periods of **recession,** to try to attract more business.

b. The department store laid off twenty workers during the **recession,** but it rehired them when business improved.

Matching Words and Definitions

Check your understanding of the ten words by matching each word with its definition. Look back at the sentences in "Ten Words in Context" as needed to decide on the meaning of each word.

_____	1. **concurrent**	a.	to make up; be the parts of
_____	2. **confiscate**	b.	to fail do something required
_____	3. **constitute**	c.	most common or noticeable
_____	4. **decipher**	d.	something required beforehand
_____	5. **default**	e.	to take or seize with authority
_____	6. **hypothetical**	f.	to interpret or read (something confusing or hard to make out)
_____	7. **nominal**	g.	slight; very small compared to what might be expected
_____	8. **predominant**	h.	happening or existing at the same time
_____	9. **prerequisite**	i.	a temporary decline in business
_____	10. **recession**	j.	supposed for the sake of argument or examination; based on something assumed for the sake of argument; make-believe

CAUTION: Do not go any further until you are sure the above answers are correct. If you have studied the "Ten Words in Context," you will know how to match each word. Then you can use the matches to help you in the following practices. Your goal is to reach a point where you don't need to check definitions at all.

➢*Sentence Check 1*

Complete each sentence below with the most suitable word from the box. Use each word once.

concurrent	**confiscate**	**constitute**	**decipher**	**default**
hypothetical	**nominal**	**predominant**	**prerequisite**	**recession**

1. The ____________________ clothing style in our high schools is jeans and T-shirts.
2. Although the two robberies were ____________________, one man had planned them both.
3. One hundred senators and 435 members of the House of Representatives ____________________ the United States Congress.
4. A ____________________ for taking the driver-education class is passing a written test on the driving laws.
5. The town library charges only a ____________________ fine for late books but a higher fine for late videotapes.
6. Derek has such terrible handwriting that his wife couldn't ____________________ his message saying she should meet him at the restaurant.
7. The town went into a ____________________ when the shoe factory closed because the laid-off workers had no money to spend in local businesses.
8. The phone company refused to install a phone in Glen's new apartment because he had ________________(e)d in paying a bill on his last account.
9. In 1988, the United States government tried to seize any boat carrying drugs. The Coast Guard even ____________________(e)d a yacht carrying less than a tenth of an ounce of marijuana.
10. To teach young children safety, many parents ask them ____________________ questions, such as "What would you do if a stranger asked you to go for a ride in a car?"

Now check your answers to these questions by turning to page 164. Going over the answers carefully will help you prepare for the next two checks, for which answers are not given.

➢Sentence Check 2

Complete each sentence below with two words from the box. Use each word once.

concurrent	**confiscate**	**constitute**	**decipher**	**default**
hypothetical	**nominal**	**predominant**	**prerequisite**	**recession**

1-2. In the summer, local children can sign up for art or music lessons for the __________ fee of $3. It's impossible to take both, though, since the classes will be __________.

3-4. Although cancer and heart disease __________ the leading threats to life in the U.S., car accidents are the __________ cause of death for teenagers.

5-6. "It seems as if a degree in accounting is a __________ for understanding our tax laws," said Ken. "Who else can really __________ the tax codes?"

7-8. The small print for my farm mortgage loan stated that if I should __________ on payments, the bank had the right to __________ the farm.

9-10. When Ms. Howe was being interviewed for the job of store manager, the regional manager said, "Here is a __________ question. What would you do to increase sales if our business were in a __________?"

➤*Final Check:* Money Problems

Here is a final opportunity for you to strengthen your knowledge of the ten words. First read the following passage carefully. Then fill in each blank with a word from the box at the top of this page. (Context clues will help you figure out which word goes in which blank.) Use each word once.

"My car has been stolen!" My neighbor, Martha, ran into my house crying and angry. "I saw them take it."

I called the police for her, and she told an officer the license number and car model. "The (1)__________ color of the car is brown," she added, "but it has a black roof. I saw two men steal it. They just towed it away."

"You saw them tow it?" the officer asked. "Have you (2)__________(e)d in paying your car loan?"

"What do you mean?" Martha asked.

"If you haven't been making your payments, the bank or dealer has the right to (3)__________ the car."

Martha admitted that she hadn't paid her loan in three months. Later she told me she'd gotten notices in the mail but threw them away because their language was too complicated to (4)__________. She also said she was having money problems. (5)__________ with the car loan was a big home improvement loan. She also had five credit-card bills and regular living expenses to pay. To top it all off, her income was down because the neighborhood her beauty parlor was in was suffering a (6)__________. She was about $12,000 in debt.

At my suggestion, Martha visited a debt counselor who helped her develop a plan to pay her bills. The only (7)__________s for receiving this free service were a regular job and a willingness to pay one's debts in full. The counselor told her what would (8)__________ a reasonable budget, based on her income and expenses. They then wrote to the companies she owed to arrange to pay a (9)__________ amount each month until the whole debt was paid. They also discussed what she would do in several (10)__________ situations, such as if her refrigerator died or her income changed.

Now, Martha is getting back on her feet again—in more ways than one, since she never got the car back.

SCORES: Sentence Check 2 ______% Final Check ______%

Enter your scores above and in the vocabulary performance chart on the inside back cover of the book.

CHAPTER

10

Previewing the Words

Find out how many of the ten words in this chapter you already know. Try to complete each sentence with the most suitable word from the list below. Use each word once.

Leave a sentence blank rather than guessing at an answer. Your purpose here is just to get a sense of the ten words and what you may know about them.

degenerate	**implausible**	**incoherent**	**intercede**	**intricate**
sanctuary	**scrutiny**	**sinister**	**suffice**	**vulnerable**

1. The class discussion on abortion soon ____________________(e)d into a shouting match.
2. Because they tend to have brittle bones, the elderly are ____________________ to fractures.
3. It's ____________________ that a college student could party every night and still make the dean's list.
4. In the movie, a mad scientist thought up the ____________________ scheme of releasing a deadly virus. His evil plot failed when he died from the virus himself.
5. Ken's cartoons ____________________ for the school newspaper, but they wouldn't be good enough for the city papers.
6. My brother talks a lot in his sleep, but he's so ____________________ that we can never figure out what he's saying.
7. Federal agents kept the house of the suspected terrorists under ____________________ for weeks, but no unusual behavior was observed.
8. My bedroom is a(n) ____________________ from the constant noises of the television and stereo throughout our apartment.
9. At the concert, I sat behind a woman with a(n) ____________________ hairstyle. Numerous intertwined braids wound about the back of her head.
10. Ever since Sandy's parents divorced, they have expected her to ____________________ in their petty disagreements, which they refuse to work out on their own.

Now check your answers by turning to page 164. Fix any mistakes and fill in any blank spaces by writing in the correct answers. By doing so, you will complete this introduction to the ten words.

You're now ready to strengthen your knowledge of the words you already know and to master the words you're only half sure of, or don't know at all. Turn to the next page.

Ten Words in Context

Figure out the meanings of the following ten words by looking *closely and carefully* at the context in which the words appear. Doing so will prepare you for the matching test and practices on the two pages that follow.

1 degenerate (di-jen'-ər-āt') *-verb*

a. Mr. Freedman's family was called to the nursing home when the old man's condition began to **degenerate**.

b. Mel's relationship with his parents **degenerated** when he dropped out of school and became a bartender.

2 implausible (im-plô'-zə-bəl) *-adjective*

a. As **implausible** as it may sound, Southern Florida sometimes does get snow.

b. Insurance companies hear such **implausible** excuses for auto accidents as "I hit the telephone pole when I was blinded by the lights of a flying saucer."

3 incoherent (in'-kō-hîr'-ənt) *-adjective*

a. If Mitch drinks much more, he'll become completely **incoherent**. His slurred speech is already difficult to understand.

b. In a terrible nightmare, a huge red spider is about to leap on my husband, but my warning is so **incoherent** that he doesn't understand me.

4 intercede (in'-tər-sēd') *-verb*

a. It's hard for parents to know when to **intercede** in their children's quarrels and when to let the children settle things themselves.

b. A negotiator was hired to **intercede** between the management of the match-book factory and the striking workers.

5 intricate (in'-tri-kit) *-adjective*

a. *War and Peace* is a long, **intricate** novel that weaves together the detailed life stories of many individuals.

b. It's amazing to see the **intricate** gold and silver jewelry that ancient Indians made with only simple tools. It obviously required great patience and skill to create such complex ornaments.

6 sanctuary (sangk'-cho͞o-er'-ē) *-noun*

a. Old, unused trains in Grand Central Station serve as a nighttime **sanctuary** for some of New York City's homeless.

b. When the houseful of children becomes too noisy, Ned finds the laundry room to be a **sanctuary**, a place where he can read in quiet.

7 scrutiny (skro͞ot'-ən-ē) *-noun*

a. Store security guards keep people with large bags under careful **scrutiny**, since the bags may be used to shoplift.

b. Before being published, a book comes under the **scrutiny** of a proofreader, who examines it for grammar and spelling errors.

8 sinister (sin'-is-ter) *-adjective*

a. Actor Edward G. Robinson often played such **sinister** characters as gangsters and Nazi spies.

b. The novel *Rosemary's Baby* concerns the **sinister** plans of a group of devil-worshippers.

9 suffice (sə-fīs') *-verb*

a. The amount of research you've done may **suffice** for a high school term paper, but not for a college one.

b. The lift I get from attending the mid-winter flower show will have to **suffice** until springtime.

10 vulnerable (vul'-nər-ə-bəl) *-adjective*

a. Homes in heavily wooded areas are especially **vulnerable** to termites.

b. Alligators are most **vulnerable** in their soft underbellies.

Matching Words and Definitions

Check your understanding of the ten words by matching each word with its definition. Look back at the sentences in "Ten Words in Context" as needed to decide on the meaning of each word.

_____	1. **degenerate**	a. having many parts arranged in a complicated way; complex
_____	2. **implausible**	b. to be enough; be good enough
_____	3. **incoherent**	c. to worsen; deteriorate
_____	4. **intercede**	d. a place of safety, protection, or relief
_____	5. **intricate**	e. to come between in order to produce agreement; mediate
_____	6. **sanctuary**	f. open to injury or harm; sensitive; susceptible
_____	7. **scrutiny**	g. difficult to believe
_____	8. **sinister**	h. evil; wicked
_____	9. **suffice**	i. close inspection; careful examination
_____	10. **vulnerable**	j. not connected in an orderly, logical manner; unable to speak in an orderly, logical way

CAUTION: Do not go any further until you are sure the above answers are correct. If you have studied the "Ten Words in Context," you will know how to match each word. Then you can use the matches to help you in the following practices. Your goal is to reach a point where you don't need to check definitions at all.

➢Sentence Check 1

Complete each sentence below with the most suitable word from the box. Use each word once.

degenerate	**implausible**	**incoherent**	**intercede**	**intricate**
sanctuary	**scrutiny**	**sinister**	**suffice**	**vulnerable**

1. The leftover meatloaf will ____________________ for tomorrow's lunch.
2. The Joker's name is misleading, for he's a(n) ____________________ man who takes pleasure in doing evil.
3. People who live in big cities are more ____________________ to muggings than are residents of small towns.
4. The leaves outside the window created a(n) ____________________ lacy shadow on my bedroom wall.
5. Although it seems ____________________, the seemingly dead desert really does blossom after a rainstorm.
6. People who open their home as a ____________________ to an escaped convict may face criminal charges themselves.
7. My husband was so upset that he was ____________________. It wasn't until he calmed down that I understood he had been fired.
8. Unclaimed bags at airports undergo careful ____________________ by security officers watching for drugs or explosives.
9. When I don't have company over, my apartment tends to ____________________ into a jumble of papers, clothes, and school supplies.
10. When Dad informed my little sister that she had to be home from her date no later than 10 o'clock, Mom ____________________(e)d and got her a midnight curfew.

Now check your answers to these questions by turning to page 164. Going over the answers carefully will help you prepare for the next two checks, for which answers are not given.

➤ *Sentence Check 2*

Complete each sentence below with two words from the box. Use each word once.

degenerate	**implausible**	**incoherent**	**intercede**	**intricate**
sanctuary	**scrutiny**	**sinister**	**suffice**	**vulnerable**

1-2. Birds feel ____________ to attack when they are out in the open. To attract them to your birdfeeder, put it near a ____________ of trees and large bushes.

3-4. To get into the party, Mitch made up a(n) ____________ story about having lost our invitations in a fire. Surprisingly, the unlikely tale ____________(e)d to get us in.

5-6. When a complicated musical piece is played by a talented orchestra, audiences can appreciate its ____________ structure. But when poor musicians try the piece, it ____________s into nothing more than noise.

7-8. The bank clerk had been so frightened by the ____________ appearance of the armed man in a ski mask that her report of the event was ____________. Only after she calmed down did the police fully understand her story.

9-10. The children's eager ____________ of the carefully arranged candies and cookies brought a warning from their mother: "Look, but don't touch!" However, their grandmother ____________(e)d and convinced their mother to let them take a few.

➤ *Final Check:* The New French Employee

Here is a final opportunity for you to strengthen your knowledge of the ten words. First read the following passage carefully. Then fill in each blank with a word from the box at the top of this page. (Context clues will help you figure out which word goes in which blank.) Use each word once.

One summer, Nan worked in a factory with an employee recently arrived from France, a young man named Jean-Louis. He spoke little English, but Nan's basic French (1)____________(e)d for simple conversations and helpful translations.

However, one day when she was called to the foreman's office, she wished she knew no French at all. FBI agents were there with Jean-Louis. After explaining that Jean-Louis may have been more (2)____________ than the innocent young man he appeared to be, the foreman left her there to translate for the agents. The agents said Jean-Louis had been on the run since several jewel thefts in France. Nan struggled to translate their questions, which were often too (3)____________ for her limited vocabulary. At times, she became so nervous that her speech was nearly (4)____________. When the message got across, Jean-Louis claimed he was being mistaken for his no-good twin brother, a story the angry FBI agents found (5)____________. The conversation soon (6)____________d until everyone was shouting at poor Nan. When her boss heard the racket, he (7)____________d and got the agents to excuse her.

Nan then went to the ladies' room, a (8)____________ from the agents and Jean-Louis, should they try to find her. After they left, she calmed down and went back to work. But she felt (9)____________ for days as she wondered if she were under the (10)____________ of jewel thieves who might blame her for Jean-Louis' arrest.

SCORES: Sentence Check 2 ________% Final Check ________%

Enter your scores above and in the vocabulary performance chart on the inside back cover of the book.

CHAPTER 11

Previewing the Words

Find out how many of the ten words in this chapter you already know. Try to complete each sentence with the most suitable word from the list below. Use each word once.

Leave a sentence blank rather than guessing at an answer. Your purpose here is just to get a sense of the ten words and what you may know about them.

blatant	**blight**	**contrive**	**garble**	**gaunt**
gloat	**immaculate**	**plagiarism**	**qualm**	**retaliate**

1. Let's ________________ a way to get backstage to see Michael Jackson.
2. My twin cousins are not identical. Don is short and chubby, and Henry is tall and ________________.
3. Trash is a(n) ________________ on this neighborhood. The streets and sidewalks are filthy.
4. A good scrubbing with baking soda got my tea-stained mug ________________.
5. I no longer feel any ________________s about the times I skipped high school to go to the movies.
6. My daughter ________________(e)d Alex's message so badly that I went to meet him at the wrong place and time.
7. The boy's dislike of the food was all too ________________. He told the hostess it tasted "like burnt dirt."
8. When Mary told about Flo's secret love affair, Flo ________________(e)d by telling their friends about Mary's affair.
9. "It's bad enough that you always beat me at bowling," one player told the other. "Then when you ________________, you hurt my pride again."
10. Not only was Tyler wrong to commit ________________, but he was also foolish to choose to copy into his report parts of the class textbook.

Now check your answers by turning to page 164. Fix any mistakes and fill in any blank spaces by writing in the correct answers. By doing so, you will complete this introduction to the ten words.

You're now ready to strengthen your knowledge of the words you already know and to master the words you're only half sure of, or don't know at all. Turn to the next page.

Ten Words in Context

Figure out the meanings of the following ten words by looking *closely and carefully* at the context in which the words appear. Doing so will prepare you for the matching test and practices on the two pages that follow.

1 **blatant**
(blā'-tənt)
-adjective

a. Scott's smoking habit is **blatant**. His clothes smell of smoke, and nicotine has stained his fingers.

b. The company's disregard of the environment is **blatant**. It makes no effort to stop polluting coastal waters with garbage.

2 **blight**
(blīt)
-noun

a. Nothing has hurt our country more than the **blight** of drugs.

b. Is TV mainly a **blight** that dulls minds or a valuable source of information?

3 **contrive**
(kən-trīv')
-verb

a. My eight-year-old son can write a book titled *101 Ways I Have **Contrived** to Stay Up Past My Bedtime*.

b. Jill has to **contrive** a way to get a day off from work for her friend's wedding. She's already used up her vacation time.

4 **garble**
(gar'-bəl)
-verb

a. The typesetter accidentally **garbled** the newspaper story, giving the reader only a mixed-up article.

b. The company had **garbled** the bike's assembly instructions so badly that we were constantly confused about which step to do next.

5 **gaunt**
(gônt)
-adjective

a. Abraham Lincoln's beard made his **gaunt** face look more full.

b. Sharon's eating disorder has made her so **gaunt** that she looks like a walking skeleton.

6 **gloat**
(glōt)
-verb

a. The coach told his team, "There's only one thing worse than a sore loser, and that's a mean winner. Don't **gloat**."

b. Neil's sister always tattles on him and then **gloats** when he's punished.

7 **immaculate**
(i-mak'-yə-lit)
-adjective

a. It's amazing that Carolyn always appears **immaculate**, yet her apartment often seems very dirty.

b. Don't expect a child to come home from a birthday party with **immaculate** clothing.

8 **plagiarism**
(plā'-jə-riz'-əm)
-noun

a. When the author saw a movie with the same plot as one of her novels, she sued for **plagiarism**.

b. The teacher warned her students that using an author's exact words as one's own is **plagiarism**.

9 **qualm**
(kwom)
-noun

a. Larry had no **qualms** about stealing from the cafeteria cash register. He didn't even feel guilty when someone else was blamed.

b. After hiding Lori's bike as an April Fool's joke, I began to have **qualms**. What if she thought it was stolen and called the police?

10 **retaliate**
(ri-tal'-ē-āt')
-verb

a. When I broke my sister's Prince record, she **retaliated** by cutting the cord of my Sony Walkman earphones.

b. After the Baker brothers squirted some girls with soda, the girls **retaliated** by spraying the boys with cologne.

Matching Words and Definitions

Check your understanding of the ten words by matching each word with its definition. Look back at the sentences in "Ten Words in Context" as needed to decide on the meaning of each word.

____	1. **blatant**	a. a feeling of discomfort about a point of conscience, honor, or what is proper
____	2. **blight**	b. to mix up or confuse (as a story or message); scramble
____	3. **contrive**	c. to express or feel spiteful pleasure or self-satisfaction
____	4. **garble**	d. something that weakens, damages, or destroys
____	5. **gaunt**	e. taking someone else's writings or ideas and using them as one's own
____	6. **gloat**	f. to plan cleverly; think up
____	7. **immaculate**	g. to return injury for an injury; pay back
____	8. **plagiarism**	h. very obvious, often offensively so
____	9. **qualm**	i. perfectly clean
____	10. **retaliate**	j. thin and bony

CAUTION: Do not go any further until you are sure the above answers are correct. If you have studied the "Ten Words in Context," you will know how to match each word. Then you can use the matches to help you in the following practices. Your goal is to reach a point where you don't need to check definitions at all.

➢ *Sentence Check 1*

Complete each sentence below with the most suitable word from the box. Use each word once.

blatant	**blight**	**contrive**	**garble**	**gaunt**
gloat	**immaculate**	**plagiarism**	**qualm**	**retaliate**

1. A(n) ____________ house may be a sign that someone has nothing better to do than clean.
2. Child abuse is an awful ____________ on the physical and mental health of our youth.
3. My aunt refuses to drive Mr. Elson to bingo because he ____________s so much when he wins, which is often.
4. The F's and D's on my brother's report card are ____________ evidence of how little he has studied this term.
5. Wally still hopes to ____________ a way to get Rita to go out with him, even though she's refused him four times.
6. I bought an answering machine because my children have ____________(e)d several important phone messages.
7. Every time the Hatfields harmed the McCoys, the McCoys would ____________, so the feud went on for years.
8. After being lost at sea for nine days, the men were frighteningly ____________, but after their rescue they put on weight rapidly.
9. I would feel guilty if I called in sick when I wasn't, but no one else in the office seems to have any ____________s about doing that.
10. Mark Twain jokingly claimed that charges of ____________ were ridiculous because no one can be completely original. He wrote, "We mortals can't create—we can only copy."

Now check your answers to these questions by turning to page 164. Going over the answers carefully will help you prepare for the next two checks, for which answers are not given.

➢Sentence Check 2

Complete each sentence below with two words from the box. Use each word once.

blatant	**blight**	**contrive**	**garble**	**gaunt**
gloat	**immaculate**	**plagiarism**	**qualm**	**retaliate**

1-2. The living room looked __________ except for a lump under the carpet, a __________ sign that my son had taken a shortcut in cleaning up.

3-4. After the bully struck him, Jules wanted to __________ by throwing a rock, but he had __________s about doing anything so dangerous.

5-6. My little girl was so __________ after her illness that I carefully __________(e)d fattening meals that were sure to arouse her appetite.

7-8. "At least I know you aren't guilty of __________," said my teacher. "Nobody else would have __________(e)d the report so badly that it's impossible to follow."

9-10. Willie is a __________ on the school's good name. Not only does he start fights with opposing players on the basketball court, but he also __________s after he's benched, as if he's proud of causing trouble.

➢*Final Check:* A Cruel Teacher

Here is a final opportunity for you to strengthen your knowledge of the ten words. First read the following passage carefully. Then fill in each blank with a word from the box at the top of this page. (Context clues will help you figure out which word goes in which blank.) Use each word once.

It has been twenty years since I was in Mr. Brill's tenth grade biology class, but I still get nervous thinking about it. Mr. Brill was a tall, (1)__________ man who resembled the skeleton at the back of the room. His meanness was (2)__________. He would call on the shyest kids to answer the most difficult questions, and when they nervously (3)__________(e)d their answers, he would clearly (4)__________. He seemed to (5)__________ situations just to make us miserable. For example, if our fingernails were not (6)__________, we were sent out of class. As if we needed clean hands to dissect a frog! One time I worked extremely hard on a paper for class, but he accused me of (7)__________. He said I must have copied it because I was too dumb to write anything that good. Without a (8)__________, he gave me an F. All of us students would imagine ways to get even with him, but we were too afraid to (9)__________. In all these years since, I've never met a person who was such a (10)__________ on the personal growth of students.

SCORES: Sentence Check 2 ________% Final Check ________%

Enter your scores above and in the vocabulary performance chart on the inside back cover of the book.

CHAPTER

12

Previewing the Word Parts

Common word parts—also known as *prefixes, suffixes,* and *roots*—are used in forming many words in English. This page will introduce you to ten common word parts.

Try to match each word part on the left with its definition on the right.Use the words in parentheses as hints to help you guess the meanings. If you can't decide on an answer, leave the space blank. Your purpose here is just to get a sense of the ten word parts and what you may know about them. (You'll have another chance to try this exercise after considering the word parts in context.)

	Word Parts	Definitions
_____	1. **-ate** (irritate, fascinate)	a. bend
_____	2. **bio-** (biology, biography)	b. half; partly
_____	3. **claim, clam** (claim, exclamation)	c. life
_____	4. **fin** (final, refinish)	d. father
_____	5. **flex, flect** (reflex, reflect)	e. cause to become
_____	6. **forc, fort** (force, effort)	f. in the direction of
_____	7. **hum** (humanity, humane)	g. declare; cry out
_____	8. **pater, patri-** (paternity, patriot)	h. strong
_____	9. **semi-** (semifinalist, semicircle)	i. person; having to do with people
_____	10. **-ward** (upward, homeward)	j. end

Now go on to "Ten Word Parts in Context" on the next page. Working through this chapter will help you to strengthen your knowledge of the word parts you already know and to master the word parts you're only half sure of, or don't know at all.

Keep in mind that learning word parts can pay several dividends. Word parts can help with the spelling and pronunciation of many words. They can also help you to unlock the meanings of unfamiliar words.

Ten Word Parts in Context

Figure out the meanings of the following ten word parts by looking *closely and carefully* at the context in which they appear. Doing so will prepare you for the matching test and practices on the two pages that follow.

1 **-ate**

a. Teachers often find it difficult to **motivate** students to learn eagerly.

b. The TV history series **fascinated** viewers with such details as a 17th-century English children's hospital that gave each child two gallons of beer per week.

2 **bio-**

a. Helen Keller wrote a touching **autobiography** titled *The Story of My Life*.

b. **Biology** is the science of living things, both plant and animal.

3 **claim, clam**

a. In 1965, American movie critics **acclaimed** *The Sound of Music* as the best picture of the year.

b. The **exclamation** point emphasizes passionate, sudden, and surprised outcries.

4 **fin**

a. The **final** word in many prayers is *amen*, which means "May it be so."

b. All the dancers who had appeared in the recital came back on stage for the **finale**, a tap dance performed to "Goodnight, Irene."

5 **flex, flect**

a. Gymnasts must be extremely **flexible** so that they can bend their bodies into many positions.

b. When they enter church, Catholics **genuflect**—that is, they bend one knee, as a sign of worship.

6 **forc, fort**

a. The burglar **forcibly** entered the home by breaking the kitchen window.

b. The children made a high wall of pressed snow to **fortify** themselves against a snowball attack by the kids across the street.

7 **hum**

a. "We have done all that is **humanly** possible to save your grandmother's life," said the doctor.

b. A resident of the shelter for the homeless complained, "The treatment here is not **humane**. We want to be treated like people, not objects."

8 **pater, patri-**

a. Kara filed a **paternity** suit against Mike, to prove he was her baby's father.

b. **Patriotism** was so strong that soldiers willingly risked their lives to defend their fatherland.

9 **semi-**

a. Last night, the thin curve of moon looked like a silver **semicircle**.

b. I use **semisweet** chocolate in my frosting to keep it from being too bitter or too sweet.

10 **-ward**

a. Everyone at the fair looked **skyward** in horror as the colorful hot-air balloon exploded.

b. The children tried walking to school **backward** but gave up before even reaching the end of their block.

Matching Word Parts and Definitions

Check your understanding of the ten word parts by matching each with its definition. See also the suggestions on page 4.

_____	1. **-ate**	a. bend*
_____	2. **bio-**	b. half; partly
_____	3. **claim, clam**	c. life
_____	4. **fin**	d. father
_____	5. **flex, flect**	e. cause to become
_____	6. **forc, fort**	f. in the direction of
_____	7. **hum**	g. declare; cry out
_____	8. **pater, patri-**	h. strong
_____	9. **semi-**	i. person; having to do with people
_____	10. **-ward**	j. end

**The first printing mistakenly contained the definition "many" here.*

CAUTION: Do not go any further until you are sure the above answers are correct. If you have studied the "Ten Word Parts in Context," you will know how to match each word part. Then you can use the matches to help you in the following practices. Your goal is to reach a point where you don't need to check definitions at all.

➢Sentence Check 1

Complete each partial word in the following sentences with a word part from the box. Use each word part only once. You may want to check off each word part as you use it.

-ate	**bio-**	**claim**	**fin**	**flex**
forc	**hum**	**patri-**	**semi-**	**-ward**

1. Little Jesse loudly (*ex . . . ed*) ____________________ that his father was the strongest man on the block.
2. A (*. . . rhythm*) ____________________ is any cycle of periodic changes in life, such as daily changes in body temperature.
3. The jury found the disturbed young man guilty of (*. . . cide*) ____________________, for shooting his father.
4. After a cold, rainy weekend of camping, the Boy Scouts were relieved to head (*home . . .*) ________________.
5. My mother was so (*in . . . ible*) ____________________ that she never once bent the rule and let me stay out past curfew.
6. The candidate's (*. . . eful*) ____________________ speech in favor of reduced military spending made a powerful impression on me.
7. Uncle Ken was in a (*. . . private*) ____________________ room in the hospital. The other man in the room had also suffered a heart attack.
8. We feared we would have to sit there for (*in . . . ity*) ____________________ listening to the principal's endless lecture about good manners.
9. Bishop Desmond Tutu of South Africa received the Nobel Peace Prize for his (*. . . anitarian*) ____________________ efforts to bring justice to his country's people.
10. In 1961, administrators of New York's Museum of Modern Art were (*humili . . . d*) ____________________ to learn that a painting had been displayed upside down for weeks.

Now check your answers to these questions by turning to page 164. Going over the answers carefully will help you prepare for the next two checks, for which answers are not given.

➢ *Sentence Check 2*

Complete each partial word in the sentences below with a word part from the box. Use each word part once. If there are two forms of a word part, use the *first* one for this practice.

-ate	**bio-**	**clam, claim**	**fin**	**flex**
forc, fort	**hum**	**pater-**	**semi-**	**-ward**

1-2. I looked (*down . . .*) ________________ and watched the doctor tap my knee to see if its (*re . . .*) ________________ was normal.

3-4. My boss, Mr. Kane, is (*. . . nal*) ________________. He (*en . . . es*) ________________ the rules in a fatherly way—firmly but kindly.

5-6. After the accident, my brother was (*. . . conscious*) ________________ for several hours. (*. . . ally*) ________________, around midnight, he became fully alert.

7-8. When the teacher asked students to write a (*. . . graphy*) ________________, she meant the life story of a (*. . . an*) ________________. But Harry wrote about Tarzan, his pet snake.

9-10. In 1863, Abraham Lincoln issued a (*pro . . . ation*) ________________ to free the slaves. But it would be almost 100 years after his announcement before real efforts were made to (*integr . . .*) ________________ black people into society's mainstream.

➢ *Final Check:* It's Never Too Late

Here is a final opportunity for you to strengthen your knowledge of the ten word parts. First read the following passage carefully. Then complete each partial word in the parentheses below with a word part from the box at the top of this page. If there are two forms of a word part, use the *second* one in this practice. Context clues will help you figure out which word part goes in which blank. Use each word part once.

I almost fell out of my chair last night when my father (*pro . . . ed*) (1)________________, "I quit my job today. I'm going to college." He says he's tired of his (*. . . skilled*) (2)________________ work in a factory and wants a job that requires more skill and training. Both of my (*. . . nal*) (3)________________ grandparents died when Dad was a child, so he and his brothers were forced to quit school early to work. Dad finished high school at night. Now, he says, he is going to (*educ . . .*) (4)________________ himself further. He still isn't sure what his major will be, but he has always liked science. He definitely wants to take a (*. . . logy*) (5)________________ course because all living things interest him. He'd like to focus his (*ef . . . s*) (6)________________ in a field that benefits (*. . . anity*) (7)________________, so he's considering physical therapy. He's also thinking about nursing. Most men of his generation think of nursing as women's work, so Dad's interest in this field shows me he is more (*. . . ible*) (8)________________ in his thinking than I ever realized. Whatever his choice, he is looking (*for . . .*) (9)________________ to classes with great enthusiasm. I know that when he (*. . . ishes*) (10)________________ his schooling, no one will be prouder of him than I already am.

SCORES: Sentence Check 2 ________% Final Check ________%

Enter your scores above and in the vocabulary performance chart on the inside back cover of the book.

UNIT TWO: Test 1

PART A

Choose the word that best completes each sentence and write it in the space provided.

	Choices	Sentence
1.	**incoherent** **immaculate** **nocturnal** **obstacle**	According to legend, vampires are ____________________ creatures who fear daylight.
2.	**rehabilitate** **contrive** **ponder** **exemplify**	The counseling program to __________________ addicts includes job training.
3.	**retaliate** **degenerate** **confiscate** **decipher**	Unless figure skaters practice regularly, their skills will __________________.
4.	**implausible** **gaunt** **mobile** **nominal**	It may sound __________________, but a camel can drink 25 gallons of water at a time.
5.	**flagrant** **hypothetical** **incoherent** **concurrent**	Movie subtitles should be __________________ with the spoken words they are translating.
6.	**sinister** **immaculate** **incoherent** **intricate**	Even the most _________________ people have microscopic creatures clinging to their hair.
7.	**blight** **plagiarism** **qualm** **prerequisite**	Measles remains a serious ________________ worldwide, killing over a million people each year.
8.	**discern** **garble** **dispatch** **default**	The Peace Corps continues to _________________ American volunteers to live and work in developing nations.
9.	**prerequisite** **sanctuary** **calamity** **qualm**	The sinking of the ship *Titanic*, which struck an iceberg, was a _________________ in which nearly 1,600 people died.
10.	**suffice** **attest** **intercede** **default**	The government student loan program is in serious trouble because many students _________________ on their payments.

11. **flagrant** **hypothetical** **conventional** **immaculate**

In a 1901 race across New Jersey, drivers traveling up to 30 miles an hour were arrested for their _______________ disregard of the speed limit, which was 8 miles an hour.

12. **vulnerable** **nominal** **mobile** **comprehensive**

Although our college library charges only a _______________ fee to use a typewriter or computer, I don't think it should charge students any fee at all.

13. **sanctuary** **attribute** **enigma** **recession**

The thousands of oak leaves that covered the ground in a Scottish town in 1889 remain a(n) _______________. The nearest oak trees were eight miles away.

PART B

Circle **C** if the italicized word is used **correctly**. Circle **I** if the word is used **incorrectly**.

C **I** 14. Ocean plants *constitute* about 85 percent of all the greenery on Earth.

C **I** 15. Jesse Jackson is often praised for his *garbled* speeches.

C **I** 16. It's healthier to stay the same weight than to *fluctuate* up and down.

C **I** 17. Elise enjoys *intricate* jigsaw puzzles, such as those of detailed flower displays.

C **I** 18. Vince *gloated* when he learned his girlfriend was moving to another state.

C **I** 19. Every day, people *enhance* the tropical rainforests by destroying some 20,000 acres.

C **I** 20. A *prerequisite* for getting the health insurance policy is a satisfactory exam by a company physician.

C **I** 21. Adult dolphins often form a protective ring around young ones to keep them *vulnerable* from attack.

C **I** 22. Each year, thousands of Americans who think themselves too *gaunt* have some fat surgically removed.

C **I** 23. Felix's teacher suspected him of *plagiarism* because his last paper was written so much better than his others.

C **I** 24. Before leaving for Antarctica, a team of explorers packed such *conventional* equipment as twenty hula hoops.

C **I** 25. In a *blatant* case of injustice, a wealthy and influential North Carolina man received no punishment when he was caught selling cocaine.

SCORE: (Number correct) ________ x 4 = ________ %

Enter your scores above and in the vocabulary performance chart on the inside back cover of the book.

UNIT TWO: Test 2

PART A

Complete each sentence with a word from the box. Use each word once.

attribute	**comprehensive**	**confiscate**	**decipher**
exemplify	**orient**	**persevere**	**qualm**
recession	**retaliate**	**scrutiny**	**sinister**
suffice			

1. Marathon runners must ___________________ beyond the point at which they start to feel pain.
2. People who can't read must ___________________ themselves in a city by relating to familiar places, not signs.
3. A hint to my daughter to take out the garbage won't ___________________. She needs to be told to do so.
4. I don't know who sent me the birthday card because I couldn't ______________________ the signature.
5. A shortage of a single product, such as sugar, could cause a(n) ___________________ in several industries.
6. Don't buy a used car unless you examine it closely and also have a mechanic give it careful ___________________.
7. The Russian Communists, who opposed private wealth, ___________________(e)d the property of wealthy landowners.
8. In some religions, gods and goddesses represent various human ___________________s, such as strength, beauty, and wisdom.
9. Through the years, people with ___________________s about having cheated on their income taxes have sent gifts of money to the IRS.
10. The Rumanian people ____________________(e)d against their Communist dictator, who had ordered mass murders, by executing him.
11. One of the oddest ___________________ plots of all time was the one thought up by a wealthy Frenchman. He fed his victims rich foods until they died of overeating.
12. To get a bachelor's degree from some universities, students must take a ___________________ exam that tests their overall knowledge of their major field.
13. Lightning bolts, which travel at millions of miles an hour and produce five times the heat of the sun's surface, ___________________ Nature's tremendous energy.

PART B

Circle C if the italicized word is used **correctly**. Circle I if the word is used **incorrectly**.

C I 14. The Olympic swimmer *pondered* across the pool in record time.

C I 15. It's hard to *discern* the differences between the Fields twins.

C I 16. The man *attested* to his crime, pleading innocent to all charges.

C I 17. The *turmoil* of a smooth, clear lake always makes me feel a similar peace.

C I 18. Our veterinarian has a *mobile* office, a fully equipped van which she drives to patients' homes.

C I 19. When Tammy tried to *intercede* between two friends who were angry with each other, they became angry at her.

C I 20. Farm *Sanctuary* offers a safe, comfortable home to farm animals who have been rescued from cruel conditions.

C I 21. In the *hypothetical* case of Dr. Martin Luther King, Jr., nonviolence was combined with aggressive action.

C I 22. The Democratic and Republican parties are *predominant* in the U.S., but other parties are also represented on our ballots.

C I 23. Some critics think Abraham Lincoln was a literary genius because of the powerful, *incoherent* speeches he wrote.

C I 24. In my dreams, I *venture* to perform feats that I would never dare when awake, such as leaping from roof to roof down a row of houses.

C I 25. Shortly before his birthday, Bruce *contrived* to get his parents to walk past the toy store so that he could point out the Nintendo game displayed in the window.

SCORE: (Number correct) ________ x 4 = ________ %

Enter your scores above and in the vocabulary performance chart on the inside back cover of the book.

UNIT TWO: Test 3

PART A

Complete each sentence in a way that clearly shows you understand the meaning of the boldfaced word. Take a minute to plan your answer before you write.

Example: Being **nocturnal** animals, raccoons ___*raid our garbage cans only at night.*___

1. The news reported a **calamity** in which ________________________________

____

2. Ray **dispatched** his younger brother ________________________________

____

3. When I take a bath, I often **ponder** ________________________________

____

4. When Carolyn saw her essay grade, she **gloated,** saying, "________________________________

____

5. My apartment is so **immaculate** that ________________________________

____

6. Three personal **attributes** that I possess are ________________________________

____

7. The novel's main character is a **sinister** doctor who ________________________________

____

8. When my neighbor cut lilacs off my bush for her home, I **retaliated** by ________________________________

____

9. One advantage of a **mobile** library might be ________________________________

____

10. I plan to **persevere** in ________________________________

____

PART B

After each boldfaced word are a *synonym* (a word that means the same as the boldfaced word), an *antonym* (a word that means the opposite of the boldfaced word), and a word that is neither. Mark the antonym with an *A*.

Example:	**nominal**	_____ personal	_A_ enormous	_____ slight
11.	**confiscate**	_____ give	_____ seize	_____ combine
12.	**enhance**	_____ improve	_____ lead	_____ weaken
13.	**comprehensive**	_____ limited	_____ broad	_____ irregular
14.	**intricate**	_____ complicated	_____ musical	_____ simple
15.	**persevere**	_____ look	_____ stop	_____ persist

PART C

Use five of the following ten words in sentences. Make it clear that you know the meaning of the word you use. Feel free to use the past tense or plural form of a word.

blight	**decipher**	**fluctuate**	**implausible**	**predominant**
qualm	**rehabilitate**	**sanctuary**	**turmoil**	**vulnerable**

16. ______________________________

____

17. ______________________________

____

18. ______________________________

____

19. ______________________________

____

20. ______________________________

SCORE: (Number correct) ________ x 5 = ________ %

Enter your scores above and in the vocabulary performance chart on the inside back cover of the book.

UNIT TWO: Test 4 (Word Parts)

PART A

Listed in the left-hand column below are ten common word parts, along with words in which the parts are used. In each blank, write in the letter of the correct definition on the right.

	Word Parts		Definitions
____	1. **-ate**	motivate, liberate	a. father
____	2. **bio-**	biologist, biography	b. declare; cry out
____	3. **claim, clam**	exclaim, proclamation	c. half; partly
____	4. **fin**	final, finish	d. end
____	5. **flex, flect**	flexible, reflect	e. cause to become
____	6. **forc, fort**	force, effort	f. in the direction of
____	7. **hum**	humanity, humane	g. having to do with people
____	8. **pater, patri-**	paternal, patricide	h. strong
____	9. **semi-**	semicircle, semiprivate	i. bend
____	10. **-ward**	backward, skyward	j. life

PART B

Find the word part that correctly completes each word. Then write the full word in the blank space. Not every word part will be used.

-ate	**bio-**	**clam**	**fin**	**flex**
fort	**hum**	**patri-**	**semi-**	**-ward**

11. To (*activ . . .*) ____________________ yeast, put it in a warm liquid.

12. When I meditate, I focus (*in . . . ly*) ____________________ by mentally repeating a nonsense word.

13. In the 17th century, England (*. . . ified*) ____________________ its weakening wool trade by passing a law that all corpses must be buried in wool.

14. The French king Louis XIV's (*. . . al*) ____________________ words were to his servants: "Why do you weep? Did you think I was immortal?"

15. Why are robots often given a (*. . . anoid*) ____________________ appearance? Are we more comfortable with "smart" machines that resemble us?

PART C

Use your knowledge of word parts to determine the meaning of the boldfaced words. Circle the letter of each meaning.

16. The dining club is **semipublic**.

a. fully public b. partly public c. private

17. A **patriarchy** is a form of social organization in which families are headed by

a. the strongest. b. the oldest. c. a father.

18. My chemistry instructor also teaches **biochemistry**, which is the chemistry of

a. life processes. b. lakes. c. weather.

19. Albert Einstein **claimed** that his brain was his laboratory.

a. denied b. stated c. wished

20. The company I work for has decided to experiment with employee **flextime**.

a. longer work hours b. shorter work hours c. adjustable work hours

SCORE: (Number correct) _______ x 5 = _______ %

Enter your scores above and in the vocabulary performance chart on the inside back cover of the book.

Unit Three

CHAPTER

13

Previewing the Words

Find out how many of the ten words in this chapter you already know. Try to complete each sentence with the most suitable word from the list below. Use each word once.

Leave a sentence blank rather than guessing at an answer. Your purpose here is just to get a sense of the ten words and what you may know about them.

curtail	**devastate**	**digress**	**incentive**	**incorporate**
indispensable	**intermittent**	**rigor**	**squander**	**succumb**

1. My girlfriend is usually cheerful, but she experiences ________________ periods of depression.
2. The showing of our home movies was __________________(e)d when the projector broke halfway through.
3. Bert's grades were so poor because he ________________(e)d much of his time playing games in the arcade at the mall.
4. The insurance company offers the ________________ of a free vacation to salespeople who reach a certain sales figure.
5. The news that their young daughter had been on the plane that crashed ________________(e)d the Crains.
6. When you're writing a paper, a good dictionary is ________________ for checking the spelling and definitions of words.
7. The ________________s of highway construction work include working on hot days and constantly breathing in gas fumes.
8. Max is a strong-willed man. Once he makes up his mind to do something, I don't think he'll ________________ to temptation.
9. Since my brother and I live next door to each other, we've __________________(e)d our back yards into one big playground for our children.
10. The novel lost my interest whenever the author ________________(e)d from the plot to explain some of the customs of the period in which the story takes place.

Now check your answers by turning to page 164. Fix any mistakes and fill in any blank spaces by writing in the correct answers. By doing so, you will complete this introduction to the ten words.

You're now ready to strengthen your knowledge of the words you already know and to master the words you're only half sure of, or don't know at all. Turn to the next page.

Ten Words in Context

Figure out the meanings of the following ten words by looking *closely and carefully* at the context in which the words appear. Doing so will prepare you for the matching test and the practices on the two pages that follow.

1 curtail (kər-tāl') *-verb*

a. Upon hearing reports of a tornado, our boss **curtailed** the meeting so we all could go home early.

b. I need to **curtail** my volunteer activities so that I can spend more time earning money to pay back a loan.

2 devastate (dev'-əs-tāt') *-verb*

a. Learning that their son had been arrested for armed robbery **devastated** the Huttons.

b. Vera is so fond of Andy. She'll be **devastated** to hear he has cancer.

3 digress (di-gres') *-verb*

a. Professor Rubin never **digresses** during a lecture. Even his jokes relate to the day's topic.

b. I tried teaching my three-year-old his phone number, but we **digressed** to a discussion of whether Winnie the Pooh has a telephone.

4 incentive (in-sen'-tiv) *-noun*

a. "As an **incentive** to call now," said the TV salesman, "the first 500 callers will receive this genuine imitation-leather handbag!"

b. The thought of myself in a bathing suit next summer provides me with adequate **incentive** to exercise.

5 incorporate (in-kôr'-pər-āt') *-verb*

a. Jerry **incorporated** all of his favorite desserts into one: a chocolate-covered banana-cream pecan pie.

b. Since the number of young children has gone down in my neighborhood, the two elementary schools have been **incorporated** into one.

6 indispensable (in'-di-spen'-sə-bəl) *-adjective*

a. Because there's no bus or train service nearby, a car is **indispensable** in my neighborhood.

b. When you're broke, you find that many things you thought were **indispensable** were merely nice to have around.

7 intermittent (in'-tər-mit'-ənt) *-adjective*

a. You have to work steadily with your dog to train him well. **Intermittent** practice won't work.

b. Dora realized that weight loss would be **intermittent** when she dieted, so she didn't give up when the losses stopped and started.

8 rigor (rig'-ər) *-noun*

a. New Marines must go through the **rigors** of boot camp.

b. The **rigor** of working two part-time jobs while going to school proved too much for Joseph. Exhausted, he dropped both jobs.

9 squander (skwon'-dər) *-verb*

a. It's sad to see such a wonderful artist **squander** her talent designing labels for baked-bean cans.

b. The company lunchroom now closes promptly at one o'clock so that workers can't **squander** time on long lunch breaks.

10 succumb (sə-kum') *-verb*

a. Leah **succumbed** to her daughter's begging and bought her a pet lizard for her birthday.

b. Once the suspect was arrested, he quickly **succumbed** and confessed to stealing the car stereo.

Matching Words and Definitions

Check your understanding of the ten words by matching each word with its definition. Look back at the sentences in "Ten Words in Context" as needed to decide on the meaning of each word.

_____	1. **curtail**	a. to waste; spend or use up excessively or with no gain, need, or purpose
_____	2. **devastate**	b. to cut short; reduce
_____	3. **digress**	c. something that moves one to take action or work harder; encouragement
_____	4. **incentive**	d. to turn aside or stray, especially from the main topic in speaking or writing
_____	5. **incorporate**	e. great hardship or difficulty; harshness; severity
_____	6. **indispensable**	f. to upset; disappoint greatly
_____	7. **intermittent**	g. to give in; give up resisting
_____	8. **rigor**	h. necessary
_____	9. **squander**	i. to unite into a single whole; combine
_____	10. **succumb (to)**	j. starting and stopping from time to time; off-and-on

CAUTION: Do not go any further until you are sure the above answers are correct. If you have studied the "Ten Words in Context," you will know how to match each word. Then you can use the matches to help you in the following practices. Your goal is to reach a point where you don't need to check definitions at all.

➢*Sentence Check 1*

Complete each sentence below with the most suitable word from the box. Use each word once.

curtail	**devastate**	**digress**	**incentive**	**incorporate**
indispensable	**intermittent**	**rigor**	**squander**	**succumb**

1. ____________________ rain kept interrupting the ballgame.
2. The sight of her bandaged husband in an oxygen tent ____________________(e)d Claire.
3. Someone has managed to ____________________ a tomato and a potato into one plant.
4. A home computer and a telephone are ____________________ tools for many self-employed people.
5. Airlines offer "frequent flyer credits" toward free trips as ____________________s to people who fly often.
6. Many teenagers don't foresee such ____________________s of parenthood as staying up all night with a sick child.
7. By examining her last two months of spending, Coretta discovered that she ____________________(e)d money on too many expensive meals.
8. The man on the corner offered to sell me a watch, but he quickly ____________________(e)d his sales pitch when he saw a police officer approach.
9. Because our history teacher loved to gab, we often could get him to ____________________ from the lesson to talk about school athletics or school politics.
10. Carl resisted Lola's charms for months, thinking she was too young for him, but he finally ____________________(e)d and asked her out to dinner.

Now check your answers to these questions by turning to page 164. Going over the answers carefully will help you prepare for the next two checks, for which answers are not given.

➢Sentence Check 2

Complete each sentence below with two words from the box. Use each word once.

curtail	devastate	digress	incentive	incorporate
indispensable	intermittent	rigor	squander	succumb

1-2. Duane feels he ________________(e)d too many years in inactivity, so now he welcomes the ________________s of an exercise program.

3-4. The company decided to ________________ the construction of its new plant until the architects could decide on how to ________________ an employee gym into the new building.

5-6. My aunt has only ________________ success in quitting smoking. Every few months she ________________s to temptation, and then she has to quit all over again.

7-8. As Leo explained a failed business deal that once ________________(e)d him, he ________________(e)d into the even more interesting tale of his romance with Molly, his business partner.

9-10. The vitamin saleswoman offered me free samples, 90-day trials, and every other ________________ she could think of to get me to buy. Her sales pitch was so convincing that I was starting to believe her products were ________________ to my well-being.

➤*Final Check:* Learning to Study

Here is a final opportunity for you to strengthen your knowledge of the ten words. First read the following passage carefully. Then fill in each blank with a word from the box at the top of this page. (Context clues will help you figure out which word goes in which blank.) Use each word once.

Linda never had to work very hard to make good grades in high school. But it was different in college, where the (1)________________s of studying were greater. It was also much easier in college for Linda to (2)________________ time on dates and parties. She didn't realize how badly she was doing until she saw her mid-term grades, which (3)________________(e)d her. She knew she had to make some changes right away. As a(n) (4)________________ to study more, she tried studying with her friend Denise. But that didn't work; their conversation would (5)________________ from European history to personal topics, such as dates or favorite singers.

Linda decided she'd have to go it alone. She began to skip weekday parties and also to (6)________________ the time she spent talking with friends. She discovered that finding a good place to study was (7)________________ to her new study habits. In the silence of the library's third floor, there were no temptations to which she could (8)________________. At first, the improvement in Linda's grades was only (9)________________—A's and B's alternated with C's and D's. But little by little, she learned to (10)________________ a social life with serious study and get grades she was proud of.

SCORES: Sentence Check 2 ________%	Final Check ________%

Enter your scores above and in the vocabulary performance chart on the inside back cover of the book.

CHAPTER

14

Previewing the Words

Find out how many of the ten words in this chapter you already know. Try to complete each sentence with the most suitable word from the list below. Use each word once.

Leave a sentence blank rather than guessing at an answer. Your purpose here is just to get a sense of the ten words and what you may know about them.

alleviate	**benefactor**	**covert**	**cynic**	**demise**
infamous	**intrinsic**	**revulsion**	**speculate**	**virile**

1. I took some aspirin to ____________________ my pounding headache.
2. Knowing that his ____________________ could come at any time, Mack had his will made out.
3. Lassie has the qualities of loyalty and affection that seem ____________________ to all dogs.
4. The wealthy ____________________ who paid for the child's operation prefers to remain anonymous.
5. Filled with ____________________ by all the killings, I walked out in the middle of the horror movie.
6. Typhoid Mary is ____________________ for knowingly spreading typhoid by taking jobs that involved working with food.
7. The therapist asked Cassy to ____________________ on what might happen if she told Ralph her true feelings.
8. My brother likes to wear sleeveless "muscle shirts." He thinks they make him look more ____________________.
9. The public knew the woman as an international business leader. Only a few CIA officials knew her ____________________ role as an international spy.
10. George Bernard Shaw, unashamed of being a(n) ____________________, once said that people who do the right thing usually do so for the wrong reason.

Now check your answers by turning to page 164. Fix any mistakes and fill in any blank spaces by writing in the correct answers. By doing so, you will complete this introduction to the ten words.

You're now ready to strengthen your knowledge of the words you already know and to master the words you're only half sure of, or don't know at all. Turn to the next page.

Ten Words in Context

Figure out the meanings of the following ten words by looking *closely and carefully* at the context in which the words appear. Doing so will prepare you for the matching test and practices on the two pages that follow.

1 **alleviate** (ə-lē'-vē-āt') *-verb*

a. To **alleviate** his loneliness, the widower moved closer to his daughter and her family.

b. After a long game in the August heat, the young baseball players **alleviated** their thirst with ice-cold lemonade.

2 **benefactor** (ben'-ə-fak'-tər) *-noun*

a. The Second Street Bank is a long-time **benefactor** of the arts. This year it will sponsor a series of free jazz concerts in the parks.

b. Many famous composers, including Mozart, would not have been able to compose very much without the financial support of royal **benefactors**.

3 **covert** (kuv'-ərt) *-adjective*

a. Miriam and David's relationship is so **covert** that they never eat out. Even Miriam's parents don't know she is seeing him.

b. If you enjoy **covert** activities, become a secret agent.

4 **cynic** (sin'-ik) *-noun*

a. Libby's parents' nasty divorce has made her a **cynic** about marriage.

b. Mr. Bryant was a **cynic** until he stumbled on a street corner and several strangers rushed to his aid.

5 **demise** (di-mīz') *-noun*

a. Drugs have led to the **demise** of numerous athletes, such as basketball great Len Bias.

b. In 1567, a beard caused a man's **demise**. Hans Steininger's beard was so long that he stepped on it while climbing a staircase, lost his balance, fell down the steps, and died.

6 **infamous** (in'-fə-məs) *-adjective*

a. King Henry VIII of England was **infamous** for executing two of his six wives.

b. Visitors to the dungeons of ancient castles always want to see the instruments of torture, including the **infamous** Iron Maiden—a body-shaped box with spikes inside.

7 **intrinsic** (in-trin'-sik) *-adjective*

a. Trust is **intrinsic** to any good friendship.

b. Because Lian has an **intrinsic** desire to learn, she doesn't need the reward of good grades to motivate her studies.

8 **revulsion** (ri-vul'-shən) *-noun*

a. Whenever I read about child abuse in the newspaper, I am filled with such **revulsion** that I often cannot finish the article.

b. When Sharon met the man who had cheated her father, she was overcome with **revulsion**.

9 **speculate** (spek'-yə-lāt') *-verb*

a. It's interesting to **speculate** how history might have been different if Abraham Lincoln had lived a few years longer.

b. Scientists **speculate** that the reason birds don't give birth to live young is that a bird's high body heat would harm a developing fetus.

10 **virile** (vîr'-əl) *-adjective*

a. Men who are unsure about their masculinity sometimes try to "prove" they are **virile** by being overly aggressive.

b. When a male heron stamps his feet and sticks his neck out, and then drops his head and says "plop-buzz," the female finds him very **virile**. In fact, that behavior is how the male attracts a mate.

Matching Words and Definitions

Check your understanding of the ten words by matching each word with its definition. Look back at the sentences in "Ten Words in Context" as needed to decide on the meaning of each word.

_____	1. **alleviate**	a. secret; hidden
_____	2. **benefactor**	b. a person who believes the worst of people's behavior and motives; someone who believes people are motivated only by selfishness
_____	3. **covert**	c. belonging to a person or thing by its very nature (and thus not dependent on circumstances)
_____	4. **cynic**	d. having a very bad reputation; widely known for being vicious, criminal, or deserving of contempt
_____	5. **demise**	e. a person or organization that gives help, especially financial aid
_____	6. **infamous**	f. manly; masculine
_____	7. **intrinsic**	g. death
_____	8. **revulsion**	h. to come up with ideas or theories about a subject; theorize
_____	9. **speculate**	i. to relieve; make easier to bear
_____	10. **virile**	j. great disgust or distaste

CAUTION: Do not go any further until you are sure the above answers are correct. If you have studied the "Ten Words in Context," you will know how to match each word. Then you can use the matches to help you in the following practices. Your goal is to reach a point where you don't need to check definitions at all.

➢Sentence Check 1

Complete each sentence below with the most suitable word from the box. Use each word once.

alleviate	**benefactor**	**covert**	**cynic**	**demise**
infamous	**intrinsic**	**revulsion**	**speculate**	**virile**

1. Problems are ____________________ to life; they're unavoidable.
2. My hunger isn't fully satisfied, but the apple ________________________(e)d it somewhat.
3. Teenage guys usually welcome a deepening voice and a thickening beard as signs they are becoming more ____________________.
4. The selfless work of the nuns in the slums of India is enough to touch the hearts of most hardened ____________________s.
5. Though she was tried and found not guilty, Lizzie Borden is still ____________________ for killing her parents with a hatchet.
6. The children loved the ____________________ activities involved in preparing their mother's surprise party.
7. The mass murderer's neighbors were overcome with ____________________ when they learned what their "friend" had been doing in his basement.
8. "As no group has claimed responsibility, we can only ____________________ on the motives for the bombing," said the newscaster.
9. Roger Novak had been a well-known ____________________ of AIDS research, so it was no surprise that he left a lot of money for the research in his will.
10. It's a good idea for married couples to discuss their plans in case of each other's ____________________. For example, do they wish to be buried or cremated?

Now check your answers to these questions by turning to page 164. Going over the answers carefully will help you prepare for the next two checks, for which answers are not given.

➢ Sentence Check 2

Complete each sentence below with two words from the box. Use each word once.

alleviate	**benefactor**	**covert**	**cynic**	**demise**
infamous	**intrinsic**	**revulsion**	**speculate**	**virile**

1-2. Nursing is a good career for Dee because it's a(n) ________________ part of her personality to try to ________________ people's pain.

3-4. Although everything about the Nazis filled the Dutch spy with ________________, his ________________ assignment was to make friends with top Nazi scientists.

5-6. The ________________s in town said that Joyce Lester's sorrow over her husband's ________________ was much less than her joy in getting the money from his insurance policy.

7-8. Young men who are bullies usually think of themselves as________________, but a ________________ of the weak is far more manly than someone who takes advantage of weakness.

9-10. With all the wild stories told about Jesse James, the Dalton Gang and other ________________ figures of the Wild West, we can only ________________ as to how much is fact and how much is fiction.

➢ *Final Check:* The Mad Monk

Here is a final opportunity for you to strengthen your knowledge of the ten words. First read the following passage carefully. Then fill in each blank with a word from the box at the top of this page. (Context clues will help you figure out which word goes in which blank.) Use each word once.

Shortly before the Russian Revolution, a man named Rasputin became (1)________________ as the "mad monk." Because he dressed like a peasant, drank heavily, and rarely bathed, the nobility often felt (2)________________ when they first met him.

Yet despite his outward appearance, Rasputin possessed a(n) (3)________________ charm that drew many to him, including the Russian Empress. She thought him a great man of God and a special (4)________________ to her seriously ill son, whose condition she felt Rasputin (5)________________d.

Many (6)________________s believed otherwise. To them, Rasputin was no healer but a man concerned only with his own power and pleasure. Some critics even dared to (7)________________ that the monk and the Empress were romantically involved. This theory was strengthened by the fact that the Empress's "holy man" pursued many women and boasted about how (8)________________ he was.

Finally, a group of Russian noblemen made (9)________________ plans to kill Rasputin. Somehow, the secret must have gotten out, for a Russian official warned Rasputin of a plot against him. He nevertheless accepted the noblemen's invitation to a dinner party, where they served him poisoned wine and cake. When Rasputin seemed unaffected by the poison, his enemies hastened his (10)________________ by shooting and stabbing him and then dumping him into an icy river. An autopsy revealed that he had died by drowning.

SCORES: Sentence Check 2 ________% Final Check ________%

Enter your scores above and in the vocabulary performance chart on the inside back cover of the book.

CHAPTER

15

Previewing the Words

Find out how many of the ten words in this chapter you already know. Try to complete each sentence with the most suitable word from the list below. Use each word once.

Leave a sentence blank rather than guessing at an answer. Your purpose here is just to get a sense of the ten words and what you may know about them.

abstain	**affiliate**	**agnostic**	**aspire**	**benevolent**
deficit	**dissent**	**diversion**	**lucrative**	**mandatory**

1. Muriel is a(n) ____________ who prays when she's in trouble, just in case God exists.
2. That computer business is so ____________ that its profits rose almost 200 percent last year.
3. After conquering his alcoholism, Michael felt it was safest to ____________ from all forms of alcohol, including dinner wine.
4. Millions of young people ____________ to be professional athletes, but only a few will succeed.
5. Diane is neither a Democrat nor a Republican. She hasn't ____________(e)d with any political party.
6. "Since automobile insurance is ____________," Dad said, "you have no choice but to pay the high rates."
7. The dictator permitted people to agree with his policies or keep silent about them, but not to express ____________.
8. When I foolishly overspent last year, I quickly made up the ____________ by taking a part-time job for a few months.
9. While practicing the piano is my sister's favorite ____________, I have to be forced to put in even 15 minutes at the keyboard.
10. Henry Burton, in a poem, gave good advice on being ____________: "Have you had a kindness shown? Pass it on."

Now check your answers by turning to page 165. Fix any mistakes and fill in any blank spaces by writing in the correct answers. By doing so, you will complete this introduction to the ten words.

You're now ready to strengthen your knowledge of the words you already know and to master the words you're only half sure of, or don't know at all. Turn to the next page.

Ten Words in Context

Figure out the meanings of the following ten words by looking *closely and carefully* at the context in which the words appear. Doing so will prepare you for the matching test and practices on the two pages that follow.

1 **abstain** (ab-stān') *-verb*

a. Although Lou has given up cigarettes, he doesn't **abstain** from tobacco. Now he chews it.

b. My sister called off her engagement to Clayton because he wouldn't **abstain** from dating other women.

2 **affiliate** (ə-fil'-ē-āt') *-verb*

a. Jack's boss pressured him to **affiliate** with the "right" politicians.

b. The young singer could have earned more if she had **affiliated** with the musicians' union, but she couldn't afford the membership dues.

3 **agnostic** (ag-nos'-tik) *-noun*

a. Iris believes there is a God, and Marcia feels sure there isn't. Jean, an **agnostic**, feels that we can't be certain one way or the other.

b. My uncle, who was an **agnostic**, used to say, "Humans cannot understand a flower, let alone whether or not there's a God."

4 **aspire** (ə-spīr') *-verb*

a. Derek, who loves drawing buildings, **aspires** to be a great architect.

b. Horatio Nelson, one of history's great naval commanders, **aspired** to a goal he never reached—overcoming his seasickness.

5 **benevolent** (bə-nev'-ə-lənt) *-adjective*

a. My grandmother is one of the most **benevolent** people I know. She's always doing something kind.

b. In 19th-century London, William Booth founded a **benevolent** association to help the poor, the Salvation Army.

6 **deficit** (def'-ə-sit) *-noun*

a. The U.S. has spent so much more than it has taken in that it now has a huge budget **deficit**.

b. Residents are asked not to water their lawns because a **deficit** of rain has dangerously lowered the water supply.

7 **dissent** (di-sent') *-noun*

a. The committee was so torn by **dissent** that its members could not even agree on whether or not to schedule another meeting.

b. There was **dissent** between principals and the school board over whether or not the public schools should be in session all year round.

8 **diversion** (də-vûr'-zhən) *-noun*

a. My history teacher says that one of her favorite **diversions** is reading historical novels.

b. Skip works hard, but he also enjoys such **diversions** as playing video games, watching baseball, and reading humorous stories.

9 **lucrative** (lo͞o'-krə-tiv) *-adjective*

a. Investments in the stock market can be **lucrative**. However, they can also result in great financial loss.

b. "Teaching at a small college isn't **lucrative**," Professor Baum admitted, "but I've never felt the need to make lots of money."

10 **mandatory** (man'-də-tôr'-ē) *-adjective*

a. Members of the basketball team have to follow strict rules. For example, it's **mandatory** that each player attend at least 80 percent of the practices.

b. "A research paper isn't **mandatory**," the instructor said, "but if you write one, you'll get extra credit."

Matching Words and Definitions

Check your understanding of the ten words by matching each word with its definition. Look back at the sentences in "Ten Words in Context" as needed to decide on the meaning of each word.

_____	1. **abstain (from)**	a. to strongly desire (a condition or goal); long for something
_____	2. **affiliate (with)**	b. profitable; well-paying
_____	3. **agnostic**	c. a shortage; a lack in amount or quality
_____	4. **aspire (to)**	d. to voluntarily do without; hold oneself back from doing something
_____	5. **benevolent**	e. kind; charitable
_____	6. **deficit**	f. a person who believes we cannot know whether or not there is a God
_____	7. **dissent**	g. required
_____	8. **diversion**	h. an amusement or pastime; anything that relaxes or amuses
_____	9. **lucrative**	i. to connect or associate oneself; join
_____	10. **mandatory**	j. disagreement

CAUTION: Do not go any further until you are sure the above answers are correct. If you have studied the "Ten Words in Context," you will know how to match each word. Then you can use the matches to help you in the following practices. Your goal is to reach a point where you don't need to check definitions at all.

➢*Sentence Check 1*

Complete each sentence below with the most suitable word from the box. Use each word once.

abstain	**affiliate**	**agnostic**	**aspire**	**benevolent**
deficit	**dissent**	**diversion**	**lucrative**	**mandatory**

1. The greatest goal to which my kid brother ____________________s is the Pinball Championship of the World.
2. The ____________________ fund at my church collects money to help the needy.
3. My parents enjoy card games, but my sister and I like electronic ____________________s, such as computer games and music videos.
4. An entrance fee wasn't ____________________, but a museum sign suggested that visitors make a donation.
5. Because Hank needs to lose weight, his doctor recommended that he ____________________ from all sweets and fatty foods.
6. We could overcome a ____________________ of organs if more people would agree to have their organs transplanted after they die.
7. Otto could have joined the all-male club, but he prefers to ____________________ with organizations that welcome both men and women.
8. There was no ____________________ in the family on whether or not to start a vegetable garden this year. We all agreed it was a great idea.
9. "When someone who believes in God marries someone who does not," the comic asked, "do they give birth to a(n) ____________________?"
10. Acting is ____________________ for only a small percentage of performers. The rest need additional sources of income, such as waiting on tables or driving a cab.

Now check your answers to these questions by turning to page 165. Going over the answers carefully will help you prepare for the next two checks, for which answers are not given.

➤ *Sentence Check 2*

Complete each sentence below with two words from the box. Use each word once.

abstain	affiliate	agnostic	aspire	benevolent
deficit	dissent	diversion	lucrative	mandatory

1-2. My uncle decided to splurge and __________________ with a country club because golf is his main __________________.

3-4. Gale didn't __________________ from smoking cigarettes at the office until her employer made non-smoking __________________.

5-6. "Although I'm a(n) __________________," said Stan, "I still hope that there's a God who's __________________ and loving."

7-8. The __________________ in the township treasury is causing a lot of __________________ over whether or not taxes should be raised.

9-10. Because my father __________________s to make enough money to send his children to college, he's working hard to make his auto repair business as __________________ as possible.

➤ *Final Check:* Conflict over Holidays

Here is a final opportunity for you to strengthen your knowledge of the ten words. First read the following passage carefully. Then fill in each blank with a word from the box at the top of this page. (Context clues will help you figure out which word goes in which blank.) Use each word once.

While Jeanne and Paul are generally a happily married couple, they do struggle over one point of (1)__________________. They disagree as to how their family should observe religious holidays. Jeanne feels that the emphasis on holiday presents and parties has made the season (2)__________________ to merchants while leaving an unnecessarily large (3)__________________ in people's budgets. She complains that exchanging presents at Christmas is practically (4)__________________, whether or not one believes in the holiday's religious significance. Jeanne (5)__________________s to keep her home free of all such nonreligious customs and thus wants her children to (6)__________________ from traditions such as gift-giving and dyeing Easter eggs. She feels the family's money would be better spent if it were donated to a (7)__________________ organization for helping the poor. Some of Jeanne's neighbors assume that she is a(n) (8)__________________ because of her lack of holiday spirit. They are wrong, however. Jeanne believes deeply in God and (9)__________________s with a church. While Paul understands Jeanne's concerns, he enjoys the (10)__________________s that are connected with the holiday, such as visits to Santa Claus and Easter egg hunts. He sees them as pleasant customs that add to the joy of the year.

SCORES: Sentence Check 2 ________%	Final Check ________%

Enter your scores above and in the vocabulary performance chart on the inside back cover of the book.

CHAPTER

16

Previewing the Words

Find out how many of the ten words in this chapter you already know. Try to complete each sentence with the most suitable word from the list below. Use each word once.

Leave a sentence blank rather than guessing at an answer. Your purpose here is just to get a sense of the ten words and what you may know about them.

charisma	**contemporary**	**contend**	**conversely**	**extrovert**
poignant	**prevalent**	**proponent**	**quest**	**traumatic**

1. Fear was ____________________ throughout the town until the escaped murderer was captured and put safely behind bars.
2. Beth likes ____________________ furniture, but her husband prefers older styles.
3. Many scientists worldwide are active in the ____________________ for a cure for cancer.
4. My father ____________________s that David Letterman is the funniest, most creative comedian in television today.
5. I cried when I read the ____________________ story about the dying girl who gave away all her dolls to "poor children."
6. My sister thinks that being an attorney is an exciting career. ____________________, I believe that most of a lawyer's work is dry and boring.
7. Lucy has such ____________________ that when she ran for class president, almost every person in the tenth grade voted for her.
8. Getting lost in the subway when I was only five years old was a(n) ____________________ experience. Even now, it upsets me to recall the event.
9. Arnie is a(n) ____________________ of the Equal Rights Amendment. He believes the law should give women the same rights as men.
10. "I wish I were more of a(n) ____________________," Miko told her counselor. "I'm so shy that sometimes I can barely talk to people."

Now check your answers by turning to page 165. Fix any mistakes and fill in any blank spaces by writing in the correct answers. By doing so, you will complete this introduction to the ten words.

You're now ready to strengthen your knowledge of the words you already know and to master the words you're only half sure of, or don't know at all. Turn to the next page.

Ten Words in Context

Figure out the meanings of the following ten words by looking *closely and carefully* at the context in which the words appear. Doing so will prepare you for the matching test and practices on the two pages that follow.

1 **charisma**
(kə-riz'-mə)
-noun

a. John Kennedy's **charisma**, perhaps even more than his policies, brought him widespread support.

b. Her numerous loyal fans worldwide show that Great Britain's Princess Diana certainly has **charisma**.

2 **contemporary**
(kən-tem'-pə-rer'-ē)
-adjective

a. I prefer "golden oldie" movies to most **contemporary** films.

b. My grandfather says that compared to kids in his day, **contemporary** youth are soft and lazy.

3 **contend**
(kən-tend')
-verb

a. The defense attorney **contended** that his client was insane and therefore could not be held responsible for the murder.

b. Scientists **contend** that no two snowflakes are identical, but how can they possibly prove it?

4 **conversely**
(kən-vûrs'-lē)
-adverb

a. Ron, who is basically bored by food, eats in order to live. **Conversely**, Nate so loves food that he seems to live in order to eat.

b. Mary drives her children to school whenever it rains. **Conversely**, I make my kids walk as usual because I think a little rain never hurt anyone.

5 **extrovert**
(ek'-strə-vûrt')
-noun

a. Surprisingly, not all performers are **extroverts**. When offstage, many are quiet and shy.

b. My boss was looking for someone to greet and chat with her clients, so I recommended Robert for the job because he's such an **extrovert**.

6 **poignant**
(poin'-yənt)
-adjective

a. The service honoring American soldiers missing in action was touching. A speech by a friend of one of the soldiers was particularly **poignant**.

b. *It's a Wonderful Life* is the **poignant** story of how one man learns that his caring actions have made a big difference in other people's lives. Viewers love to cry during this film each holiday season.

7 **prevalent**
(prev'-ə-lənt)
-adjective

a. Unemployment was **prevalent** during America's Great Depression. By 1932, over 12 million people were out of work.

b. Television sets are more **prevalent** in the U.S. than bathtubs. Over half of American homes have two or more TV's. Far fewer homes have more than one bathtub.

8 **proponent**
(prō-pō'-nənt)
-noun

a. I voted for Senator Williams, a **proponent** of improved services for the elderly, because I feel many older people need greater assistance.

b. Elaine is a **proponent** of employer-supported day care. She believes every big company should help provide care for its workers' children.

9 **quest**
(kwest)
-noun

a. During Carlo's **quest** for the perfect pizza, he sampled the cheese pizza at 27 different restaurants.

b. Ponce de Leon's **quest** was for the Fountain of Youth; what he found instead was Florida.

10 **traumatic**
(trô-mat'-ik)
-adjective

a. Divorce can be less **traumatic** for children if their fears and feelings are taken into account as the divorce takes place.

b. My cousin has had nightmares ever since his **traumatic** experience of being trapped in a coal mine.

Matching Words and Definitions

Check your understanding of the ten words by matching each word with its definition. Look back at the sentences in "Ten Words in Context" as needed to decide on the meaning of each word.

_____	1. **charisma**	a. in a reversed way; in an opposite or contrary manner
_____	2. **contemporary**	b. the quality of a leader which captures great popular devotion; personal magnetism; charm
_____	3. **contend**	c. a search; hunt
_____	4. **conversely**	d. widespread; common
_____	5. **extrovert**	e. to state to be so; claim
_____	6. **poignant**	f. modern; up-to-date
_____	7. **prevalent**	g. someone who supports a cause
_____	8. **proponent (of)**	h. emotionally moving; touching
_____	9. **quest**	i. causing painful emotions, with possible long-lasting psychological effects
_____	10. **traumatic**	j. an outgoing, expressive person

CAUTION: Do not go any further until you are sure the above answers are correct. If you have studied the "Ten Words in Context," you will know how to match each word. Then you can use the matches to help you in the following practices. Your goal is to reach a point where you don't need to check definitions at all.

➢*Sentence Check 1*

Complete each sentence below with the most suitable word from the box. Use each word once.

charisma	contemporary	contend	conversely	extrovert
poignant	prevalent	proponent	quest	traumatic

1. I study best in the morning. __________________, my sister concentrates better at night.
2. Nancy is a(n) __________________ by nature, but since she's become depressed, she has been avoiding other people.
3. At the airport, I was very moved by the __________________ reunion of family members who had been separated for years.
4. Underage drinking was so __________________ in the fraternity house that college officials ordered the house closed for a year.
5. "This woman __________________s that she was here before you," said the supermarket checkout clerk. "Is it her turn now?"
6. Neal is a(n) __________________ of exercising for good health. He even encourages his young children to swim or cycle every day.
7. Although some movie stars are short on talent, they have a(n) __________________ that makes people want to see their films.
8. Abby didn't like the apartment with the old-fashioned tub and radiators. She preferred a more __________________ place.
9. Repeating third grade was __________________ for my brother. It still pains him to think about it, even though he's a successful businessman now.
10. In the past 300 years, several people have gone on a(n) __________________ for Noah's Ark. Some have looked for it in northwestern Turkey, on Mount Ararat, 16,000 feet above sea level.

Now check your answers to these questions by turning to page 165. Going over the answers carefully will help you prepare for the next two checks, for which answers are not given.

➢Sentence Check 2

Complete each sentence below with two words from the box. Use each word once.

charisma	**contemporary**	**contend**	**conversely**	**extrovert**
poignant	**prevalent**	**proponent**	**quest**	**traumatic**

1-2. Many people are surprised to learn how ____________________ poverty is in ____________________ America. Today, millions live below the poverty line.

3-4. A(n) ____________________, Judy chooses work that brings her in heavy contact with others. ____________________, Marty prefers jobs in which he mainly works alone.

5-6. Ever since the ____________________ experience of finding her 12-year-old son dead from a drug overdose, Sophie has been a strong ____________________ of drug education for all ages.

7-8. My mother ____________________s that *Romeo and Juliet* is the most ____________________ story ever written, but my sister claims *Love Story* is more moving.

9-10. Mahatma Gandhi's ____________________ and vision inspired millions of fellow Indians to join him enthusiastically in the ____________________ for peaceful solutions to national problems.

➤*Final Check:* Dr. Martin Luther King, Jr.

Here is a final opportunity for you to strengthen your knowledge of the ten words. First read the following passage carefully. Then fill in each blank with a word from the box at the top of this page. (Context clues will help you figure out which word goes in which blank.) Use each word once.

(1)____________________ youth may be able to list the many accomplishments of the Reverend Dr. Martin Luther King, Jr. They may know he was a civil-rights leader who was a(n) (2)____________________ of peaceful but direct action. They may know he fought the discrimination against blacks that was more (3)____________________ in our country in the 1950's and 1960's. They may also know he was the founder of the Southern Christian Leadership Conference and that he won a Nobel Peace Prize. They may even (4)____________________ that he is the most important social reformer in the history of our nation.

But can the young really know the (5)____________________, the powerful personal magnetism of this man? When Dr. King spoke, people listened. The warmth of his voice reflected the outwardly directed energy of the (6)____________________. He had such a forceful, yet (7)____________________ way of speaking that those who heard him felt his message deep within. For most, this meant a stronger belief in and respect for the man and his ideals. (8)____________________, for bigots, it meant a hatred and fear of what he stood for.

Dr. King's (9)____________________ for equal rights for all was clear when he said, "I have a dream that this nation will rise up and live out the true meaning of its creed: 'We hold these truths to be self-evident; that all men are created equal.'" He gave his time, leadership, and, in the end, his life. His murder was a(n) (10)____________________ event in the lives of many Americans, who will never fully recover from that awful day. But because of Martin Luther King, Americans live with greater dignity. And many have taken up his fight for the betterment of all.

SCORES: Sentence Check 2 ________% Final Check ________%

Enter your scores above and in the vocabulary performance chart on the inside back cover of the book.

CHAPTER

17

Previewing the Words

Find out how many of the ten words in this chapter you already know. Try to complete each sentence with the most suitable word from the list below. Use each word once.

Leave a sentence blank rather than guessing at an answer. Your purpose here is just to get a sense of the ten words and what you may know about them.

congenial	**flippant**	**impasse**	**perception**	**prompt**
prone	**rapport**	**rationale**	**relentless**	**reprisal**

1. My sister is more ________________ to complaining about her homework than to simply doing it and getting it over with.
2. Our coworkers are very ________________ except for Walter, who has remained cool and unfriendly towards everyone.
3. When there's a teenager in the house, the ringing of the telephone seems to be ________________.
4. The mountain climbers panicked when they reached a(n) ________________. They couldn't go up any farther, but they couldn't go back down either.
5. When asked to explain the ________________ behind his decision to divorce, Ed had two strong reasons—his wife's two affairs.
6. The general's policy was that every attack on the army was to be followed by immediate ________________.
7. Don's boss knows more about business than he does about people. His ________________s of his staff's thoughts and feelings are often inaccurate.
8. Many companies ________________ people to buy their products by giving them money-saving coupons.
9. When, for the third time, I told my son to clean his room, he gave this ________________ response: "Why should I? I just cleaned it last month."
10. Since Barbara broke up with her fiance last year, she has had a hard time developing a(n) ________________ with other men. She's afraid to get close again.

Now check your answers by turning to page 165. Fix any mistakes and fill in any blank spaces by writing in the correct answers. By doing so, you will complete this introduction to the ten words.

You're now ready to strengthen your knowledge of the words you already know and to master the words you're only half sure of, or don't know at all. Turn to the next page.

Ten Words in Context

Figure out the meanings of the following ten words by looking *closely and carefully* at the context in which the words appear. Doing so will prepare you for the matching test and practices on the two pages that follow.

1 **congenial**
(kən-jēn'-yəl)
-adjective

a. You don't find Anita to be **congenial,** but she's pleasant and friendly with me.

b. I was nervous being at a party where I didn't know anyone, but the other guests were so **congenial** that I soon felt at ease.

2 **flippant**
(flip'-ənt)
-adjective

a. "Don't give me a **flippant** answer," George's father told him. "Your financial situation is a serious matter."

b. Kim stayed after school a half hour for not bringing her homework and another half hour for her **flippant** excuse—"My goldfish ate it."

3 **impasse**
(im'-pas)
-noun

a. The jurors had reached an **impasse.** No decision could be reached because some thought the defendant was the murderer and others were sure he was innocent.

b. If you think you've reached an **impasse** when trying to solve a problem, take a break. After a while, you might think of a solution.

4 **perception**
(pər-sep'-shən)
-noun

a. Brenda's **perceptions** of others are usually accurate. She is able to size people up quickly.

b. Our **perceptions** of the problem differ. Rob thinks money is the main issue, but I believe it's a question of who controls the purse strings.

5 **prompt**
(prompt)
-verb

a. To **prompt** Byron to get a job, I put the want ads under his pillow.

b. Fast-food clerks **prompt** customers to buy more by asking such questions as "Would you like cookies or apple pie with that?"

6 **prone**
(prōn)
-adjective

a. Mr. Walker is **prone** to high blood pressure, so he limits his salt intake.

b. **Prone** to fits of laughter during class, Chris sometimes controls the sound by biting into his pen.

7 **rapport**
(ra-por')
-noun

a. In high school, I had such good **rapport** with my gym teacher that our close relationship continues to this day.

b. If no **rapport** develops between you and your therapist after a month or two, start looking for another counselor who makes you feel comfortable.

8 **rationale**
(rash'-ə-nal')
-noun

a. Danielle's **rationale** for majoring in business was simple. "I want to make a lot of money," she said.

b. The **rationale** for raising the drinking age to 21 is that self-control and good judgment generally increase with age.

9 **relentless**
(ri-lent'-lis)
-adjective

a. The dog's **relentless** barking got on my nerves. He barked the entire two hours his owners were out.

b. In a large city, the noise of crowds and heavy traffic is so **relentless** that it can be difficult to find peace and quiet.

10 **reprisal**
(ri-prī'-zəl)
-noun

a. Settlers who took Indian land shouldn't have been surprised when, as **reprisal,** Indians attacked settlers.

b. An abused woman who fears **reprisal** may not press charges against a man who has beaten her.

Matching Words and Definitions

Check your understanding of the ten words by matching each word with its definition. Look back at the sentences in "Ten Words in Context" as needed to decide on the meaning of each word.

_____	1. **congenial**	a. an impression; the way someone or something is viewed
_____	2. **flippant**	b. having a tendency; inclined
_____	3. **impasse**	c. persistent; continuous
_____	4. **perception**	d. the underlying reasons for something; logical basis
_____	5. **prompt**	e. disrespectful and not serious enough
_____	6. **prone (to)**	f. agreeable or pleasant in character
_____	7. **rapport**	g. to urge into action
_____	8. **rationale**	h. the paying back of one injury with another
_____	9. **relentless**	i. a situation with no way out; dead end
_____	10. **reprisal**	j. a relationship, especially a close, trusting, or sympathetic one

CAUTION: Do not go any further until you are sure the above answers are correct. If you have studied the "Ten Words in Context," you will know how to match each word. Then you can use the matches to help you in the following practices. Your goal is to reach a point where you don't need to check definitions at all.

➣*Sentence Check 1*

Complete each sentence below with the most suitable word from the box. Use each word once.

congenial	**flippant**	**impasse**	**perception**	**prompt**
prone	**rapport**	**rationale**	**relentless**	**reprisal**

1. Nan is ____________________ to accidents, so her car insurance rates are quite high.
2. You will get along better in life if you are usually ____________________, rather than unpleasant.
3. My brother hides his lack of confidence by being ____________________. He rarely treats anything seriously.
4. It took a magazine article about women who help handicapped children to ____________________ me to do the same.
5. There was an instant ____________________ between Duke and Otis. They talked as if they'd known each other for years.
6. At the movie's climax, the bad guys reached a(n) ____________________. On one side of them was the police; on the other was a tiger.
7. During April and May, the rain was so ____________________ that we thought we might have to start building an ark.
8. Floyd's ____________________ of human nature is strongly colored by some bad experiences. He thinks everyone is basically selfish.
9. When Lacey and John divorced, she tried to get over half his income. In ____________________, he tried to deny her any income from him at all.
10. The ____________________ behind encouraging pregnant women to gain about 25 pounds is that low weight gain can lead to dangerously low birth weights.

Now check your answers to these questions by turning to page 165. Going over the answers carefully will help you prepare for the next two checks, for which answers are not given.

➢Sentence Check 2

Complete each sentence below with two words from the box. Use each word once.

congenial	**flippant**	**impasse**	**perception**	**prompt**
prone	**rapport**	**rationale**	**relentless**	**reprisal**

1-2. Wade is so ____________________, so easy to talk to, that we established a warm ____________________ the first day we met.

3-4. ____________________ to anger, my mother was quick to punish any of her children who spoke to her in a ____________________ way.

5-6. Although the company president explained the ____________________ behind the pay cuts, his announcement ____________________(e)d an employee protest.

7-8. My ____________________ of the situation is that talks between the factory management and union officials reached a(n) ____________________ because neither side would compromise on salaries.

9-10. Abby could put up with a little teasing, but her brother's teasing was often ____________________, going on for weeks at a time. Sick of it all, she finally planned a(n) ____________________ that would embarrass him in front of his friends.

➢*Final Check:* Relating to Parents

Here is a final opportunity for you to strengthen your knowledge of the ten words. First read the following passage carefully. Then fill in each blank with a word from the box at the top of this page. (Context clues will help you figure out which word goes in which blank.) Use each word once.

How do you respond when your parents deny you permission to do something? For example, if you want to travel and work around the country for the summer but your parents say you're too young, do you yell and demand your rights? Do you plan a(n) (1)____________________, vowing to ruin their summer because they've ruined yours? Or do you explain the (2)____________________ behind your request, so that your parents will understand your reasoning?

The way you behave when you and your parents reach a(n) (3)____________________ on an issue can have a big effect on how they view you. Sure, you could say, "Fine. Just fine. I'll go buy a leash so you can really run my life." But if you are consistently (4)____________________ like that, you'll just strengthen their (5)____________________ of you as too immature to be on your own. Also, if you are (6)____________________ in your begging, asking 300 times a day, "But WHY won't you let me go?" they may tell you where to go, and it won't be on a cross-country trip.

Instead, approach your parents in a (7)____________________ way and try to develop a strong, friendly (8)____________________ with them. A warm relationship will make them more (9)____________________ to see things your way. Even if you can't (10)____________________ them to change their minds about this summer's plans, your chances will be better the next time you want to try something new.

SCORES: Sentence Check 2 ________% Final Check ________%

Enter your scores above and in the vocabulary performance chart on the inside back cover of the book.

CHAPTER

18

Previewing the Word Parts

Common word parts—also known as *prefixes, suffixes,* and *roots*—are used in forming many words in English. This page will introduce you to ten common word parts.

Try to match each word part on the left with its definition on the right. Use the words in parentheses as hints to help you guess the meanings. If you can't decide on an answer, leave the space blank. Your purpose here is just to get a sense of the ten word parts and what you may know about them. (You'll have another chance to try this exercise after considering the word parts in context.)

	Word Parts	**Definitions**
_____	1. **cor, cour** (cordial, courtesy)	a. great; large
_____	2. **di-, du-** (divorce, duel)	b. cause to be or become; make
_____	3. **-dom** (boredom, wisdom)	c. forward; forth; in favor of
_____	4. **-fy** (simplify, terrify)	d. fear; dislike
_____	5. **im-, il-** (impossible, illogical)	e. two; double
_____	6. **-ish** (boyish, greenish)	f. resembling; like; characteristic of
_____	7. **magni-, magn-** (magnify, magnate)	g. heart
_____	8. **phob** (phobia, phobic)	h. mental processes; mind
_____	9. **pro-** (propel, prolabor)	i. condition; quality; region of authority
_____	10. **psych-, psycho-** (psychiatrist, psychology)	j. not

Now go on to "Ten Word Parts in Context" on the next page. Working through this chapter will help you to strengthen your knowledge of the word parts you already know and to master the word parts you're only half sure of, or don't know at all.

Keep in mind that learning word parts can pay several dividends. Word parts can help with the spelling and pronunciation of many words. They can also help you to unlock the meanings of unfamiliar words.

Ten Word Parts in Context

Figure out the meanings of the following ten word parts by looking *closely and carefully* at the context in which they appear. Doing so will prepare you for the matching test and practices on the two pages that follow.

1 **cor, cour**

a. I felt truly welcomed by my **cordial** hosts. Their kindness and generosity were heartfelt.

b. Emmy was **courageous** enough to face the bully without backing down. I'm too chicken-hearted to do the same.

2 **di-, du-**

a. When we got **divorced,** we had to spend a difficult day dividing our household possessions into two groups.

b. One of the three band members didn't show up, so only a **duo** played at the dance.

3 **-dom**

a. A few actors achieve overnight success, but for most, the road to **stardom** is long and difficult.

b. Kings and queens invested in exploring the New World with hopes of expanding their **kingdoms**.

4 **-fy**

a. Would it **simplify** matters if I held your baby while you go into the dressing room to try on the slacks?

b. First **liquefy** the ice cream over heat. Then mix in the strawberry jam.

5 **im-, il-**

a. My brother-in-law is so **immature** that he often acts as if he is 16 instead of a married man of 26.

b. Nita doesn't seem to care that it's **illegal** to park in front of a fire hydrant.

6 **-ish**

a. My **devilish** brother once videotaped me huffing and puffing my way through aerobics, and now he shows the tape to every new friend I bring home.

b. Of all the girls at school, Jessy was the most **stylish,** wearing only the latest clothing featured in the fashion magazine.

7 **magni-, magn-**

a. My grandmother uses a **magnifying** glass to read small newsprint.

b. Eight years after starting Standard Oil in 1870, oil **magnate** John D. Rockefeller controlled about 85 percent of the country's oil industry.

8 **phob**

a. One of the most unusual **phobias** is the fear of peanut butter sticking to the roof of one's mouth.

b. Marilyn's mother has developed **agoraphobia** to the point that she fears even going to the mailbox at the end of the driveway.

9 **pro-**

a. **Proceed** down to the end of this hallway, make a left, and you will see the x-ray department.

b. During the Civil War, most southern states were **proslavery**. The northern states favored freeing the slaves.

10 **psych-, psycho-**

a. A **psychiatrist** is a medical doctor who specializes in treating mental disorders.

b. A **psychologist** specializes in mental and emotional processes.

Matching Word Parts and Definitions

Check your understanding of the ten word parts by matching each with its definition. See also the suggestions on page 4.

_____ 1. **cor, cour** a. great; large

_____ 2. **di-, du-** b. cause to be or become; make

_____ 3. **-dom** c. forward; forth; in favor of

_____ 4. **-fy** d. fear; dislike

_____ 5. **im-, il-** e. two; double

_____ 6. **-ish** f. resembling; like; characteristic of

_____ 7. **magni-, magn-** g. heart

_____ 8. **phob** h. mental processes; mind

_____ 9. **pro-** i. state of being; quality; region of authority

_____ 10. **psych-, psycho-** j. not

CAUTION: Do not go any further until you are sure the above answers are correct. If you have studied the "Ten Word Parts in Context," you will know how to match each word part. Then you can use the matches to help you in the following practices. Your goal is to reach a point where you don't need to check definitions at all.

➢Sentence Check 1

Complete each partial word in the following sentences with a word part from the box. Use each word part only once. You may want to check off each word part as you use it.

cour	du-	-dom	-fy	im-
-ish	magni-	phob	pro-	psycho-

1. Despite her (*boy . . .*) ____________________ hairdo, Paula looks very feminine.
2. (*Wis . . .*) ____________________ is what we gain when we learn from our mistakes.
3. The family was greatly (*dis . . . aged*) ____________________ when every attempt to find their son failed.
4. To keep the accident victim (*. . . mobile*) ____________________, the paramedics tied her to a stretcher.
5. The reason these life-size dolls are so expensive is that only 100 are (*. . . duced*) ____________________ each year.
6. The funhouse mirror (*. . . fied*) ____________________ my reflection so that I looked 50 pounds heavier.
7. I always (*. . . plicate*) ____________________ important papers and letters so that if the original gets lost, I still have the copy.
8. Barb's (*. . . analyst*) ____________________ asked her to write down her dreams, as they might be helpful in understanding her problems.
9. If you want to find a job before all the graduates start looking for employment next month, you'd better (*intensi . . .*) ____________________ your job search.
10. It's lucky Santa Claus doesn't have (*claustro . . . ia*) ____________________. Otherwise, he would be too frightened of confined spaces to come down the chimney.

Now check your answers to these questions by turning to page 165. Going over the answers carefully will help you prepare for the next two checks, for which answers are not given.

➢ *Sentence Check 2*

Complete each partial word in the sentences below with a word part from the box. Use each word part once. If there are two forms of a word part, use the *first* one for this practice.

cour	**du-, di-**	**-dom**	**-fy**	**im-, il-**
-ish	**magni-**	**phob**	**pro-**	**psycho-**

1-2. The purpose of (. . . *therapy*) ____________ is to (. . . *mote*) ____________ mental health.

3-4. Everyone has fears, but (. . . *ic*) ____________ people need to gain (*free*. . .) ____________ from extreme fears.

5-6. The apartment the realtor showed us was (. . . *ficent*) ____________ but (. . . *practical*) ____________ for us. Not only was it too large, but it would also make an uncomfortable dent in our budget.

7-8. Florence and I felt (*fool* . . .) ____________ when we sang a (. . . *et*) ____________ of "Silent Night" and forgot the words halfway through.

9-10. The mayor didn't allow racial tensions to (*dis* . . . *age*) ____________ him. He just made more of an effort to (*uni* . . .) ____________ the city.

➤ *Final Check:* Held Back by Fears

Here is a final opportunity for you to strengthen your knowledge of the ten word parts. First read the following passage carefully. Then complete each partial word in the parentheses below with a word part from the box at the top of this page. If there are two forms of a word part, use the *second* one in this practice. Context clues will help you figure out which word part goes in which blank. Use each word part once.

At age 24, Gina is facing a major (. . . *lemma*) (1)____________: to give in to her fears or to fight them. She desperately wants to live and work beyond her hometown, but she is prevented from traveling by her (. . . *ias*) (2)____________. She suffers from (. . . *logical*) (3)____________ but intense fears of bridges and airplanes. Gina is convinced that if she doesn't fall off a bridge or crash in an airplane, the mere possibility will so (*terri* . . .) (4)____________ her that she'll have a heart attack.

For some time now, Gina's friends have tried to convince her to start seeing a (. . . *logist*) (5)____________. They believe the problem will only increase in (. . . *tude*) (6)____________ if she doesn't get help. But her family says she is just being (*child* . . .) (7)____________. Her brothers tease her, calling her "baby" and "chicken." They say if she only had a little more (. . . *age*) (8)____________, she would be able to go places. They don't realize that if she could have controlled her fears by now, she would have. She is seriously considering her friends' advice. She hopes she will make rapid (. . . *gress*) (9)____________ in gaining (*free*. . .) (10)____________ from her fears so that she can start to live a full life.

SCORES: Sentence Check 2 ________% Final Check ________%

Enter your scores above and in the vocabulary performance chart on the inside back cover of the book.

UNIT THREE: Test 1

PART A

Choose the word that best completes each sentence and write it in the space provided.

1. **alleviated** **speculated** **dissented** **contended** — The muscle ointment _______________ the pain of my sprained neck.

2. **flippant** **poignant** **relentless** **infamous** — It was _______________ to see the bear immediately adopt the orphaned cub.

3. **virile** **intermittent** **congenial** **flippant** — In irregular bursts of energy, dying stars give off _______________ radio signals.

4. **speculate** **digress** **detract** **squander** — Scientists _______________ that the average life span of a dinosaur was probably 100 to 120 years.

5. **impasse** **quest** **incentive** **cynic** — Freud, being a(n) _______________, believed that all people are driven primarily by selfish desires.

6. **diversion** **charisma** **perception** **demise** — The _______________ of a Connecticut man was strange indeed. He died when his 500-pound wife sat on him.

7. **prompted** **curtailed** **contended** **dissented** — A power failure _______________ our viewing of the TV mystery, so we never found out who had committed the murder.

8. **covert** **traumatic** **virile** **congenial** — The CIA's _______________ activities often include "bugging" people's telephone lines with tiny, hidden microphones.

9. **Quests** **Incentives** **Proponents** **Rigors** — _______________ of gun control point out that gun accidents in American homes result in over a thousand deaths each year.

10. **affiliate** **abstain** **contend** **aspire** — Alcohol is involved in nearly half of all U.S. traffic deaths, so _______________ from drinking when you need to drive.

11. **benefactor** **rapport** **diversion** **impasse**
The talks between the two countries reached a(n) ________________ when each side claimed the oil-rich border area as its own.

12. **Virile** **Lucrative** **Prone** **Covert**
________________ to oversleeping, Sherman keeps his alarm clock across the room so he has to get out of bed to turn it off.

13. **charisma** **perception** **dissent** **deficit**
If you are never able to pay off your credit-card bills, why not avoid the permanent ________________ by tearing up the cards and paying with cash?

PART B

Circle **C** if the italicized word is used **correctly**. Circle **I** if the word is used **incorrectly**.

C I 14. The *benevolent* boss laid workers off without even giving them a week's pay.

C I 15. A typewriter or word processor is *indispensable* for preparing a college term paper.

C I 16. The beautiful sunset, with dramatic red swirls in a pink sky, filled us with *revulsion.*

C I 17. Since baldness is a masculine trait, why don't more men view it as attractively *virile?*

C I 18. Priests, rabbis, and other *agnostics* signed the petition asking for aid to the homeless.

C I 19. Eric has often had cats, but never dogs. *Conversely,* Joan has often had dogs, but never cats.

C I 20. A course in American history isn't *mandatory* at most colleges, but our school does require first-year students to take one.

C I 21. I don't consider retirement benefits a sufficient *incentive* to stick with a job I dislike.

C I 22. Fran often *squanders* her money by walking through rain or snow instead of paying for a cab.

C I 23. The children *incorporated* their money so they could afford a nicer anniversary gift for their parents.

C I 24. At the restaurant, Kevin *prompted* me to save room for dessert by saying, "They make the world's best chocolate layer cake here."

C I 25. Halloween has *contemporary* roots. Annually, the ancient Irish would dress as demons and witches to frighten away ghosts who might otherwise claim their bodies.

SCORE: (Number correct) ________ x 4 = ________ %

Enter your scores above and in the vocabulary performance chart on the inside back cover of the book.

UNIT THREE: Test 2

PART A

Complete each sentence with a word from the box. Use each word once.

benefactor	**contend**	**devastate**	**extrovert**
flippant	**lucrative**	**prevalent**	**quest**
rapport	**rationale**	**reprisal**	**rigor**
succumb			

1. Jill was ___________________(e)d when she lost her job and, with it, her hopes of affording a house.

2. I have an excellent ___________________ with my brother, but I haven't spoken to my sister for years.

3. Rudy is such a(n) ___________________ that he makes friends with most of the customers at his beauty salon.

4. Before the turn of the century, the _________________s of prizefighting included boxing without gloves.

5. The owner of the restaurant ___________________(e)d to public pressure and established a non-smoking section.

6. My ___________________ for using cloth napkins is that they result in fewer trees being cut down for paper napkins.

7. With violent crime so ___________________, some newspaper reporters now wear bulletproof vests when they cover a story.

8. Halloween is ___________________ for candy manufacturers. The holiday brings in about a billion dollars a year for them.

9. In some fairy tales, the hero searches far and wide, on a ___________________ for some precious object or missing person.

10. The high school's chief ___________________ has offered to pay all college costs for any low-income student who graduates from high school.

11. When her brother took her bike without asking, Meg's ___________________ was simply not to warn him that one of the tires was going flat.

12. The street's residents ___________________ that they complained for months about the open garbage dump before the city government did anything about it.

13. When the principal asked Randy why he had spilled milk on some girls in the lunchroom, his ___________________ response was: "Because they were thirsty."

PART B

Circle **C** if the italicized word is used **correctly**. Circle **I** if the word is used **incorrectly**.

C I 14. Our English teacher said, "Be sure to *digress.* A short essay needs a tight focus."

C I 15. For two weeks, the newspapers reported on the crimes of the *infamous* serial killer.

C I 16. The *relentless* beat of my neighbor's stereo gave me an equally persistent headache.

C I 17. When its ratings fell, the detective show was *aspired* to a new time slot on a different evening.

C I 18. Whenever it snowed, the *congenial* boy next door would throw tightly packed snowballs at me.

C I 19. Groucho Marx once joked that he wouldn't want to *affiliate* with any club that would accept him as a member.

C I 20. Bob's near-fatal auto accident was so *traumatic* for him that, a year later, he still refuses to get inside a car.

C I 21. The candidate lost the TV debate partly because of his *charisma,* which included sweating and stammering.

C I 22. The student meeting went smoothly. There was full *dissent* to give the retiring art teacher a set of fine oil paints.

C I 23. The desire to aid others seems *intrinsic* to many animals. Baboons, for example, will try to free other baboons who are caged.

C I 24. Vanessa's current *diversion* is as a night-shift clerk in a supermarket. She took the part-time job temporarily to pay off some bills.

C I 25. Fashion designers influence our *perceptions* of what is attractive. For example, who would have thought a few years ago that jeans filled with holes would be considered good looking?

SCORE: (Number correct) ________ x 4 = ________ %

Enter your scores above and in the vocabulary performance chart on the inside back cover of the book.

UNIT THREE: Test 3

PART A

Complete each sentence in a way that clearly shows you understand the meaning of the boldfaced word. Take a minute to plan your answer before you write.

Example: As an **incentive** to work better, the company *awards bonuses to workers who show special effort.*

1. One sight that makes me feel **revulsion** is ______________________________

____

2. A good way to **squander** your money is to ______________________________

____

3. Jon, who is a **proponent** of daily exercise, advised me, " ______________________________

____

4. At our school, it is **mandatory** to ______________________________

____

5. I **aspire** to ______________________________

____

6. During the math class, the teacher **digressed** by ______________________________

____

7. Our father told us how **traumatic** it was for him to ______________________________

____

8. My **rationale** for going to college is ______________________________

____

9. The reason the plan was **covert** was that ______________________________

____

10. When asked by the restaurant owner to pay his bill, the young man's **flippant** reply was: "______________

____

PART B

After each boldfaced word are a *synonym* (a word that means the same as the boldfaced word), an *antonym* (a word that means the opposite of the boldfaced word), and a word that is neither. Mark the antonym with an *A*.

Example:	**contemporary**	_____ modern	_____ rapid	__*A*__ ancient
11.	**benevolent**	_____ evil	_____ gifted	_____ kind
12.	**alleviate**	_____ relieve	_____ worsen	_____ raise
13.	**indispensable**	_____ essential	_____ expensive	_____ unnecessary
14.	**prevalent**	_____ heavy	_____ rare	_____ common
15.	**congenial**	_____ disagreeable	_____ clever	_____ pleasant

PART C

Use five of the following ten words in sentences. Make it clear that you know the meaning of the word you use. Feel free to use the past tense or plural form of a word.

affiliate	**contend**	**curtail**	**cynic**	**diversion**
perception	**rapport**	**relentless**	**squander**	**virile**

16. ____

____

17. ____

____

18. ____

____

19. ____

____

20. ____

SCORE: (Number correct) ________ x 5 = ________ %

Enter your scores above and in the vocabulary performance chart on the inside back cover of the book.

UNIT THREE: Test 4 (Word Parts)

PART A
Listed in the left-hand column below are ten common word parts, along with words in which the parts are used. In each blank, write in the letter of the correct definition on the right.

Word Parts		**Definitions**
____ 1. **cor, cour**	cordial, encourage	a. two; double
____ 2. **du-, di-**	duet, divorce	b. mental processes; mind
____ 3. **-dom**	boredom, wisdom	c. not
____ 4. **-fy**	fortify, simplify	d. fear; dislike
____ 5. **im-, il-**	immoral, illegal	e. heart
____ 6. **-ish**	girlish, bearish	f. forward; forth; in favor
____ 7. **magni-, magn-**	magnified, magnitude	g. great; large
____ 8. **phob**	claustrophobia, phobic	h. state of being; quality; region of authority
____ 9. **pro-**	pro-British, progress	i. cause to be or become; make
____10. **psych-, psycho-**	psychiatrist, psychological	j. resembling; like; characteristic of

PART B
Find the word part that correctly completes each word. Then write the full word in the blank space. Not every word part will be used.

cour	**du-**	**-dom**	**-fy**	**il-**
-ish	**magni-**	**phob**	**pro-**	**psycho-**

11. Considering all the books, movies, and TV programs in everyday life, there's no reason for (*bore . . .*) ____________________

12. Identical twins have (*. . . plicate*) ____________________ gene patterns.

13. Bacteria (*puri . . .*) ____________________ soil in which bodies are buried by destroying germs.

14. The (*nightmar . . .*) ____________________ experience of constantly hiccuping can be stopped with drugs.

15. A victim of (*acro . . . ia*) ____________________, a fear of heights, Diane refused any job that required working higher than the second floor.

PART C

Use your knowledge of word parts to determine the meaning of the boldfaced words. Circle the letter of each meaning.

16. The governor is **progambling.**

    a. against gambling b. a gambler c. in favor of gambling

17. A blue moon is **improbable.**

    a. shocking b. unlikely c. beautiful

18. We bought a **magnum** of champagne.

    a. large bottle b. medium-sized bottle c. little bottle

19. Ken's report emphasized the **core** of the plan.

    a. details b. background c. central part

20. Belle suffered from a **psychosis.**

    a. a physical disease b. a mental disorder c. a heart problem

SCORE: (Number correct) ________ x 5 = ________ %

Enter your scores above and in the vocabulary performance chart on the inside back cover of the book.

Unit Four

CHAPTER

19

Previewing the Words

Find out how many of the ten words in this chapter you already know. Try to complete each sentence with the most suitable word from the list below. Use each word once.

Leave a sentence blank rather than guessing at an answer. Your purpose here is just to get a sense of the ten words and what you may know about them.

benign	**blase**	**comprise**	**condescend**	**facade**
glib	**haughty**	**libel**	**pseudonym**	**redundant**

1. Although the ____________ of the hotel was dull and plain, the inside was fit for royalty.
2. The first-grade teacher's ____________ smile was encouraging to her new students.
3. My shampoo ____________s 22 ingredients, from herbs to Yellow Dye Number 5.
4. I'm sorry I snored in church, but the repetition in the minister's ____________ sermon put me to sleep.
5. Although everyone else in the office took turns making coffee, Bill would not ____________ to perform "such a lowly task."
6. Scarlett O'Hara was a ____________ young woman who became very annoyed if every man in the room did not admire her beauty.
7. The ____________ car salesman smoothly claimed that he was giving me the best deal ever, but he never really answered any of my questions.
8. A well-known political writer signed a humorous essay he wrote with a ____________. He didn't want readers who knew him to expect a serious piece.
9. In the winter, the very thought of a barbecue is exciting. But by Labor Day, we feel ____________ about cooking over charcoal again.
10. Most magazine editors double-check the facts they publish about a person. That way, if they are accused of ____________, they can prove they stated only the truth.

Now check your answers by turning to page 165. Fix any mistakes and fill in any blank spaces by writing in the correct answers. By doing so, you will complete this introduction to the ten words.

You're now ready to strengthen your knowledge of the words you already know and to master the words you're only half sure of, or don't know at all. Turn to the next page.

Ten Words in Context

Figure out the meanings of the following ten words by looking *closely and carefully* at the context in which the words appear. Doing so will prepare you for the matching test and practices on the two pages that follow.

1 **benign**
(bi-nīn')
-adjective

a. Finding a stranger on our doorstep startled me, but the **benign** expression on his face told me not to worry.

b. Gorilla mothers, usually loving and **benign,** become abusive to their babies when caged with them.

2 **blase**
(bla-zā')
-adjective

a. The new staff members were active and enthusiastic at their weekly meetings, but the old-timers were pretty **blase**.

b. No matter how many games I see, I will never become **blase** about baseball. Each game is new and exciting to me.

3 **comprise**
(kom-prīz')
-verb

a. The United Kingdom **comprises** England, Scotland, Wales and Northern Ireland.

b. Saliva **comprises** about sixty ingredients, including minerals that help repair tooth enamel.

4 **condescend**
(kon-di-send')
-verb

a. The snobby millionaire wouldn't **condescend** to associate with anyone of only middle or lower income.

b. The company president would occasionally **condescend** and eat lunch with the factory workers. His attitude showed that he really felt they were beneath him.

5 **facade**
(fə-sod')
-noun

a. The **facade** of the old department store was cleaned this summer. Now the store's brick front is an inviting bright orange-red.

b. Kevin puts on a macho **facade,** but inside he's really a kind and gentle man.

6 **glib**
(glib)
-adjective

a. Always ready with a slick promise, the **glib** politician smoothly talked his way into being re-elected.

b. The man thought his **glib** conversation would impress Sandra, but she found him insincere.

7 **haughty**
(hô'-tē)
-adjective

a. My Aunt Rose remained **haughty** even in her 70s. She refused to wear glasses because she felt they were unattractive, and she insisted that her children dress up to dine with her.

b. After being promoted to manager, Gil was **haughty** with his old office buddies, saying he now had more important things to do than gab with them.

8 **libel**
(lī'-bəl)
-noun

a. When Nick saw his name listed in the article as a gang member, he was furious. "That's **libel,**" he yelled. "How dare they print such a lie about me?"

b. One editor refused to print anything critical about anyone because he was afraid of being sued for **libel**. Another editor said, "Let them sue. We tell it like it is."

9 **pseudonym**
(sōō'-də-nim')
-noun

a. When writing a personal story for a family magazine, Bev used a **pseudonym**. She didn't want everyone in town to know about her problems.

b. Author Stephen King uses a **pseudonym** on some of his books so that readers won't be aware that many of the horror novels on the market are his.

10 **redundant**
(ri-dun'-dənt)
-adjective

a. The TV ad for a headache medicine was so **redundant** that it gave me a headache! The name of the product was repeated at least a dozen times.

b. Eric's teacher wrote "**redundant**" in several spots in his essay where he was wordy and too repetitive.

Matching Words and Definitions

Check your understanding of the ten words by matching each word with its definition. Look back at the sentences in "Ten Words in Context" as needed to decide on the meaning of each word.

_____	1. **benign**	a.	a false name used by an author
_____	2. **blase**	b.	to do something one feels is beneath oneself
_____	3. **comprise**	c.	unexcited or bored about something already experienced repeatedly
_____	4. **condescend**	d.	the front of a building; a false appearance
_____	5. **facade**	e.	wordy or needlessly repetitive
_____	6. **glib**	f.	kindly; gentle
_____	7. **haughty**	g.	the publishing of false information that harms a person's reputation
_____	8. **libel**	h.	proud of one's appearance or accomplishments to the point of looking down on others; arrogant
_____	9. **pseudonym**	i.	to consist of
_____	10. **redundant**	j.	characterized by a smooth, ready manner of speaking that often suggests insincerity and thoughtlessness; spoken in a smooth, ready manner

CAUTION: Do not go any further until you are sure the above answers are correct. If you have studied the "Ten Words in Context," you will know how to match each word. Then you can use the matches to help you in the following practices. Your goal is to reach a point where you don't need to check definitions at all.

➢*Sentence Check 1*

Complete each sentence below with the most suitable word from the box. Use each word once.

benign	**blase**	**comprise**	**condescend**	**facade**
glib	**haughty**	**libel**	**pseudonym**	**redundant**

1. An igloo ____________________s blocks of ice or hard snow.
2. My aunt's letters are annoyingly ____________________, always repeating the "news" of previous letters.
3. Since becoming a fashion model, Nora has been very ____________________, even snubbing some of her old, unglamorous friends.
4. One actress sued a magazine for ____________________ because it printed a false and damaging story about her being drunk in public.
5. Harry, always ready with some made-up excuse, is ____________________ enough to talk himself out of any difficulty at the snap of a finger.
6. In his usual ____________________ manner, my neighbor carefully picked up the ant in his kitchen, brought it outside, and gently put it down on the sidewalk.
7. When my sister first got her job at the recording studio, she was thrilled to go to work each day. Now, after 10 years, she's ____________________ about her work and wants to change jobs.
8. When he's not being a hero, Superman puts on the ____________________ of a bumbling, fearful reporter named Clark Kent.
9. The conceited young baseball player wouldn't ____________________ and talk to his fans until an old-timer reminded him that the fans are the ones who made him a star.
10. Samuel Langhorne Clemens wasn't the first author to use the ____________________ Mark Twain. A newspaper writer of the time used the same pen name.

Now check your answers to these questions by turning to page 165. Going over the answers carefully will help you prepare for the next two checks, for which answers are not given.

➢Sentence Check 2

Complete each sentence below with two words from the box. Use each word once.

benign	blase	comprise	condescend	facade
glib	haughty	libel	pseudonym	redundant

1-2. Believing he was better than everyone else at the supermarket, Dan was so ____________________ that he would rarely ____________________ to speak to the other cashiers.

3-4. One author was accused of ____________________ when he wrote a damaging article about the governor's wife. After that, he used a ____________________, so others wouldn't know he was the author whose facts were in doubt.

5-6. At first Joanne thought Barry was too ____________________, that his smooth talk was all show. As she got to know him better, however, she found that his easy manner reflected a friendly and ____________________ nature.

7-8. The scenery crew for the summer theatre ____________________(e)d three artists and a set designer. Last year they built a beautiful stage model of the ____________________ of a palace, with towers and a golden door.

9-10. Mr. Edwards quit teaching writing when he realized he had become ____________________ from repeatedly seeing the same student problems: careless organization, lack of focus, and writing so ____________________ that paragraphs held only a sentence of meaning.

➢*Final Check:* Interview with a Rude Star

Here is a final opportunity for you to strengthen your knowledge of the ten words. First read the following passage carefully. Then fill in each blank with a word from the box at the top of this page. (Context clues will help you figure out which word goes in which blank.) Use each word once.

When a famous actress arrived in town to work on a movie, an editor asked me to interview her. Since this was my first interview assignment, I felt far from (1)____________________ about it. Instead, I was both excited and scared. Would a star (2)____________________ to see me, an unknown, inexperienced reporter?

When I arrived at the movie set, I saw the actress standing in front of the painted (3)____________________ of a mansion. During a break in the filming, I approached her and introduced myself. "Well, let's get this over with," she said, clearly annoyed.

The interview went terribly. Although it (4)____________________(e)d carefully thought-out questions, she sighed or rolled her eyes at every one of them. And no matter how (5)____________________ my manner, she seemed to view me as some sort of threat. At one point, she completely lost her temper and yelled, "Don't be (6)____________________! I don't have time to answer the same question twice." When I asked her about serious issues, she was totally (7)____________________ in her answers, which were insincere and shallow.

Now that the interview is over, I have to write about her. Should I say that she's a (8)____________________, rude woman who thinks only of herself and expects others to do the same? If I do, she might sue me for (9)____________________. I wonder if the editor would let me write under a (10)____________________, so my real name won't be on an article about this miserable woman.

SCORES: Sentence Check 2 ________% Final Check ________%

Enter your scores above and in the vocabulary performance chart on the inside back cover of the book.

CHAPTER 20

Previewing the Words

Find out how many of the ten words in this chapter you already know. Try to complete each sentence with the most suitable word from the list below. Use each word once.

Leave a sentence blank rather than guessing at an answer. Your purpose here is just to get a sense of the ten words and what you may know about them.

averse	**detract**	**disdain**	**divulge**	**elation**
endow	**expulsion**	**mortify**	**nullify**	**ominous**

1. It's against the law to ask people to ____________________ their age at a job interview.
2. The enormous amount of makeup that Sara wears ____________________s from her natural beauty.
3. Although Gene was overjoyed and proud to have won the Senate race, he was too tired to show ____________________.
4. One student faces permanent ____________________ from high school for continually stealing from other people's lockers.
5. My little brother used to be ____________________ to any foreign food, but now he enjoys Chinese, Indian, and African dishes.
6. A soft drink company decided to ____________________ its contract with a well-known athlete because he was arrested for drunk driving.
7. One of my classmates is ____________________(e)d with such musical talent that at six she could hear a tune once and then play it on the piano.
8. Steve feared Lorna might view his rusting old car with ____________________ until he pulled up to her house and saw a car in even worse condition.
9. The horror movie opened with a view of a(n) ____________________ old house. Its dark shadows and location high on a cliff seemed to warn of some evil to come.
10. I doubt anything will ever ____________________ me more than the streamer of toilet paper that clung to my shoe as I returned from the ladies' room to rejoin my date in a fancy restaurant.

Now check your answers by turning to page 165. Fix any mistakes and fill in any blank spaces by writing in the correct answers. By doing so, you will complete this introduction to the ten words.

You're now ready to strengthen your knowledge of the words you already know and to master the words you're only half sure of, or don't know at all. Turn to the next page.

Ten Words in Context

Figure out the meanings of the following ten words by looking *closely and carefully* at the context in which the words appear. Doing so will prepare you for the matching test and practices on the two pages that follow.

1 **averse**
(ə-vûrs')
-adjective

a. My son was once so **averse** to tomatoes that the very sight of them made him gag.

b. Being **averse** to screaming crowds, I'd rather stay home and listen to a record than go to a rock concert.

2 **detract**
(di-trakt')
-verb

a. Julius thinks the scar on his cheek **detracts** from his good looks, but it's barely noticeable.

b. All of the litter in the park certainly **detracts** from the beauty of the trees and flowers.

3 **disdain**
(dis-dān')
-noun

a. The snobby waiter in the French restaurant viewed Tanya with **disdain** because she couldn't pronounce anything on the menu.

b. I was afraid my request to see the state senator would be treated with **disdain**. Instead, the senator's secretary politely made an appointment for me.

4 **divulge**
(di-vulj')
-verb

a. My father wouldn't **divulge** the type of car he had bought, saying only, "It's a surprise."

b. Unaware that his hairpiece is obvious, Ted has never **divulged** that he's bald, even to his closest friends.

5 **elation**
(i-lā'-shən)
-noun

a. The principal shouted with **elation** when the school team scored the winning touchdown.

b. Roy had expected to feel **elation** at his graduation. Instead, he felt sadness at the thought of parting with some of his high school friends.

6 **endow**
(en-dou')
-verb

a. Nature has **endowed** hummingbirds with the ability to fly backward.

b. Oscar Wilde was **endowed** with the ability to find humor in any situation. While dying, he said of the ugly wallpaper in his hotel room, "One of us had to go."

7 **expulsion**
(eks-pul'-shən)
-noun

a. The theater manager told us we risked **expulsion** from the theater if we continued to talk during the movie.

b. **Expulsion** from school is intended as a punishment, but some students may consider not having to attend classes to be a reward.

8 **mortify**
(môr'-tə-fī')
-verb

a. It would **mortify** me if my voice were to crack during my choir solo.

b. James was completely **mortified** when he proposed and Carla just laughed in his face.

9 **nullify**
(nul'-ə-fī')
-verb

a. The college will **nullify** my student ID at the end of the term unless I update it with a new sticker.

b. The dead woman's will was **nullified** when her daughter proved that the signature on it had been faked by the woman's lover.

10 **ominous**
(om'-ə-nəs)
-adjective

a. To many, cemeteries have an **ominous** quality, particularly at night or on Halloween, when the threat of ghosts can seem very real.

b. The sore's failure to heal was **ominous**, a possible sign of cancer.

Matching Words and Definitions

Check your understanding of the ten words by matching each word with its definition. Look back at the sentences in "Ten Words in Context" as needed to decide on the meaning of each word.

_____	1. **averse (to)**	a.	to provide with a talent or quality
_____	2. **detract (from)**	b.	an attitude or feeling of contempt; scorn
_____	3. **disdain**	c.	the act or condition of being dismissed or sent away
_____	4. **divulge**	d.	threatening evil or harm; menacing
_____	5. **elation**	e.	to reveal; make known
_____	6. **endow**	f.	having a feeling of dislike or distaste for something, thus tending to avoid it
_____	7. **expulsion**	g.	to humiliate or embarrass
_____	8. **mortify**	h.	to lessen what is admirable or worthwhile about something
_____	9. **nullify**	i.	a feeling of great joy or pride
_____	10. **ominous**	j.	to make legally ineffective; cancel

CAUTION: Do not go any further until you are sure the above answers are correct. If you have studied the "Ten Words in Context," you will know how to match each word. Then you can use the matches to help you in the following practices. Your goal is to reach a point where you don't need to check definitions at all.

➢*Sentence Check 1*

Complete each sentence below with the most suitable word from the box. Use each word once.

averse	**detract**	**disdain**	**divulge**	**elation**
endow	**expulsion**	**mortified**	**nullified**	**ominous**

1. People talking in a movie theater greatly _____________________ from the experience of watching a film.
2. Because of the dark, _____________________ storm clouds, we cancelled the softball game.
3. I'm _____________________ to speaking in public since I don't enjoy making a fool of myself.
4. When he received the college scholarship, my brother felt such _____________________ that he wept with joy.
5. The results of the mayor's election were _____________________ after the townspeople found evidence of voting fraud.
6. The American water shrew is _____________________(e)d with feet that have air pockets, enabling the small animal to walk on water.
7. Some want a law calling for the _____________________ of illegal immigrants. Others want all immigrants to be allowed to stay in the U.S.
8. Vinnie's repeated boasts about his muscle-building backfired. They caused his date to look at him with _____________________, not admiration.
9. Labels on American foods must list the product's ingredients, but many other countries don't require that a product's contents be _____________________(e)d.
10. The reporter was _____________________ when he was told that he had delivered much of his news story facing away from the operating TV camera.

Now check your answers to these questions by turning to page 165. Going over the answers carefully will help you prepare for the next two checks, for which answers are not given.

➢Sentence Check 2

Complete each sentence below with two words from the following list. Use each word once.

averse	detract	disdain	divulge	elation
endow	expulsion	mortified	nullified	ominous

1-2. Some people are so ____________________ to living near a nuclear plant that they want the the plant's license to be ____________________.

3-4. Shannon is ____________________(e)d with beautiful curly red hair, but her self-image is so low that she feels her hair ____________________s from her looks.

5-6. When someone ____________________(e)d to college officials that a certain student was selling drugs, an investigation began that led to that student's ____________________ from college.

7-8. Amy was ____________________ by the low grade she received for her class speech, a grade she considered a sign of the teacher's ____________________ for her.

9-10. Marty had believed his headaches and blurred vision were ____________________ signs of some terrible disease, so he felt ____________________ when he learned that he simply needed glasses.

➢*Final Check:* The Nightmare of Gym

Here is a final opportunity for you to strengthen your knowledge of the ten words. First read the following passage carefully. Then fill in each blank with a word from the box at the top of this page. (Context clues will help you figure out which word goes in which blank.) Use each word once.

I was not (1)____________________(e)d with athletic ability. In a frequent nightmare, I'm still trying to pass gym so that I can graduate from high school. The situation always looks grim. For one thing, the teacher has threatened me with (2)____________________ from school for refusing to take a group shower. Also appearing in my dream is the terrifying vault horse, the very sight of which (3)____________________s from my mental health. I run toward the horse, leap, and nose-dive into the mat. Ignoring my despair, the rest of the gym class laughs. Once again, I am (4)____________________ by my athletic performance.

Next, a single (5)__________________ rope threatens overhead, where it hangs from the ceiling. Wondering if anyone has ever died from rope burn, I struggle to climb it. Almost to the top, I sweat so much that I slide back to the floor, landing at the gym teacher's feet. "What a loser," the teacher mutters with an expression of total (6)____________________.

Because I've always been (7)____________________ to square-dancing, that too appears in the nightmare. Having forgotten my sneakers, I'm forced to dance in my socks. I slip, rather than dance, around the polished floor. During one high-speed turn, I go sliding—right into the men's locker room, where the smell causes me to pass out.

The only pleasant part of the dream comes near the end. With amazement and (8)____________________, I learn that I will graduate after all.

But then, the principal (9)____________________s the terrible truth. I haven't managed to pass gym. My graduation depends on my agreeing to take four more years of gym when I get to college. If I don't, my high school diploma will be (10)____________________.

SCORES: Sentence Check 2 ________% Final Check ________%

Enter your scores above and in the vocabulary performance chart on the inside back cover of the book.

CHAPTER

21

Previewing the Words

Find out how many of the ten words in this chapter you already know. Try to complete each sentence with the most suitable word from the list below. Use each word once.

Leave a sentence blank rather than guessing at an answer. Your purpose here is just to get a sense of the ten words and what you may know about them.

credible	**cursory**	**designate**	**deviate**	**improvise**
interim	**latent**	**secular**	**shun**	**simulate**

1. Jean's allergies force her to ____________________ many foods she used to enjoy, including chocolate.
2. The church library has a surprising number of ____________________ books on its shelves.
3. The presidential candidate gets to ____________________ who will run for vice president.
4. "Playing possum" is not just a myth. When it is threatened, the possum really does ____________________ dying.
5. During the ____________________ between 2 to 4 p.m., the house is fairly peaceful because that's when the baby takes her nap.
6. By exposing students to a variety of subjects, schools help young people discover their ____________________ talents.
7. When I got to the last essay question of the test, time was almost up, so all I could write was a(n) ____________________ answer.
8. As ____________________ as Mr. Bower's resume may seem, I don't think you should hire him without checking that it really is truthful.
9. "We will not ____________________ from our protest until our demands are met!" declared the union leader.
10. On the piano, Nadia can ____________________ accompaniments to songs she's never heard before. I don't know how she plays so well without any preparation or sheet music.

Now check your answers by turning to page 165. Fix any mistakes and fill in any blank spaces by writing in the correct answers. By doing so, you will complete this introduction to the ten words.

You're now ready to strengthen your knowledge of the words you already know and to master the words you're only half sure of, or don't know at all. Turn to the next page.

Ten Words in Context

Figure out the meanings of the following ten words by looking *closely and carefully* at the context in which the words appear. Doing so will prepare you for the matching test and practices on the two pages that follow.

1 **credible**
(kred'-ə-bəl)
-adjective

a. The jurors must have found the state's witnesses **credible,** for they found the defendant guilty.

b. I lent money to a friend with a **credible** hard-luck story, but I began to suspect the story was false when I saw her driving a new car.

2 **cursory**
(kûr'-sə-rē)
-adjective

a. Most people do only a **cursory** job of brushing their teeth. To avoid cavities, however, you must take the time to brush carefully.

b. Because I had to work late, I had only enough time to give my apartment a **cursory** cleaning before my parents arrived.

3 **designate**
(dez'-ig-nāt')
-verb

a. At the party, Betty drank soda rather than beer, so her friends **designated** her driver for the trip home.

b. A co-worker was **designated** to give Vonnie the "Employee of the Year" award at the banquet.

4 **deviate**
(dē'-vē-āt')
-verb

a. Having taken the wrong exit off the highway, I **deviated** somewhat from the route marked on the map.

b. If you **deviate** even a little from the test's directions, you might hurt your grade.

5 **improvise**
(im'-prə-vīz')
-verb

a. Stand-up comics sometimes **improvise** routines based on themes suggested by the audience.

b. When I rang the doorbell, I wasn't expecting Ellen's father to come to the door, so I had to quickly **improvise** an explanation for my visit.

6 **interim**
(in'-tər-im)
-noun

a. Cassie hadn't seen her nephews for years. In the **interim,** they had grown from rascals into serious young men.

b. In the **interim** between the secretary leaving and our boss hiring someone new, we had to do our own typing.

7 **latent**
(lāt'-ənt)
-adjective

a. Certain viruses, such as the one for AIDS, can be **latent** in the body for years before symptoms appear.

b. After he retired, my father discovered his **latent** artistic talent. He took up oil painting and now sells much of his work.

8 **secular**
(sek'-yə-lər)
-adjective

a. In addition to the **secular** public school, there are several church-related high schools in town.

b. The Hindu holy man denied himself many **secular** pleasures and devoted himself to a life of prayer.

9 **shun**
(shun)
-verb

a. I used to see a lot of Tracy, but since our argument, she **shuns** me whenever possible.

b. The Amish live without many modern conveniences. For example, they **shun** automobiles and electric lights.

10 **simulate**
(sim'-yo͞o-lāt')
-verb

a. The tan plastic of our kitchen table, with its wood-grain design, **simulates** oak.

b. Equipment that **simulates** a human heart can keep someone alive only temporarily, until an actual heart can be substituted.

Matching Words and Definitions

Check your understanding of the ten words by matching each word with its definition. Look back at the sentences in "Ten Words in Context" as needed to decide on the meaning of each word.

_____	1. **credible**	a.	to compose, perform, or provide without preparation
_____	2. **cursory**	b.	believable
_____	3. **designate**	c.	the period of time in between; meantime
_____	4. **deviate**	d.	to name to an office or duty; appoint
_____	5. **improvise**	e.	to act or look like; imitate
_____	6. **interim**	f.	not directly related to religion
_____	7. **latent**	g.	done quickly and without attention to detail
_____	8. **secular**	h.	to keep away from; avoid consistently
_____	9. **shun**	i.	present but hidden or inactive
_____	10. **simulate**	j.	to turn aside or stray, as from a path, direction, or standard

CAUTION: Do not go any further until you are sure the above answers are correct. If you have studied the "Ten Words in Context," you will know how to match each word. Then you can use the matches to help you in the following practices. Your goal is to reach a point where you don't need to check definitions at all.

➢Sentence Check 1

Complete each sentence below with the most suitable word from the box. Use each word once.

credible	**cursory**	**designate**	**deviate**	**improvise**
interim	**latent**	**secular**	**shun**	**simulate**

1. My daughter's ____________________ talent for sarcasm became apparent when she turned 12.
2. Presidents ____________________ as Supreme Court justices people who share their political views.
3. What caused Andy to ____________________ from his college-bound course and drop out of high school?
4. Because his "flat tire" story sounded ________________, my parents allowed the stranger to use our telephone.
5. In the ____________________ between applying to college and getting the letter of acceptance, I spent a lot of time worrying.
6. Margo couldn't identify the driver of the car. She'd given him only a(n) ____________________ glance at the time of the accident.
7. The chorus is known for its gospel music, but it also performs ____________________ compositions, including show tunes.
8. When the actor forgot his lines, he was forced to ____________________ until the stage manager whispered to him from offstage.
9. Tony found the hardest part of kicking his addiction was learning to ____________________ people and places that would tempt him to use drugs again.
10. The zoo's exhibits ________________ the natural environments of its animals. The orangutans, for example, live in a space that looks much like an Asian rain forest.

Now check your answers to these questions by turning to page 165. Going over the answers carefully will help you prepare for the next two checks, for which answers are not given.

➢Sentence Check 2

Complete each sentence below with two words from the box. Use each word once.

credible	cursory	designate	deviate	improvise
interim	latent	secular	shun	simulate

1-2. In the ________ between 7th and 8th grades, my ________ interest in girls began to surface.

3-4. Although it's a Catholic university, the school gives much more than ________ attention to ________ subjects. The popular math courses, for example, are taught at a high level.

5-6. Matt told his mother he was late because he had fallen while running home. To make his lie more ________, he had scratched his knee with a rock to ________ an injury from a fall.

7-8. Della wanted to be a cheerleader, but she willingly ________(e)d from that goal when she was ________(e)d class mascot and got to wear a polar bear costume to all the games.

9-10. The psychology teacher asked several students to come to the head of the class and ________ a scene in which several snobbish students ________ a quiet student who is trying to be friendly.

➤*Final Check:* Skipping Church

Here is a final opportunity for you to strengthen your knowledge of the ten words. First read the following passage carefully. Then fill in each blank with a word from the box at the top of this page. (Context clues will help you figure out which word goes in which blank.) Use each word once.

How well I remember the time my mother's back injury prevented her from going to church with my brother and me. For five weeks we were to go by ourselves. Zack and I then preferred (1)________ activities to church-going, so we decided to (2)________ church while Mom was recovering. We (3)________(e)d the church-goers she wanted us to be by getting dressed in our church clothes and leaving home and returning at the right times. We spent the (4)________ at a restaurant or the movies. Of course, we knew Mom would question us about the service. Each week we would (5)________ one of us to invent a sermon. I thought Zack's sermons sounded not only (6)________, but inspiring. I, in contrast, tended to (7)________ on the spot and didn't sound so believable. But Mom never seemed to notice how weak my sermons were or how (8)________ our answers were when she asked whom we'd seen and what news we'd heard.

Finally, she was ready to attend church again. Over dinner Saturday evening, she began what seemed to be an innocent conversation. Gently, but showing a previously (9)________ talent for cross-examination that could have made her a star attorney, she questioned us about our "church-going." The more she asked, the more Zack and I stumbled and (10)________(e)d from our official story. We eventually concluded we were caught and blurted out the truth. We felt pretty foolish when we realized she'd known all along.

SCORES: Sentence Check 2 ________% Final Check ________%

Enter your scores above and in the vocabulary performance chart on the inside back cover of the book.

CHAPTER

22

Previewing the Words

Find out how many of the ten words in this chapter you already know. Try to complete each sentence with the most suitable word from the list below. Use each word once.

Leave a sentence blank rather than guessing at an answer. Your purpose here is just to get a sense of the ten words and what you may know about them.

commemorate	**complacent**	**consensus**	**deplete**	**diligent**
empathy	**menial**	**niche**	**transcend**	**waive**

1. The fox terrier was so ____________________ in his digging that he soon escaped under the fence.
2. We ____________________ the late Martin Luther King, Jr., on his birthday, now a national holiday.
3. Many people believe that Shakespeare's works continue to ____________________ those of all other authors.
4. According to the survey, the community ____________________ is that a swimming pool is needed more than a new parking lot.
5. Dom spent the years after college moving restlessly from job to job, never finding a comfortable ____________________ for himself.
6. I'd like to help you out with a loan, but some unexpected car repairs have managed to ______________ my bank account.
7. Because adults were once kids, they often have ____________________ for children. Kids, on the other hand, rarely identify with adults.
8. Victor seems to think my summer job delivering pizza is too____________________, but I'm enjoying learning my way around the city.
9. The old man decided to ____________________ any claim he had to the family fortune, preferring to see the money go to the younger generation.
10. The restaurant got off to a good start, but then the owners became ____________________ about their success and stopped trying to attract new customers.

Now check your answers by turning to page 165. Fix any mistakes and fill in any blank spaces by writing in the correct answers. By doing so, you will complete this introduction to the ten words.

You're now ready to strengthen your knowledge of the words you already know and to master the words you're only half sure of, or don't know at all. Turn to the next page.

Ten Words in Context

Figure out the meanings of the following ten words by looking *closely and carefully* at the context in which the words appear. Doing so will prepare you for the matching test and practices on the two pages that follow.

1 **commemorate** (kə-mem'-ə-rāt') *-verb*

a. Thomas devoted his life to feeding the hungry. So on the anniversary of his death it seems wrong to **commemorate** him with a fancy dinner party that only the rich can attend.

b. Each year, my parents **commemorate** their first date by dancing to some of the same songs they danced to that night.

2 **complacent** (kəm-plā'-sənt) *-adjective*

a. Elected officials cannot afford to be overly **complacent** about winning an election. Before long, they'll have to campaign again for the voters' support.

b. Getting all A's hasn't made Ivy **complacent**. She continues to work hard at school.

3 **consensus** (kən-sen'-səs) *-noun*

a. A vote revealed strong agreement among the teachers. The **consensus** was that they would strike if the school board did not act quickly to raise their pay.

b. A vote revealed the family **consensus** was that we should go camping again this summer. Ray was the only one who wanted to do something else for a change.

4 **deplete** (di-plēt') *-verb*

a. No one **depletes** my supply of sympathy faster than my brother. He's always asking for pity.

b. In order not to **deplete** their small quantity of canned food, the survivors of the shipwreck searched the island for plants they could eat.

5 **diligent** (dil'-ə-jənt) *-adjective*

a. I wish I had been more **diligent** about practicing piano when I was younger. It would be nice to be able to play well now.

b. Diane was lazy when she first joined the family business, but now she's become so **diligent** that she inspires others to work harder.

6 **empathy** (em'-pə-thē) *-noun*

a. Families who have lost loved ones in the Vietnam War have **empathy** for one another because of their shared grief.

b. Ms. Allan is an excellent career counselor partly because of her great **empathy**. She understands each student's feelings and point of view.

7 **menial** (mē'-nē-əl) *-adjective*

a. At summer camp, everyone shares in the **menial** work. Even the counselors clean bathrooms and mop floors.

b. Every job can be done with pride. Even such **menial** jobs as washing windows or scrubbing floors can be performed with care.

8 **niche** (nich) *-noun*

a. Although her degree was in accounting, Laura decided her **niche** was really in business management, so she went back to school for more training.

b. Chet felt his sister's household provided a good **niche** for him since he was a bachelor who enjoyed having people of all ages around.

9 **transcend** (tran-send') *-verb*

a. The psychic convinced her clients that she could **transcend** the restrictions of time and space and talk directly with the dead.

b. Yoga exercises are supposed to help one **transcend** the cares of the world and reach a state of relaxation.

10 **waive** (wāv) *-verb*

a. The defendant decided to **waive** his right to an attorney and, instead, speak for himself in court.

b. Since Lin had studied so much math on her own, the school **waived** the requirement that she take high school algebra.

Matching Words and Definitions

Check your understanding of the ten words by matching each word with its definition. Look back at the sentences in "Ten Words in Context" as needed to decide on the meaning of each word.

_____	1. **commemorate**	a.	not requiring special skills or higher intellectual abilities; lowly
_____	2. **complacent**	b.	the ability to share in someone else's feelings or thoughts
_____	3. **consensus**	c.	to rise above or go beyond the limits of; exceed
_____	4. **deplete**	d.	to honor the memory of someone or something, as with a ceremony; celebrate; observe
_____	5. **diligent**	e.	to willingly give up (as a claim, privilege, or right); do without; forgo
_____	6. **empathy**	f.	an opinion held by most or all involved
_____	7. **menial**	g.	self-satisfied; feeling too much satisfaction with oneself or one's accomplishments
_____	8. **niche**	h.	steady, determined, and careful in work
_____	9. **transcend**	i.	an activity or place especially suited to a person
_____	10. **waive**	j.	to use up

CAUTION: Do not go any further until you are sure the above answers are correct. If you have studied the "Ten Words in Context," you will know how to match each word. Then you can use the matches to help you in the following practices. Your goal is to reach a point where you don't need to check definitions at all.

➢ Sentence Check 1

Complete each sentence below with the most suitable word from the box. Use each word once.

commemorate	**complacent**	**consensus**	**deplete**	**diligent**
empathy	**menial**	**niche**	**transcend**	**waive**

1. Amber offered to ____________________ her turn on the swing so the younger kids could use it.
2. The American Inventors Association gathered at a banquet to ____________________ Thomas Edison.
3. The old man is weak, so it doesn't take much effort for him to ____________________ the little energy he has.
4. Fans of gymnastics believe it is an art form that ____________________s the ordinary world of sports.
5. If society becomes ____________________ about its situation, it will never move toward solving its problems.
6. Several sessions with a career counselor helped Suzanne consider what her ____________________ in the working world might be.
7. When the children help out at the family restaurant, they perform ____________________ tasks such as mopping and cleaning tables.
8. Arnie has been ____________________ in his German studies because he hopes to speak the language with his relatives from Germany when they visit next summer.
9. I had hoped the restaurant would be good, but our group's ____________________ was that the food was only so-so and the service was even worse.
10. Dr. Grange is a brilliant mathematician, but she has little ____________________ for her students. She doesn't understand how they can find some problems so difficult.

Now check your answers to these questions by turning to page 165. Going over the answers carefully will help you prepare for the next two checks, for which answers are not given.

➢Sentence Check 2

Complete each sentence below with two words from the following list. Use each word once.

commemorate	complacent	consensus	deplete	diligent
empathy	menial	niche	transcend	waive

1-2. Lynn begged the bank to ________________ the overdraft charge, telling them that the $20 would entirely ________________ her savings.

3-4. In high school, Victor was voted "Most Likely to Become a Psychologist." It was the ________________ of his classmates that he was the student with the most ________________ for other people.

5-6. My mother could have stayed in her comfortable ________________ as part of the secretarial pool, but she wanted to ________________ the limits of that job and become an executive herself.

7-8. "On this, our 100th anniversary celebration," said the company president, "I'd like to ________________ our founder with a toast. He ran the company from top to bottom, doing even such ________________ jobs as emptying garbage cans."

9-10. Dr. Roberts and Dr. Krill practice medicine very differently. Roberts is ________________ about reading journals and learning new techniques, while Krill, more ________________, never tries anything new.

➢*Final Check:* A Model Teacher

Here is a final opportunity for you to strengthen your knowledge of the ten words. First read the following passage carefully. Then fill in each blank with a word from the box at the top of this page. (Context clues will help you figure out which word goes in which blank.) Use each word once.

At Eastman High School reunions, the conversation usually gets around to the question: "Which teacher do you remember best?" And year after year, the (1)________________ of the graduates is Mr. MacDonald. Many remember Joe MacDonald as the teacher against whom they measured all others.

He had started his professional life as a highly paid attorney, but never at home with that work, he left the law and found his (2) ________________ as an English teacher in the shabby classrooms at Eastman. Mr. MacDonald somehow helped his students (3)________________ their broken-down surroundings until they, too, could experience the magic in the words of Shakespeare, Dickinson, or Frost. Even those who tended to avoid reading began to think there might be something to this literature stuff after all.

Mr. MacDonald never (4)________________(e)d his enthusiasm for teaching or for students. Other teachers became (5)________________ about their work and didn't put much time into lesson preparation. But Mr. MacDonald was as (6)________________ as an eager first-year teacher. He could often be found talking with students after school, as his great (7)________________ had given him the reputation of being someone who understood students' problems. He was fun, too. On the first really beautiful spring day of each year, he'd (8)________________ his lesson plan and take the class out into the sunshine to sit under the blue sky and talk about literature. And no task was too (9)________________ for him. He was often seen picking up trash from the grounds or even pulling stray weeds from around a shrub.

After Mr. MacDonald's retirement, his former students wanted to honor him in some way. They thought about a statue, but decided to (10)________________ his teaching in the way that he'd like best, with a college scholarship for an Eastman student, which was established in his name.

SCORES: Sentence Check 2 ________% Final Check ________%

Enter your scores above and in the vocabulary performance chart on the inside back cover of the book.

CHAPTER

23

Previewing the Words

Find out how many of the ten words in this chapter you already know. Try to complete each sentence with the most suitable word from the list below. Use each word once.

Leave a sentence blank rather than guessing at an answer. Your purpose here is just to get a sense of the ten words and what you may know about them.

bizarre	conducive	falter	flaunt	frenzy
gist	hamper	paradox	repertoire	viable

1. We asked Alex to skip the details and get right to the ____________________ of the argument.
2. Frequent partying is not ____________________ to one's earning high grades.
3. After losing 68 pounds, Pat wanted to ____________________ her new figure in a tight size-10 dress.
4. I was in a ____________________ because I had locked my keys in the car and I was already 20 minutes late for work.
5. My young son quickly learned that using plastic tape is not a ____________________ solution to mending a broken vase.
6. Vince ____________________(e)d on the first few notes of his piano piece, but then played the rest without hesitation.
7. Teenaged mothers learn all too quickly that babies can ____________________ a young parent's freedom to socialize and pursue an education.
8. Every time my Aunt Zelda and her children visited, she made them perform their entire ____________________ of songs and dances.
9. The woman's ____________________ makeup included white lipstick and eyebrow pencil lines that could have been drawn on with Magic Markers.
10. When Joan kept postponing her decision about whether or not to go back to school, I reminded her of the ____________________ "No decision is also a decision."

Now check your answers by turning to page 166. Fix any mistakes and fill in any blank spaces by writing in the correct answers. By doing so, you will complete this introduction to the ten words.

You're now ready to strengthen your knowledge of the words you already know and to master the words you're only half sure of, or don't know at all. Turn to the next page.

Ten Words in Context

Figure out the meanings of the following ten words by looking *closely and carefully* at the context in which the words appear. Doing so will prepare you for the matching test and practices on the two pages that follow.

1 **bizarre**
(bi-zor')
-adjective

a. Some mentally ill people have **bizarre** ideas. For example, they may think the TV is talking to them or that others can steal their thoughts.

b. Wally's outfits may seem **bizarre**, but if you see him with his even stranger-looking friends, his dress looks quite ordinary.

2 **conducive**
(kən-dōō'-siv)
-adjective

a. A deliciously warm and sunny April day is **conducive** to a bad case of spring fever.

b. Learning to budget an allowance at a young age is **conducive** to good spending habits later in life.

3 **falter**
(fôl'-tər)
-verb

a. Although the flower girl was only three years old, she didn't **falter** even once as she walked down the aisle.

b. Even public speakers who now sound smooth and confident must have **faltered** when giving their first speeches.

4 **flaunt**
(flônt)
-verb

a. Instead of enjoying their wealth quietly, the Stewarts **flaunt** every new thing they buy in front of their poor relatives.

b. Cindy never **flaunted** her high grades. In fact, I didn't know that she was first in her class until she received the highest awards at graduation.

5 **frenzy**
(fren'-zē)
-noun

a. When I couldn't find my little son in the department store, I went into a **frenzy** and didn't calm down until I knew he was safe.

b. The holiday season always includes a **frenzy** of last-minute shopping.

6 **gist**
(jist)
-noun

a. The **gist** of the novel is that a family got stranded on an island and had to struggle to survive.

b. I don't know Spanish well, but if you speak slowly enough, I'll get the **gist** of what you're saying.

7 **hamper**
(ham'-pər)
-verb

a. "We never meant to **hamper** your struggle for independence," Tom's parents said. "From now on, we'll let you handle your own life, including your laundry and meals."

b. Hank used to swim in cut-off jeans. But when he noticed they **hampered** his speed, he switched to sleek swimming trunks.

8 **paradox**
(par'-ə-doks')
-noun

a. My mother used to recite this **paradox** to my father: "When a husband brings his wife flowers for no reason, there's a reason."

b. When a customer tried to pull a can from the bottom of the pile, the supermarket manager muttered, "It's an unfortunate **paradox** that common sense is not so common."

9 **repertoire**
(rep'-ər-twor')
-noun

a. The actor's **repertoire** includes drama, story-telling, song, and dance.

b. In order to be successful in college, it's important to have a **repertoire** of study strategies from which to choose.

10 **viable**
(vī'-ə-bəl)
-adjective

a. The parties in the labor dispute can reach a **viable** agreement if both sides benefit equally.

b. All the king's horses and all the king's men tried to come up with a **viable** way to repair Humpty Dumpty, but nothing worked.

Matching Words and Definitions

Check your understanding of the ten words by matching each word with its definition. Look back at the sentences in "Ten Words in Context" as needed to decide on the meaning of each word.

_____	1. **bizarre**	a.	the main point or essential part of a matter; central idea
_____	2. **conducive (to)**	b.	to act or speak with uncertainty; hesitate
_____	3. **falter**	c.	to limit, interfere with, or restrict
_____	4. **flaunt**	d.	a wild outburst of excited feelings or actions
_____	5. **frenzy**	e.	workable; capable of being successful or effective
_____	6. **gist**	f.	a statement that seems contradictory yet may be true
_____	7. **hamper**	g.	a range or collection of skills or accomplishments
_____	8. **paradox**	h.	dramatically unusual, as in manner or appearance; strange; odd
_____	9. **repertoire**	i.	tending to promote or bring about
_____	10. **viable**	j.	to show off (something)

CAUTION: Do not go any further until you are sure the above answers are correct. If you have studied the "Ten Words in Context," you will know how to match each word. Then you can use the matches to help you in the following practices. Your goal is to reach a point where you don't need to check definitions at all.

➢Sentence Check 1

Complete each sentence below with the most suitable word from the box. Use each word once.

bizarre	**conducive**	**falter**	**flaunt**	**frenzy**
gist	**hamper**	**paradox**	**repertoire**	**viable**

1. Halloween offers everyone the chance to look as ____________________ as possible.
2. Dustin Hoffman's ____________________ includes both modern dramas and Shakespearian plays.
3. When a reporter asked Senator Drake a difficult question, the senator ________________(e)d for a moment.
4. For snails, heat is ____________________ to sleep. In fact, desert snails may sleep for even three or four years.
5. The ____________________ of Kelly's essay was that school should be open only four days a week, from 8 a.m. to 6 p.m.
6. Since ordinary clothes may ____________________ movement, sweat suits and leotards are recommended for the exercise class.
7. This morning, the staff could not come up with a ____________________ plan to improve business. Every suggestion had a drawback.
8. When Chun's parents said they worried when he didn't call home, he said, "Remember that well-known ____________________—no news is good news."
9. My sister was in a ____________________ because her luggage hadn't arrived at the airport and she needed the suit she had brought to wear at a job interview.
10. Lucas believed the only way he could get a date was to __________________ his wealth by driving expensive sports cars and wearing thick gold chains.

Now check your answers to these questions by turning to page 166. Going over the answers carefully will help you prepare for the next two checks, for which answers are not given.

➢ *Sentence Check 2*

Complete each sentence below with two words from the box. Use each word once.

bizarre	**conducive**	**falter**	**flaunt**	**frenzy**
gist	**hamper**	**paradox**	**repertoire**	**viable**

1-2. Although Jenny chose the songs from her ____________ that she knew best, she was afraid she would ____________ the night of the concert.

3-4. The ____________ of the lecture was that although the U.S. encourages free trade, some other countries ____________ it.

5-6. The joking and teasing at today's staff meeting wasn't ____________ to problem-solving. No one thought of a ____________ way to ease the parking problem.

7-8. Bob changes his mind so often that his rapid shifts in opinion sometimes make me furious. Once, in a ____________ of anger, I shouted this ____________: "You're always the same—always changing your mind!"

9-10. My mother took me aside at the party and said, "That looks more like a strange costume than a dress. It's bad enough your clothing looks so ____________, but do you have to ____________ it in front of all my friends?"

➢ *Final Check:* My Talented Roommate

Here is a final opportunity for you to strengthen your knowledge of the ten words. First read the following passage carefully. Then fill in each blank with a word from the box at the top of this page. (Context clues will help you figure out which word goes in which blank.) Use each word once.

"If you've got it, (1)____________ it!" That's the (2)____________ of Georgia's philosophy. Georgia is my dorm roommate. She's a dance and theatre major, and she's always showing off, always "on stage." It seems she is in constant motion, going from graceful leaps down the hall to such (3)____________ acrobatics as swinging by her knees from the clothes rod in her closet. Some days Georgia performs her entire (4)____________ right in our room. The (5)____________ "Less is more" doesn't apply to her on those occasions, when she delights by acting, singing, and dancing everything she's ever learned. The lack of space in our room never seems to (6)____________ her movements. Since Georgia's shows are not very (7)____________ to good studying on my part, I join the crowd gathering to watch her. She is so smooth and confident that I have never seen her (8)____________. She moves easily from ballet to tap to jazz. She'll sing part of an opera, perform a scene from *Romeo and Juliet*, and then tell jokes. When she finishes, her audience breaks into a (9)____________ of applause. Many drama students will probably end up in other careers, but I believe Georgia is talented enough to build a (10)____________ career in show business.

SCORES: Sentence Check 2 ________% Final Check ________%

Enter your scores above and in the vocabulary performance chart on the inside back cover of the book.

CHAPTER

24

Previewing the Word Parts

Common word parts—also known as *prefixes, suffixes,* and *roots*—are used in forming many words in English. This page will introduce you to ten common word parts.

Try to match each word part on the left with its definition on the right. Use the words in parentheses as hints to help you guess the meanings. If you can't decide on an answer, leave the space blank. Your purpose here is just to get a sense of the ten word parts and what you may know about them. (You'll have another chance to try this exercise after considering the word parts in context.)

	Word Parts	Definitions
_____	1. **astro-, aster-** (astronomy, asterisk)	a. wrongly; badly
_____	2. **contra-, contro-** (contrary, controversy)	b. straight
_____	3. **-er, -or** (painter, doctor)	c. star
_____	4. **-gamy** (bigamy, monogamy)	d. people
_____	5. **geo-** (geography, geology)	e. someone who (does something)
_____	6. **mis-** (misbehave, mistake)	f. earth; ground
_____	7. **omni-** (omnipresent, omnipotent)	g. god or God
_____	8. **pop** (populate, popular)	h. all; everywhere
_____	9. **rect** (rectangle, direct)	j. marriage
_____	10. **the, theo-** (atheist, theology)	i. against; opposing

Now go on to "Ten Word Parts in Context" on the next page. Working through this chapter will help you to strengthen your knowledge of the word parts you already know and to master the word parts you're only half sure of, or don't know at all.

Keep in mind that learning word parts can pay several dividends. Word parts can help with the spelling and pronunciation of many words. They can also help you to unlock the meanings of unfamiliar words.

Ten Word Parts in Context

Figure out the meanings of the following ten word parts by looking *closely and carefully* at the context in which they appear. Doing so will prepare you for the matching test and practices on the two pages that follow.

1 astro-, aster-

a. **Astrologers** claim to interpret the influence of heavenly bodies on our lives.

b. The **aster** is a lovely flower named for its starlike shape: its petals point outward from a yellow disk.

2 contra-, contro-

a. **Contrary** to his campaign promise, the mayor has decided to raise taxes.

b. In the 19th century, there was **controversy** over whether or not women could master academic subjects.

3 -er, -or

a. When the opera **singer** Enrico Caruso had his first professional pictures taken, his only shirt was in the laundry, so he draped a bedspread around his shoulders.

b. American **visitors** to Canadian cities are often struck by how clean the streets are.

4 -gamy

a. Jackson's wife was charged with **bigamy** after he learned she hadn't divorced her first husband.

b. King Mongut of Siam, whose story was told in the musical *The King and I*, practiced **polygamy**. He was reported to have had 9,000 wives.

5 geo-

a. Pierce County, North Dakota, has the distinction of being the **geographic** center of North America.

b. **Geophysics** is the science of the matter and forces of the earth, including oceans, volcanos, and earthquakes.

6 mis-

a. I think there must be something wrong with a child who never **misbehaves**.

b. The telephone caller **misrepresented** herself. She said she was doing a quick survey, but she really wanted to sell me life insurance.

7 omni-

a. For many years, the mobs seemed **omnipotent**. However, once the government began convicting gangsters, the mobs lost their all-powerful image.

b. Some dinosaurs ate only plants, and others ate only meat. Still others, **omnivorous** dinosaurs, ate all kinds of food.

8 pop

a. In 1770, the U.S. was not very **populous**. Only about 2 million people lived here then.

b. In order to **populate** the West, the government gave free land to people who would build on it.

9 rect

a. Whenever I play Monopoly, I manage to pick the card that reads, "Go **directly** to jail. Do not pass Go. Do not collect $200."

b. If you forget your airplane tickets at home, you can **rectify** the situation by buying new tickets at the airport and cashing in the old ones when you get home.

10 the, theo-

a. **Monotheism** is the belief there there is only one God.

b. The ancient Greeks and Romans were **polytheists**. Among the gods they believed in were those of war, rain, and love.

Matching Word Parts and Definitions

Check your understanding of the ten word parts by matching each with its definition. See also the suggestions on page 4.

_____	1. **astro-, aster-**	a. wrongly; badly
_____	2. **contra-, contro-**	b. straight
_____	3. **-er, -or**	c. star
_____	4. **-gamy**	d. people
_____	5. **geo-**	e. someone who (does something)
_____	6. **mis-**	f. earth; ground
_____	7. **omni-**	g. god or God
_____	8. **pop**	h. all; everywhere
_____	9. **rect**	j. marriage
_____	10. **the, theo-**	i. against; opposing

CAUTION: Do not go any further until you are sure the above answers are correct. If you have studied the "Ten Word Parts in Context," you will know how to match each word part. Then you can use the matches to help you in the following practices. Your goal is to reach a point where you don't need to check definitions at all.

➢Sentence Check 1

Complete each partial word in the following sentences with a word part from the box. Use each word part only once. You may want to check off each word part as you use it.

aster-	**contra-**	**-or**	**-gamy**	**geo-**
mis-	**omni-**	**pop**	**rect**	**theo-**

1. Wade, a professional (*act . . .*) ____________________, seems to play a part even when he's offstage.
2. The study of the chemical makeup of the Earth's crust is called (*. . . chemistry*) ____________________.
3. Poverty is (*. . . present*) ____________________ in large Indian cities, where people beg on every street.
4. A small starlike figure called an (*. . . isk*) ____________________ is often used in books and magazines to indicate a footnote.
5. On a movie set, the (*di . . . or*) ____________________ is the person who keeps everyone and everything running on course.
6. John Wesley was the 18th-century British (*. . . logian*) ____________________ who founded the Protestant sect of Methodism.
7. If I don't hang my car keys on a special hook in the kitchen as soon I walk into the house, I'll (*. . . place*) ____________________ them.
8. My daughter is going through a stage in which she (*. . . dicts*) ____________________ everything I say. If I say "Yes," she will certainly say "No."
9. (*Mono . . .*) ____________________ doesn't stop people from having as many husbands or wives as they like. It only requires them to marry one at a time.
10. The few places on Earth that have not yet been (*. . . ulated*) ____________________ by humans probably would not appeal to many. Who wants to live on the snowcapped peak of a mountain?

Now check your answers to these questions by turning to page 166. Going over the answers carefully will help you prepare for the next two checks, for which answers are not given.

➢Sentence Check 2

Complete each partial word in the sentences below with a word part from the box. Use each word part once. If there are two forms of a word part, use the *first* one for this practice.

astro-	contro-, contra-	-or, -er	-gamy	geo-
mis-	omni-	pop	rect	the, theo-

1-2. The kindergartners were asked to draw a (. . . *angle*) __________________, but several made a (. . . *take*) __________________ and drew a circle instead.

3-4. (*Pan . . . ists*) __________________ believe that God is not a personality but an (. . . *present*) __________________ force of nature, present throughout the universe.

5-6. (*Doct . . .*) __________________ Fisher was very (. . . *ular*) __________________ with the townspeople because she always took the time to answer their questions.

7-8. There was a (. . . *versy*) __________________ among the (. . . *nauts*) __________________ over whether or not civilians should be allowed to fly on the spaceship..

9-10. In (. . . *graphy*) __________________ class, we not only learned about the location and climate of various countries but about customs. For example, in some African nations, (*exo . . .*) __________________, or marrying outside the tribe, is not allowed.

➢*Final Check:* Fascinating Courses

Here is a final opportunity for you to strengthen your knowledge of the ten word parts. First read the following passage carefully. Then complete each partial word in the parentheses below with a word part from the box at the top of this page. If there are two forms of a word part, use the *second* one in this practice. Context clues will help you figure out which word part goes in which blank. Use each word part once.

Each semester, I like to choose one fascinating course unrelated to my major. Last fall, for example, I took a (. . . *logy*) (1)__________________ course that focused on the remarkable changes in the Earth's surface over time. Then in the spring, I took (. . . *nomy*) (2)__________________. When I looked at the stars through a telescope, I felt tiny and insignificant in (. . . *st*) (3)__________________ to the enormous sizes and distances of outer space. This experience made me wonder about God.

So this semester I'm taking a course in (. . . *logy*) (4__________________. One day we spent three hours discussing this question: If God is an (. . . *potent*) (5)__________________ being, can God make a rock so heavy that even God can't lift it? We've also talked about how much (. . . *understanding*) (6)__________________ arises in the world from people not knowing about others' beliefs. For example, I've long heard my (*minist . . .*) (7)__________________ preach that we should be true to one spouse, but I never knew that in some other religions, (*poly . . .*) (8)__________________ is quite acceptable.

If we were to take a survey of the world's (. . . *ulation*) (9)__________________, many people would probably say they look to their church for (*di . . . ion*) (10)__________________ in their lives. I've learned that there are benefits to understanding other religions as well.

SCORES: Sentence Check 2 ________% Final Check ________%

Enter your scores above and in the vocabulary performance chart on the inside back cover of the book.

UNIT FOUR: Test 1

PART A

Choose the word that best completes each sentence and write it in the space provided.

1. **ominous** **complacent** **latent** **menial** — Admiring his build in the mirror, Lee gave himself a ______________________ smile.

2. **hampered** **improvised** **flaunted** **designated** — The rain ______________________ the work of the road construction crew.

3. **transcended** **simulated** **faltered** **waived** — Suddenly dizzy from the heat, the speaker ______________________ and covered his eyes.

4. **viable** **haughty** **blase** **secular** — It's hard to become ______________________ about great music, no matter how often you hear it.

5. **comprised** **deviated** **simulated** **divulged** — In becoming a priest, Brian certainly ______________________ from his plan to become a stockbroker.

6. **benign** **secular** **ominous** **menial** — My boss asked me into his office in such a(n) ______________________ tone that I thought he was about to fire me.

7. **elation** **facade** **niche** **libel** — The ______________________ of Scott's parents was as great as his own joy and pride at winning the gymnastics competition.

8. **interim** **empathy** **consensus** **repertoire** — My nephew's ______________________ of tricks for getting his own way includes pouting, crying, and throwing tantrums.

9. **diligent** **glib** **haughty** **blase** — I'm not quick with home repairs, but I'm ______________________. I work steadily and carefully until I get the job done.

10. **paradox** **gist** **empathy** **libel** — Because the article made unproven accusations against the mayor, the editors wouldn't print it for fear of being sued for ______________________.

11. **benign** **viable** **latent** **menial** — Janet's __________________ fear of marriage surfaced when Elliot proposed, and she reacted by insisting that they end their previously happy relationship.

12. **interim** **pseudonym** **consensus** **expulsion** — We were amazed to learn that gentle, soft-spoken Professor Geyer writes horror novels under the __________________ of Trent Paterson.

13. **redundant** **mortified** **viable** **ominous** — Heather was __________________ when, after diving into the pool, she bounced back up to the surface with the top of her bathing suit around her waist.

PART B

Circle **C** if the italicized word is used **correctly**. Circle **I** if the word is used **incorrectly**.

C I 14. When I was a child, I hated broccoli, but now I'm quite *averse* to it.

C I 15. Stage scenery often shows the *facades* of buildings, painted on a flat surface.

C I 16. During meditation, heart rate slows as a person enters a state of calm *frenzy.*

C I 17. Although Dad usually *shuns* sweets, he can't resist an occasional hot fudge sundae.

C I 18. That bow tie *detracts* from Alan's appearance by making him look strangled and gift-wrapped.

C I 19. Because pollution is *conducive* to rainfall, there is a great deal more rain in downtown Manhattan than in nearby Long Island.

C I 20. Despite his great success as a singer, Robert has remained as down-to-earth and *haughty* as ever.

C I 21. The company president was so impressed with Greta's sales record that he honored her with an *expulsion.*

C I 22. My sister didn't find her *niche* until she took a computer course and discovered her great talent for programming.

C I 23. By careful saving, I managed to *deplete* my bank account from $80 to almost $1,200 by the summer's end.

C I 24. Keith is an excellent mental health counselor who feels genuine *empathy* for those who come to him for help.

C I 25. I expected my interview to last only 20 minutes or so, but the interviewer did such a *cursory* job that I was there for over an hour.

SCORE: (Number correct) ________ x 4 = ________ %

Enter your scores above and in the vocabulary performance chart on the inside back cover of the book.

UNIT FOUR: Test 2

PART A

Complete each sentence with a word from the box. Use each word once.

commemorate	**consensus**	**credible**	**designate**
divulge	**flaunt**	**gist**	**improvise**
interim	**paradox**	**secular**	**simulate**
viable			

1. It's a ____________________ that we can sometimes be more generous by giving less.
2. Authors often state the ____________________ of an article in the introductory paragraph.
3. Alonso ____________________s his good voice by singing louder than anyone else in the choir.
4. More and more nuns are wearing ____________________ clothes rather than traditional religious dress.
5. On Presidents' Day, the nation ____________________s George Washington and Abraham Lincoln.
6. I think it's selfish of Dolly not to ____________________ the secret recipe for her wonderful salad dressing.
7. Films that ____________________ the experience of riding on a roller coaster give me a genuine feeling of nausea.
8. I don't mind speaking before a group if I have time to prepare, but I'd be scared to death if I had to ____________________.
9. The only ____________________ plan for making enough money to keep up the house payments is to rent out some of its rooms.
10. Although the man's alibi at first sounded ____________________, the police doubted its truth once he started changing the details.
11. The ____________________ among the city's sports writers is that Bridgewater High will win the basketball championship this year.
12. When the church's pastor resigned, a retired minister stepped in for the ____________________ until a permanent replacement was found.
13. The boys ____________________(e)d my little brother the treasurer of their tree-house club because he's the only one who receives a regular allowance.

PART B

Circle **C** if the italicized word is used **correctly**. Circle **I** if the word is used **incorrectly**.

C I 14. Sharon is *endowed* with the gift of photographic memory.

C I 15. I admire Frank's vivid, crisp, and *redundant* writing.

C I 16. Black South Africans continue their struggle to *waive* equal rights.

C I 17. The woods near our house *comprise* oak, maple, and beech trees.

C I 18. This morning, Velma ate a *bizarre* breakfast of orange juice, cereal, and coffee.

C I 19. In my nightmare, the evil monster's *benign* eyes frightened me to death.

C I 20. The TV contract would be *nullified* if the star missed any more rehearsals.

C I 21. Wayne has *transcended* his usual good grades by failing three out of his four classes this semester.

C I 22. Because *menial* tasks require little thought, I was able to plan some of my essay while cleaning my apartment yesterday.

C I 23. The *glib* street vendor smoothly claimed that the "gold" watch was just my style and that I'd find no better bargain anywhere else.

C I 24. After working in a hospital one summer, Andy has gained *disdain* for the hard-working nurses he feels serve the patients so well.

C I 25. The host's famous sister remained in her room for most of the party, although she did *condescend* to come down and say goodnight to the other guests before they left.

SCORE: (Number correct) ________ x 4 = ________ %

Enter your scores above and in the vocabulary performance chart on the inside back cover of the book.

UNIT FOUR: Test 3

PART A

Complete each sentence in a way that clearly shows you understand the meaning of the boldfaced word. Take a minute to plan your answer before you write.

Example: Charles **flaunted** his new convertible by *driving it back and forth past the school with its top down.*

1. My favorite **secular** holiday is ______________________________

____

2. An author might use a **pseudonym** because ______________________________

____

3. A stiff arm **hampers** ______________________________

____

4. My father showed his **elation** at the news by ______________________________

____

5. The children are so **blase** about fireworks that ______________________________

____

6. In our office, the secretary's job includes such **menial** tasks as ______________________________

____

7. I find it **detracts** from a restaurant meal when ______________________________

____

8. Lamont is **averse** to city life because ______________________________

____

9. One of the most **bizarre** sights I've ever seen on campus is ______________________________

____

10. I was **mortified** when ______________________________

____

PART B

After each boldfaced word are a *synonym* (a word that means the same as the boldfaced word), an *antonym* (a word that means the opposite of the boldfaced word), and a word that is neither. Mark the antonym with an *A*.

Example:	**divulge**	_____ reveal	__*A*__ conceal	_____ defend
11.	**haughty**	_____ proud	_____ humble	_____ tall
12.	**disdain**	_____ loss	_____ contempt	_____ admiration
13.	**benign**	_____ cruel	_____ broken	_____ kindly
14.	**shun**	_____ owe	_____ seek	_____ avoid
15.	**facade**	_____ back	_____ light	_____ front

PART C

Use five of the following ten words in sentences. Make it clear that you know the meaning of the word you use. Feel free to use the past tense or plural form of a word.

condescend	**consensus**	**deplete**	**deviate**	**diligent**
empathy	**gist**	**interim**	**niche**	**waive**

16. ____

____

17. ____

____

18. ____

____

19. ____

____

20. ____

SCORE: (Number correct) ________ x 5 = ________ %

Enter your scores above and in the vocabulary performance chart on the inside back cover of the book.

UNIT FOUR: Test 4 (Word Parts)

PART A

Listed in the left-hand column below are ten common word parts, along with words in which the parts are used. In each blank, write in the letter of the correct definition on the right.

Word Parts		**Definitions**
____1. **astro-, aster-**	astrology, aster	a. someone who (does something)
____2. **contra-, contro-**	contrast, controversy	b. star
____3. **-er, -or**	singer, visitor	c. all; everywhere
____4. **-gamy**	monogamy, polygamy	d. straight
____5. **geo-**	geographic, geologic	e. god or God
____6. **mis-**	misplace, misrepresent	f. against; opposing
____7. **omni-**	omnipresent, omnipotent	g. marriage
____8. **pop**	population, popular	h. earth; ground
____9. **rect**	direct, rectangle	j. people
___10. **the, theo-**	theology, monotheism	i. wrongly; badly

PART B

Find the word part that correctly completes each word. Then write the full word in the blank space. Not every word part will be used.

aster-	**contra-**	**-er**	**-gamy**	**geo-**
mis-	**omni-**	**pop**	**rect**	**theo-**

11. Vanilla ice cream is even more (. . . *ular*) __________________ among Americans than chocolate is.

12. (. . . *ry*) __________________ to what many suppose, Shakespeare made his living by acting as well as writing.

13. Circling the sun between the paths of Mars and Jupiter are thousands of (. . . *oids*) __________________, or small planets.

14. In a society with twice as many women as men, or twice as many men as women, (*bi* . . .) __________________ would be useful.

15. An interesting (. . . *graphic*) __________________ fact is that Mount Everest, the highest mountain in the world, has grown a foot taller over the last century.

PART C

Use your knowledge of word parts to determine the meaning of the boldfaced words. Circle the letter of each meaning.

16. Houses are usually **rectilinear**; they are characterized by

    a. opposing forces. b. straight lines. c. great cost.

17. Mr. Nolan is a man of many **misdeeds.**

    a. religious feelings b. girlfriends c. immoral acts

18. There will be many **exhibitors** at the state fair this year.

    a. farm exhibits b. people who exhibit c. exhibit fees

19. Throughout history, a common form of government has been **theocracy,** in which the supreme ruler is

    a. popular. b. elected. c. a god or God.

20. There's too much knowledge in the world today for any one person to claim **omniscience**.

    a. knowledge of biology b. complete knowledge c. partial knowledge

SCORE: (Number correct) ________ x 5 = ________ %

Enter your scores above and in the vocabulary performance chart on the inside back cover of the book.

Unit Five

CHAPTER

25

Previewing the Words

Find out how many of the ten words in this chapter you already know. Try to complete each sentence with the most suitable word from the list below. Use each word once.

Leave a sentence blank rather than guessing at an answer. Your purpose here is just to get a sense of the ten words and what you may know about them.

devoid	**implore**	**infuriate**	**intimidate**	**introvert**
jeopardize	**sibling**	**smug**	**sneer**	**vivacious**

1. Don't try to ____________________ me with your threats of blackmail. I don't frighten easily.
2. Being a(n) ____________________, Paul is uncomfortable at large parties.
3. Grandpa and his sister, Great-Aunt Alice, are the only survivors of eleven ____________________s.
4. At the grocery store, it ____________________s me when people with a cartload of food get in the express line.
5. Although the quiet puppy in a litter may be cute, experts say a more ____________________ animal will probably make a better pet.
6. Victor ____________________(e)d his parents over and over to let him buy a motorcycle, but they consider motorcycles too dangerous.
7. When you read about the horrors of Nazi Germany, you wonder how people can be so ____________________ of kindness.
8. I know I should congratulate Michael on being promoted to manager, but he's already so ____________________ that I hate to do it.
9. Maybe your ideas are more promising than mine, but that doesn't mean you should ____________________ at my suggestions for getting us out of debt.
10. The attorney warned his client that if he didn't stop shouting "I didn't do it" in court, he would ____________________ their chances of winning the case.

Now check your answers by turning to page 166. Fix any mistakes and fill in any blank spaces by writing in the correct answers. By doing so, you will complete this introduction to the ten words.

You're now ready to strengthen your knowledge of the words you already know and to master the words you're only half sure of, or don't know at all. Turn to the next page.

Ten Words in Context

Figure out the meanings of the following ten words by looking *closely and carefully* at the context in which the words appear. Doing so will prepare you for the matching test and practices on the two pages that follow.

1 **devoid**
(di-void')
-adjective

a. The French fries were so thin, dry, and **devoid** of taste that they seemed like splinters of wood.

b. Sometimes Carl is totally **devoid** of common sense. Once he went on vacation leaving his front door unlocked and the newspaper delivery service uncancelled.

2 **implore**
(im-plôr')
-verb

a. Please hide those Hershey bars, and don't tell me where they are no matter how much I **implore** you.

b. The princess **implored** the evil magician to spare the handsome prince's life.

3 **infuriate**
(in-fyōōr'-ē-āt')
-verb

a. Peter so **infuriated** Sheila that she slammed down the phone while he was still talking.

b. I promised myself before I went into the meeting that no matter how unreasonable the boss was, nothing she said would **infuriate** me.

4 **intimidate**
(in-tim'-ə-dāt')
-verb

a. Will's huge size **intimidates** strangers, but anyone who knows him realizes that he's a very gentle man.

b. Public speaking so **intimidates** Charlene that she would rather write four term papers than give a single oral report.

5 **introvert**
(in'-trə-vûrt')
-noun

a. Pearl is a very outgoing person, but her brother Larry is such an **introvert** that he seldom socializes at all.

b. It could be difficult for an **introvert** to succeed in sales, which involves considerable contact with the public.

6 **jeopardize**
(jep'-ər-dīz')
-verb

a. Molly is so clumsy that she **jeopardizes** every fragile item she touches. Whatever she picks up is liable to get broken.

b. Pregnant women who take drugs **jeopardize** their babies' health.

7 **sibling**
(sib'-ling)
-noun

a. Do you think twins are more similar in personality than other **siblings**?

b. It's hard enough for children to move to foster homes; it's even worse when **siblings** have to be separated.

8 **smug**
(smug)
-adjective

a. Self-confidence is a virtue, but being **smug** is self-confidence carried too far.

b. Already conceited about his good looks, Jeff became completely **smug** when he was hired to play a small part in a rock video.

9 **sneer**
(snēr)
-verb

a. Janice is terrific with little children. No matter how silly their questions are, she never **sneers** at them.

b. Instead of encouraging us when we make a mistake, our biology teacher **sneers** at us with a scornful smile or a put-down.

10 **vivacious**
(vi-vā'-shəs)
-adjective

a. My father is such a **vivacious** host that he makes his guests feel bright and lively too.

b. Between scenes, the actors might appear tired and dull, but they become **vivacious** once the camera is on.

Matching Words and Definitions

Check your understanding of the ten words by matching each word with its definition. Look back at the sentences in "Ten Words in Context" as needed to decide on the meaning of each word.

_____	1. **devoid (of)**	a. a shy or inwardly directed person
_____	2. **implore**	b. completely lacking
_____	3. **infuriate**	c. a sister or brother
_____	4. **intimidate**	d. to anger greatly
_____	5. **introvert**	e. lively; full of life and enthusiasm
_____	6. **jeopardize**	f. to beg or plead
_____	7. **sibling**	g. to smile scornfully or curl the lip in ridicule; express ridicule or contempt in speech or writing
_____	8. **smug**	h. to make timid or afraid; frighten
_____	9. **sneer**	i. overly satisfied with oneself; conceited
_____	10. **vivacious**	j. to endanger; risk loss or injury

CAUTION: Do not go any further until you are sure the above answers are correct. If you have studied the "Ten Words in Context," you will know how to match each word. Then you can use the matches to help you in the following practices. Your goal is to reach a point where you don't need to check definitions at all.

➢*Sentence Check 1*

Complete each sentence below with the most suitable word from the box. Use each word once.

devoid	**implore**	**infuriate**	**intimidate**	**introvert**
jeopardize	**sibling**	**smug**	**sneer**	**vivacious**

1. You may call Linda charming and ___________________, but to me, she's just an irritating chatterbox.
2. I ___________________ you not to mention the VCR to Stewart. I want to surprise him with it.
3. The genius who invents a chocolate ice cream that's ___________________ of calories should win a medal.
4. Working with computers all day suits my brother. He's too much of a(n) ___________________ to enjoy working much with other people.
5. I don't understand why Eileen enjoys activities that ___________________ her life, like skydiving and mountain climbing.
6. Christmas is the one time of year when my grandparents, parents, and three ___________________s are able to get together.
7. There used to be little that angered my father, but since he got laid off, it seems everything we kids do ___________________s him.
8. When he found Art selling drugs by the elementary school, the police officer ___________________(e)d at him and snarled, "You scum."
9. It's better to get children's cooperation through setting shared goals than by trying to ___________________ them with threats of punishment.
10. Jenny would be more popular if she didn't get that ___________________ look on her face every time she answers the teacher's question correctly.

Now check your answers to these questions by turning to page 166. Going over the answers carefully will help you prepare for the next two checks, for which answers are not given.

➢Sentence Check 2

Complete each sentence below with two words from the box. Use each word once.

devoid	implore	infuriate	intimidate	introvert
jeopardize	sibling	smug	sneer	vivacious

1-2. The people I love best can ___________________ me the most. No one can make me as angry as my parents and ___________________s can.

3-4. It won't do any good to ___________________ me to help you with your term paper. Since you delayed working on it for so long, I'm ___________________ of sympathy.

5-6. I think Marvin only pretends to look down on the weight-lifters in school. He ___________________s at them to hide the fact that they ___________________ him.

7-8. Among her close friends, my sister is known as a really ___________________ woman, energetic and bubbly. But she often seems like a(n) ___________________ around people she doesn't know well.

9-10. I told Seth he would ___________________ his chances of getting a date for the dance if he waited until the last minute to ask someone. But he was ___________________ enough to think that any girl he asked would be happy to break a date to go to the dance with him.

➤*Final Check:* Cal and His Sisters

Here is a final opportunity for you to strengthen your knowledge of the ten words. First read the following passage carefully. Then fill in each blank with a word from the box at the top of this page. (Context clues will help you figure out which word goes in which blank.) Use each word once.

I've never met (1)___________________s who are less alike than Cal and his sisters, Margo and Tina. Cal is smart, but he isn't very popular. He thinks he's right about everything and isn't afraid to say so. It's hard to like someone who is so (2)___________________ about his intelligence. On the other hand, everybody loves Margo, the life of any party. She's so (3)___________________ that she's always fun to be with. Tina is just the opposite. She is such a(n) (4)___________________ that you hardly know she's around. When she does speak up to voice an opinion, Cal (5)___________________s at her ideas, dismissing them as "ridiculous." Margo is too confident for Cal to (6)___________________. Even when they were little, he couldn't frighten her. But it (7)___________________s her when he is mean to Tina. She's afraid he will (8)___________________ Tina's chances of ever gaining confidence. Margo (9)___________________s Cal to be kind to Tina, but he seems (10)___________________ of sympathy for his shy sister.

SCORES:	Sentence Check 2 ________%	Final Check ________%

Enter your scores above and in the vocabulary performance chart on the inside back cover of the book.

CHAPTER

26

Previewing the Words

Find out how many of the ten words in this chapter you already know. Try to complete each sentence with the most suitable word from the list below. Use each word once.

Leave a sentence blank rather than guessing at an answer. Your purpose here is just to get a sense of the ten words and what you may know about them.

condone	**contemplate**	**feasible**	**feign**	**fiscal**
furtive	**gape**	**pathetic**	**precedent**	**punitive**

1. Two young children stepped closer to ____________________ at the clown, but when he approached them, they hid their faces.
2. Shy Dennis stole a ____________________ glance at the woman he liked, but he was afraid to approach her.
3. Our father had a ____________________ nature. He tended to spank us for every wrongdoing, however small.
4. It isn't ____________________ for Joanne to have the report done by Monday. The research alone will take two weeks.
5. As head of the hospital's ____________________ department, my brother oversees all accounting and billing.
6. I ____________________(e)d vacationing in Hawaii, but I decided that my budget wouldn't allow such an expensive trip.
7. Crystal will often ____________________ illness to avoid work. She may fool her supervisor, but she doesn't fool me.
8. I don't ____________________ Barb's habit of smoking in public because it annoys other people and threatens their health.
9. My sit-ups are ____________________. They're so weak that they look like neck-ups.
10. "I'd like to give you a day off to go to the World Series," said Calvin's boss. "But I'd be setting a ____________________ that other employees would use to go to events they'd want to see."

Now check your answers by turning to page 166. Fix any mistakes and fill in any blank spaces by writing in the correct answers. By doing so, you will complete this introduction to the ten words.

You're now ready to strengthen your knowledge of the words you already know and to master the words you're only half sure of, or don't know at all. Turn to the next page.

Ten Words in Context

Figure out the meanings of the following ten words by looking *closely and carefully* at the context in which the words appear. Doing so will prepare you for the matching test and practices on the two pages that follow.

1 **condone** (kən-dōn') *-verb*

a. "I can't stop you," Ms. Mather told her daughter, "but neither can I **condone** your plan to live with Allen without being married to him."

b. I can overlook it when you're five minutes late. But how can I **condone** your walking in to work an hour late?

2 **contemplate** (kon'-təm-plāt') *-verb*

a. Because Ben hadn't studied for the test, he **contemplated** cheating. He quickly realized, however, that the eagle-eyed teacher would spot him.

b. Whenever Anne's husband drank too much, she would **contemplate** divorce, but then she would feel guilty for thinking about leaving a sick man.

3 **feasible** (fē'-zə-bəl) *-adjective*

a. It isn't **feasible** for me to work full time and keep the house clean unless my spouse shares the cleaning chores.

b. Marilyn told her supervisor, "It just isn't **feasible** for this staff to do the work of the two people who were fired. You need to hire more people."

4 **feign** (fān) *-verb*

a. My bosses only **feigned** concern about my financial difficulties. They really didn't care.

b. You can **feign** a head cold by pretending you're too stuffed up to pronounce an *l*, *n*, or *m*. Try it by saying, "I have a code id by dose."

5 **fiscal** (fis'-kəl) *-adjective*

a. The gift shop closed due to **fiscal** problems. It simply didn't make enough money to cover costs.

b. Some states have passed laws allowing child-support payments to be taken directly from the paychecks of divorced men who ignore their **fiscal** responsibility to their children.

6 **furtive** (fûr'-tiv) *-adjective*

a. I wondered why Cathy's behavior was so **furtive** until I discovered 20 people gathered for a surprise party in my honor.

b. According to experts, teenagers who are **furtive** about where they are going and with whom may be involved with drugs.

7 **gape** (gāp) *-verb*

a. Everyone stopped to **gape** at the odd-looking sculpture in front of the library.

b. Because drivers slowed down to **gape** at an accident in the southbound lanes, northbound traffic was backed up for miles.

8 **pathetic** (pə-thet'-ik) *-adjective*

a. That plumber's work was **pathetic**. Not only does the faucet still drip, but now the pipe is leaking.

b. Health care in some areas of the world is **pathetic**. People are dying of diseases that are easily treatable with modern medicine.

9 **precedent** (pres'-i-dənt) *-noun*

a. When Jean's employer gave her three months off after her baby was born, a **precedent** was set for any other woman in the firm who became pregnant.

b. To set a **precedent**, the teacher gave the student who stole an exam an F for the entire course. "Others will think twice before they do the same," he explained.

10 **punitive** (pyōō'-ni-tiv) *-adjective*

a. Judge Starn is especially **punitive** with drunk drivers, giving every one of them a jail term.

b. Many parents find that reward is a better basis for teaching children than **punitive** action is.

Matching Words and Definitions

Check your understanding of the ten words by matching each word with its definition. Look back at the sentences in "Ten Words in Context" as needed to decide on the meaning of each word.

_____	1. **condone**	a. possible; able to be done
_____	2. **contemplate**	b. done or behaving in a secretive way
_____	3. **feasible**	c. to stare in wonder or amazement
_____	4. **feign**	d. anything that may serve as an example in dealing with later similar circumstances
_____	5. **fiscal**	e. to forgive or overlook
_____	6. **furtive**	f. giving or involving punishment; punishing
_____	7. **gape**	g. financial
_____	8. **pathetic**	h. to think about seriously
_____	9. **precedent**	i. pitifully lacking or unsuccessful; so inadequate as to be ridiculous
_____	10. **punitive**	j. to pretend; give a false show of

CAUTION: Do not go any further until you are sure the above answers are correct. If you have studied the "Ten Words in Context," you will know how to match each word. Then you can use the matches to help you in the following practices. Your goal is to reach a point where you don't need to check definitions at all.

➢Sentence Check 1

Complete each sentence below with the most suitable word from the box. Use each word once.

condone	**contemplate**	**feasible**	**feign**	**fiscal**
furtive	**gape**	**pathetic**	**precedent**	**punitive**

1. Handicapped people don't like others to ____________ at them. Instead of a stare, a simple smile would be appreciated.
2. From time to time, I ____________ attending business school, but so far I've made no firm decision.
3. Lawyers can strengthen a case by finding a useful ____________ among previous similar cases.
4. It's not ____________ for me to attend two parties on the same night, so I'll have to choose between them.
5. The principal does not ____________ hitting students. He believes every problem has a nonviolent solution.
6. At the low-cost clinic, Clayton had to give evidence of his ____________ situation, such as a tax form or current pay stub.
7. The people on the elevator didn't want to stare at the patch on my eye, but several took ____________ glances.
8. Old Mr. Hall's living conditions were ____________. There was no heat or electricity in his apartment, and the walls were crumbling.
9. When I had to give an oral report in class, I tried to ____________ confidence, but my shaking legs revealed my nervousness.
10. My mother wasn't usually ____________, but one day I pushed her too far, and she said, "If you do that one more time, I will send you to your room for the rest of your adolescence."

Now check your answers to these questions by turning to page 166. Going over the answers carefully will help you prepare for the next two checks, for which answers are not given.

➢Sentence Check 2

Complete each sentence below with two words from the box. Use each word once.

condone	contemplate	feasible	feign	fiscal
furtive	gape	pathetic	precedent	punitive

1-2. "Would it be ________ for us to buy a new copy machine? Or is our ________ situation too tight?" I asked at the office budget meeting.

3-4. Some parents take only ________ measures when children misbehave. They never take time to ________ the benefits of a gentler approach.

5-6. Several commuters stopped to ________ at the homeless man and his ________ shelter, made of cardboard and a torn blanket.

7-8. The fourth-grade teacher said, "I will not ________ any ________ behavior in my class. Rita, please read out loud the note you secretly passed to Ellen."

9-10. The ________ was set many years ago: When the winner of a beauty contest is announced, the runner-up ________s happiness for the winner, no matter how she actually feels.

➢*Final Check:* Shoplifter

Here is a final opportunity for you to strengthen your knowledge of the ten words. First read the following passage carefully. Then fill in each blank with a word from the box at the top of this page. (Context clues will help you figure out which word goes in which blank.) Use each word once.

Valerie took a (1)________ glance around her. When it seemed no one was watching, she stuffed a blue shirt into the bottom of her purse and darted out of the women's department. She walked slowly around the shoe department for a while and then left the store. "Stop! You! Stop!" shouted a guard who seemed to appear from nowhere. Then another man in street clothes grabbed her purse and pulled out the shirt.

"But... but... It's not mine. I don't know how it got there," Valerie cried.

The two men just looked at each other and laughed. The guard said, "That's what they all say. People steal without taking time to (2)________ the possible results. Then when they're caught, they (3)________ innocence."

As the guard began to phone the police, Valerie begged, "Please don't press charges. Please. This is the first time I've ever done anything like this, and I'll never do it again."

The men laughed again. "Your argument is (4)________," the man in street clothes said. "It's everyone's first time. Our store always presses charges against shoplifting. We can't set the bad (5)________ of letting a shoplifter go, as if we (6)________(e)d such crimes."

"That's right," said the guard. "This shirt only costs twenty dollars, but the twenties add up. Our (7)________ officer has reported a loss of about $150,000 worth of merchandise to shoplifters last year. So it simply isn't (8)________ to let you walk away. We have no choice but to take (9)________ action."

Soon Valerie was led to the police car. She covered her face as other shoppers stopped to (10)________ at the lovely young woman, an unlikely-looking criminal.

SCORES: Sentence Check 2 ______% Final Check ______%

Enter your scores above and in the vocabulary performance chart on the inside back cover of the book.

CHAPTER

27

Previewing the Words

Find out how many of the ten words in this chapter you already know. Try to complete each sentence with the most suitable word from the list below. Use each word once.

Leave a sentence blank rather than guessing at an answer. Your purpose here is just to get a sense of the ten words and what you may know about them.

cryptic	**deficient**	**depict**	**detrimental**	**implicit**
inhibition	**ironic**	**rupture**	**saturate**	**vindictive**

1. My cat and I have a(n) ____________________ understanding that when I open a can of sardines, she gets some too.
2. A good author can ____________________ a particular scene in a few well-chosen words.
3. It's not necessary to ________________________ your paint brush. Just pick up enough paint to coat the tip.
4. It's _______________________ that Loretta is such a strict mother because she was certainly wild in her youth.
5. My brother's ____________________(s) about women are the result of an unhappy romance he had several years ago.
6. Even something as healthy-sounding as vitamins can be ____________________ to your health when taken in large quantities.
7. Gil is ______________________ in good manners. For example, I've never heard him thank anyone for anything.
8. The bulge in the baby's stomach was caused by a muscle wall that ____________________(e)d and would have to be repaired.
9. When he was denied permission to have another cookie, the ____________________ child aimed a kick right at his aunt's weak ankle.
10. I begged Tony to tell me the big secret, but he always gave the same ____________________ reply: "It's a green world, my friend."

Now check your answers by turning to page 166. Fix any mistakes and fill in any blank spaces by writing in the correct answers. By doing so, you will complete this introduction to the ten words.

You're now ready to strengthen your knowledge of the words you already know and to master the words you're only half sure of, or don't know at all. Turn to the next page.

Ten Words in Context

Figure out the meanings of the following ten words by looking *closely and carefully* at the context in which the words appear. Doing so will prepare you for the matching test and practices on the two pages that follow.

1 **cryptic**
(krip'-tik)
-adjective

a. The Easter egg hunt featured **cryptic** clues like "You'll find a prize somewhere narrow."

b. A **cryptic** note containing the words "Not now" was found next to the dead woman's body.

2 **deficient**
(di-fish'-ənt)
-adjective

a. When people have too little iron in their blood, it sometimes means that their diet is also **deficient** in iron.

b. The living room is **deficient** in light. We need to get another lamp.

3 **depict**
(di-pikt')
-verb

a. The painting **depicts** a typical 19th-century summer day in the park.

b. Harriet Beecher Stowe's novel *Uncle Tom's Cabin* **depicted** the cruelty of slavery so forcefully that the book helped to begin the Civil War.

4 **detrimental**
(de'-trə-men'-təl)
-adjective

a. Do you think all television is **detrimental** to a child, or are some programs good for kids?

b. The gases from automobiles and factories have been so **detrimental** to the environment that some of the damage may be permanent.

5 **implicit**
(im-plis'-it)
-adjective

a. When the gangster growled, "I'm sure you want your family to stay well," Harris understood the **implicit** threat.

b. Although it's never been said, there's an **implicit** understanding that Carla will be promoted when Earl finally retires.

6 **inhibition**
(in'-hə-bish'-ən)
-noun

a. A two-year-old has no **inhibition** about running around naked.

b. Sarah's family is openly affectionate, with no **inhibitions** toward hugging or kissing in public.

7 **ironic**
(ī-ron'-ik)
-adjective

a. "Ken better get his act together" was Beth's **ironic** comment when she heard he had gotten straight A's that semester.

b. "The Gift of the Magi" is a short story with an **ironic** twist: A woman sells her long hair to buy a chain for her husband's watch, while her husband sells his watch to buy combs for her hair.

8 **rupture**
(rup'-chər)
-verb

a. If the dam were to **rupture**, the town would disappear under many feet of water.

b. Victims of the Black Death, the fatal disease that swept Europe in the mid-1300's, often developed swellings that **ruptured** near the time of death.

9 **saturate**
(sach'-ə-rāt')
-verb

a. Most people like their cereal crunchy, but Teresa lets hers sit until the milk has **saturated** every piece.

b. After studying history for three hours, my brain was so **saturated** that I couldn't have absorbed one more bit of information.

10 **vindictive**
(vin-dik'-tiv)
-adjective

a. If a woman refuses to date Leon, he becomes **vindictive**. One way he takes revenge is to insult the woman in public.

b. After she was given two weeks' notice, the **vindictive** employee intentionally jumbled the company's files.

Matching Words and Definitions

Check your understanding of the ten words by matching each word with its definition. Look back at the sentences in "Ten Words in Context" as needed to decide on the meaning of each word.

_____	1. **cryptic**	a. a holding back or block of some action, feeling, or thought
_____	2. **deficient**	b. having a vague or hidden meaning; puzzling
_____	3. **depict**	c. suggested but not directly expressed; unstated, but able to be understood
_____	4. **detrimental**	d. vengeful; inclined to seek revenge
_____	5. **implicit**	e. to represent in pictures or words; describe
_____	6. **inhibition**	f. to burst or break apart
_____	7. **ironic**	g. lacking some characteristic or element
_____	8. **rupture**	h. to soak, load, or fill as much as possible
_____	9. **saturate**	i. harmful
_____	10. **vindictive**	j. meaning the opposite of what is said; being opposite to what might be expected

CAUTION: Do not go any further until you are sure the above answers are correct. If you have studied the "Ten Words in Context," you will know how to match each word. Then you can use the matches to help you in the following practices. Your goal is to reach a point where you don't need to check definitions at all.

➢*Sentence Check 1*

Complete each sentence below with the most suitable word from the box. Use each word once.

cryptic	**deficient**	**depict**	**detrimental**	**implicit**
inhibition	**ironic**	**rupture**	**saturate**	**vindictive**

1. A person can be intelligent and yet be ____________________ in common sense.
2. When the pressure in the gas pipe became too great, the pipe ____________________(e)d.
3. Isn't it ____________________ that the richest man in town should win the million dollar lottery?
4. That ugly factory building is certainly ____________________ to the neighborhood's appearance.
5. Becky's customary lack of ____________________ was evident the time she came to class barefoot.
6. In the novel *Oliver Twist*, Charles Dickens ____________________s life in an English orphanage as being most pitiful.
7. Street gangs are ____________________. If anyone harms a member of a gang, the other members will take full revenge.
8. The fifth-grade assignment was written in double talk. Everyone laughed as the students tried to make out the teacher's ____________________ message.
9. The aroma of Gretchen's perfume so ____________________(e)d the air in the car that Steve coughed and rolled down a window.
10. While it's not written in teachers' contracts, there is a(n) ____________________ understanding that teachers will spend time preparing lessons and responding to students' work.

Now check your answers to these questions by turning to page 166. Going over the answers carefully will help you prepare for the next two checks, for which answers are not given.

➢*Sentence Check 2*

Complete each sentence below with two words from the box. Use each word once.

cryptic	deficient	depict	detrimental	implicit
inhibition	ironic	rupture	saturate	vindictive

1-2. Water balloon fights are fun until a balloon ________________s against your clothes, and they get ________________(e)d with cold water.

3-4. Most viewers find the painting, with its dozens of dots on a white background, to be ________________. However, it's possible to figure out what the painting ________________s by mentally connecting the dots.

5-6. My sister is always trying to "get even" with someone. Her ________________ attitude is ________________ to her relationships with family and friends.

7-8. It's ________________ that the book *Live Simply on Little Money* has made the author wealthy since a(n) ________________ message of the book is that the author himself requires little money.

9-10. Gerry feels people should "lose their ________________s" and do whatever they feel like doing, but I think people who are altogether ________________ in self-control have poor manners.

➤*Final Check:* A Nutty Newspaper Office

Here is a final opportunity for you to strengthen your knowledge of the ten words. First read the following passage carefully. Then fill in each blank with a word from the box at the top of this page. (Context clues will help you figure out which word goes in which blank.) Use each word once.

My therapist says it's (1)________________ to my mental health to keep my thoughts bottled up inside of me, so I'll drop all (2)________________s and tell you about the newspaper office where I work.

Let me describe my editor first. It's sort of (3)________________ that Ed is in communications because I've never met anyone harder to talk to. I'll say, "How are you doing today, Ed?" and he'll give me some (4)________________ response such as "The tidal pools of time are catching up with me." I used to think there might be some deep wisdom (5)________________ in Ed's statements, but now I just think he's a little crazy.

Then there's Seymour, our sports writer. Seymour is perfectly normal except that he has unexplained fits of crying two or three times a week. You'll be in the middle of a conversation about the Mets or something and suddenly Seymour has started to (6)________________ handfuls of Kleenex with his tears.

Now, I don't mean to (7)________________ our office as a totally depressing place. It is not entirely (8)________________ in excitement, but even our excitement is a little weird. It is usually provided by Jan, a (9)________________ typesetter who, whenever irritated by Ed, takes revenge in some horrible but entertaining way. One of her favorite ways is sneaking fictional items about him into the society column. I'll never forget the time Ed was in the hospital after his appendix (10)________________(e)d. He almost broke his stitches when he read that he was taking a vacation at a nudist colony.

SCORES: Sentence Check 2 ________% Final Check ________%

Enter your scores above and in the vocabulary performance chart on the inside back cover of the book.

CHAPTER

28

Previewing the Words

Find out how many of the ten words in this chapter you already know. Try to complete each sentence with the most suitable word from the list below. Use each word once.

Leave a sentence blank rather than guessing at an answer. Your purpose here is just to get a sense of the ten words and what you may know about them.

constrict	**exhaustive**	**fallible**	**formulate**	**genial**
habitat	**pragmatic**	**pretentious**	**reconcile**	**vile**

1. If my daughter's jeans were any tighter, they would ____________________ the blood flowing to her feet.
2. If you intend to open a restaurant, you must first ____________________ a careful business plan.
3. Everyone is ____________________, but there's no need to make the same mistakes over and over again.
4. "Hang your food bag from a pole at night," the park ranger warned. "This area is a bear ____________________."
5. After the motorcycle accident, Sheena had to ____________________ herself to the limited use of her right hand.
6. My sister loves a certain cheese that has the ____________________ odor of something that fell off a garbage truck.
7. The Chinese restaurant's menu was the most ____________________ I'd ever seen. It listed many dishes I'd never even heard of.
8. The employees who run the rides at the amusement park are very ____________________. I've never heard an unfriendly word from one of them.
9. Some wealthy people live comfortable yet simple lives, but others are quite ____________________ and never miss a chance to show off their wealth.
10. Lloyd is so concerned about looking good that sometimes he isn't at all ____________________. Once he wore a suit and a silk tie to a company softball game.

Now check your answers by turning to page 166. Fix any mistakes and fill in any blank spaces by writing in the correct answers. By doing so, you will complete this introduction to the ten words.

You're now ready to strengthen your knowledge of the words you already know and to master the words you're only half sure of, or don't know at all. Turn to the next page.

Ten Words in Context

Figure out the meanings of the following ten words by looking *closely and carefully* at the context in which the words appear. Doing so will prepare you for the matching test and practices on the two pages that follow.

1 constrict
(kən-strikt')
-verb

a. The summer highway construction will **constrict** traffic to the width of only two lanes.

b. For centuries in China, girls' feet were **constricted** with binding to keep them from growing to normal size. Women's feet were considered most attractive if they were under four inches long.

2 exhaustive
(eg-zôs'-tiv)
-adjective

a. Don't buy a used car without putting it through an **exhaustive** inspection. Check every detail, from hood to trunk.

b. My teacher recommended an **exhaustive** thousand-page biography of Freud, but who has time to read such a thorough account?

3 fallible
(fal'-ə-bəl)
-adjective

a. "I know everyone is **fallible,**" the boss told his workers. "But do you have to make so many of your mistakes on company time?"

b. When they are little, kids think their parents can do no wrong, but when they become teenagers, their parents suddenly become quite **fallible**.

4 formulate
(for'-myōō-lāt')
-verb

a. Before stepping into his boss's office, Hank had carefully **formulated** his case for a raise.

b. The author first **formulated** an outline of his plot and then began writing his mystery.

5 genial
(jēn'-yəl)
-adjective

a. I was worried about my grandmother's treatment at the nursing home, so I was relieved when the nurses and aides turned out to be very **genial**.

b. Libby found her first dance instructor so harsh and unpleasant that she changed to a more **genial** one.

6 habitat
(hab'-i-tat)
-noun

a. A growing number of people believe that wild animals should be allowed to remain in their natural **habitats** and not be captured and put in zoos.

b. Although we think of the forest as the **habitat** of raccoons, many raccoons live in cities where food is plentiful.

7 pragmatic
(prag-mat'-ik)
-adjective

a. We always called my sister "Practical Polly" because she was the most **pragmatic** member of the family.

b. When I was young and single, I spent most of my money on travel. Now that I have a family to support, I must spend my money in more **pragmatic** ways.

8 pretentious
(prē-ten'-shəs)
-adjective

a. Dana's classmates don't like him because he's so **pretentious**. It's hard to like someone who acts as if he knows it all, even if he does.

b. While most vacation homes are simply furnished, the Whites' **pretentious** "little cabin" is stuffed with expensive furniture and art, intended to impress their new neighbors.

9 reconcile
(rek'-ən-sīl')
-verb

a. When my grandfather died, we worked hard to **reconcile** Grandmother to the fact that he was really gone.

b. After his third wreck in six months, Tony **reconciled** himself to living somewhere along a bus line and doing without a car.

10 vile
(vīl)
-adjective

a. Piles of wet garbage sitting in the summer sun soon acquire a **vile** smell.

b. When I finally get around to cleaning out my refrigerator, I always find some **vile** moldy food at the back of a shelf.

Matching Words and Definitions

Check your understanding of the ten words by matching each word with its definition. Look back at the sentences in "Ten Words in Context" as needed to decide on the meaning of each word.

_____	1. **constrict**	a. to bring (oneself or someone else) to accept
_____	2. **exhaustive**	b. the natural environment of an animal or plant
_____	3. **fallible**	c. making a show of superiority, excellence, or importance; showy
_____	4. **formulate**	d. capable of making an error
_____	5. **genial**	e. to make smaller or narrower, as by squeezing or shrinking
_____	6. **habitat**	f. covering all possible details; complete; thorough
_____	7. **pragmatic**	g. friendly, pleasant, and kindly
_____	8. **pretentious**	h. offensive to the senses, feelings, or thoughts; disgusting
_____	9. **reconcile (to)**	i. to form or work out in one's mind; develop
_____	10. **vile**	j. practical

CAUTION: Do not go any further until you are sure the above answers are correct. If you have studied the "Ten Words in Context," you will know how to match each word. Then you can use the matches to help you in the following practices. Your goal is to reach a point where you don't need to check definitions at all.

➢Sentence Check 1

Complete each sentence below with the most suitable word from the box. Use each word once.

constrict	**exhaustive**	**fallible**	**formulate**	**genial**
habitat	**pragmatic**	**pretentious**	**reconcile**	**vile**

1. Our cafeteria serves the world's most ____________________ beef stew, full of big globs of fat.
2. Why is Debra acting so unfriendly today? She's usually so ____________________.
3. My mother was forced to ____________________ herself to my independence when I moved into my own apartment.
4. Bright light ____________________s the pupils of our eyes. Darkness makes them wider, letting more light in.
5. My supervisor told me that if I wished to work on an independent project, I should ____________________ a detailed plan of my idea.
6. For her term paper on orchids, Wilma did ____________________ research, covering every aspect of the flower's growth and marketing.
7. Norm's way of speaking was ____________________. He used a lot of big words because he thought that would make him sound smart.
8. Children's stories sometimes mistakenly show penguins at the North Pole. The birds' ____________________ is actually near the South Pole.
9. "It would be more ____________________," my daughter said, "if you went to the grocery once a week for a larger order rather than going daily for just a few items."
10. When the auto mechanic said, "Well, I'm ____________________ like everyone else," I responded, "Yes, but your mistake almost got me flattened by a truck."

Now check your answers to these questions by turning to page 166. Going over the answers carefully will help you prepare for the next two checks, for which answers are not given.

➢*Sentence Check 2*

Complete each sentence below with two words from the box. Use each word once.

constrict	**exhaustive**	**fallible**	**formulate**	**genial**
habitat	**pragmatic**	**pretentious**	**reconcile**	**vile**

1-2. "You want me to be perfect, but that's impossible!" my daughter cried. "__________ yourself to the fact that every one of us is __________."

3-4. Wildlife experts __________(e)d a plan by which to preserve what little remains of the gorilla's natural __________.

5-6. My roommate was not at all __________. He would spend our household money on videotapes and __________-smelling cigars and leave us without food.

7-8. When our pet python escaped, we quickly made a(n) __________ search throughout the house and grounds. We found him wrapped around our dog, about to __________ the poor mutt to death.

9-10. At the sales seminar, we were taught to be __________ with customers and never to be __________ about our products, no matter how much we know. People like warm, friendly salespeople, not ones who show off.

➤*Final Check:* Roughing It

Here is a final opportunity for you to strengthen your knowledge of the ten words. First read the following passage carefully. Then fill in each blank with a word from the box at the top of this page. (Context clues will help you figure out which word goes in which blank.) Use each word once.

"Whose brilliant idea was this anyway?" Sara asked. "If people were intended to sleep on the ground and cook over a fire, we wouldn't have invented beds and microwave ovens."

"Stop complaining," Emily said. "At least you've got dry clothes on. You didn't end up walking through some (1)__________ mud because your canoe overturned. And you didn't have a (2)__________ partner who claimed to know everything about canoeing but actually didn't know enough to steer around a rock."

"So I made a mistake," George said. "We're all (3)__________."

"Well," Emily responded, "your mistake has lost us our tent. And our sleeping bags and clothes are soaked."

Doug spoke up. "It's no big deal. Sara and I will lend you clothes, and you two can squeeze into our tent."

"Squeeze is right, " said Emily. "Four in one tent will (4)__________ us so much that we won't be able to exhale."

"It's your choice," said Doug. "Decide if you want to be in a crowded tent or sleep out in this wild-animal (5)__________."

Sara couldn't resist adding, "If you had listened to me and were more (6)__________ when planning for this trip, we wouldn't be in such a mess. You would have written a(n) (7)__________ list of what would be needed, from A to Z . Then you would have (8)__________(e)d a clear plan for who would take what. Then we wouldn't be out here with two corkscrews but no plastic to wrap our belongings in."

"Let's just stop complaining and be a little more (9)__________ with one another," said Doug. "We need to (10)__________ ourselves to the fact that we are in this mess together, and then get back to having a good time."

SCORES: Sentence Check 2 ______% Final Check ______%

Enter your scores above and in the vocabulary performance chart on the inside back cover of the book.

CHAPTER

29

Previewing the Words

Find out how many of the ten words in this chapter you already know. Try to complete each sentence with the most suitable word from the list below. Use each word once.

Leave a sentence blank rather than guessing at an answer. Your purpose here is just to get a sense of the ten words and what you may know about them.

avid	**dwindle**	**esteem**	**evoke**	**legacy**
mediate	**muted**	**nurture**	**pacify**	**transient**

1. The smells of cider, pumpkin pie, and burning leaves all ____________________ thoughts of autumn.
2. Julie wants a lasting relationship, but Evan seems interested in only ____________________ ones.
3. The day's brightness continued to ____________________ as more and more clouds blocked the sun.
4. The critics held the play in such high ____________________ that they voted it "Best Play of the Year."
5. At the party, Yoko and I kept our conversation ____________________ so that no one would overhear us.
6. The quickest way to ____________________ the angry employees was to meet their demand for higher wages.
7. Todd is a(n) ____________________ sportsman who spends much of his free time jogging and playing basketball.
8. Each of the farmers claimed the stream was part of his property. Finally, they agreed to let the town council ____________________ their conflict.
9. Some birds feed their young with fresh insects. Others ____________________ their newborn with partially digested food from their own mouths.
10. Ana's great-grandfather, grandmother, and mother were all musicians. She must have inherited the ____________________ of musical talent because she's an excellent piano and guitar player.

Now check your answers by turning to page 166. Fix any mistakes and fill in any blank spaces by writing in the correct answers. By doing so, you will complete this introduction to the ten words.

You're now ready to strengthen your knowledge of the words you already know and to master the words you're only half sure of, or don't know at all. Turn to the next page.

Ten Words in Context

Figure out the meanings of the following ten words by looking *closely and carefully* at the context in which the words appear. Doing so will prepare you for the matching test and practices on the two pages that follow.

1 **avid**
(av'-id)
-adjective

a. Rich, an **avid** reader, enjoys nothing more than a good science-fiction novel.

b. My sister is such an **avid** fan of Michael Jackson that her bedroom walls are covered with posters of him and she has taken to wearing white gloves.

2 **dwindle**
(dwin'-dəl)
-verb

a. As the number of leaves on the tree **dwindled,** the number on the ground increased.

b. The nicotine gum helped Jane's craving for cigarettes to **dwindle** down to two cigarettes a day. Soon she quit altogether.

3 **esteem**
(e-stēm')
-noun

a. When Mr. Cranston retired after teaching gym and coaching for 30 years, his admiring students gave him a gold whistle as a sign of their **esteem.**

b. In some countries, people show **esteem** with a bow from the waist or other actions, but such gestures of respect are rare in the U.S.

4 **evoke**
(ē-vōk')
-verb

a. Strangely enough, seeing my son's high school graduation picture **evoked** memories of his infancy.

b. Although the horror movie was meant to **evoke** fear, John found the purple monsters only laughable.

5 **legacy**
(leg'-ə-sē)
-noun

a. In many legends, after someone commits a terrible crime, that person's entire family is cursed for all time. This **legacy** is the victim's lasting revenge.

b. One of my mother's richest **legacies** to me was her love of nature. I've inherited her interests in growing flowers and in hiking.

6 **mediate**
(mē'-dē-āt')
-verb

a. When my sister and I used to fight, my father would refuse to **mediate.** He would say, "Settle your own fights."

b. A panel has been appointed to **mediate** the conflict between the striking pilots and the airlines, but no settlement has been reached yet.

7 **muted**
(myōō'-təd)
-adjective

a. When I put on my earplugs, the yelling from the next apartment becomes **muted** enough so that it no longer disturbs me.

b. The artist used **muted** rather than bright colors, to give the painting a soft, peaceful tone.

8 **nurture**
(nûr'-chər)
-verb

a. While I often forget to water or feed my plants, my sister carefully **nurtures** her many ferns and violets.

b. In general, female fish do not **nurture** their young by feeding and protecting them. They only lay the eggs, which are guarded by the male until hatching.

9 **pacify**
(pas'-ə-fī')
-verb

a. When I'm feeling nervous or upset, I often **pacify** myself with a soothing cup of mint tea.

b. Not only did I anger Roberta by calling her boyfriend "a creep," but I failed to **pacify** her with my note of apology: "I'm sorry I called Mel a creep. It's not always wise to tell the truth."

10 **transient**
(tran'-shənt)
-adjective

a. The drug's dangers include both **transient** side effects, such as temporarily blurred vision, and permanent brain damage.

b. Some hotels have only **transient** guests; others welcome permanent residents as well.

Matching Words and Definitions

Check your understanding of the ten words by matching each word with its definition. Look back at the sentences in "Ten Words in Context" as needed to decide on the meaning of each word.

_____	1. **avid**	a.	softened; toned down; made less intense
_____	2. **dwindle**	b.	temporary; passing soon or quickly
_____	3. **esteem**	c.	enthusiastic and devoted
_____	4. **evoke**	d.	to make calm or peaceful
_____	5. **legacy**	e.	to draw forth, as a mental image or a feeling
_____	6. **mediate**	f.	to gradually lessen or shrink
_____	7. **muted**	g.	to settle (a conflict) by acting as a go-between
_____	8. **nurture**	h.	a high regard; respect; favorable opinion
_____	9. **pacify**	i.	to promote the development of by providing nourishment, support, and protection
_____	10. **transient**	j.	something handed down from people who have come before

CAUTION: Do not go any further until you are sure the above answers are correct. If you have studied the "Ten Words in Context," you will know how to match each word. Then you can use the matches to help you in the following practices. Your goal is to reach a point where you don't need to check definitions at all.

➢*Sentence Check 1*

Complete each sentence below with the most suitable word from the box. Use each word once.

avid	**dwindle**	**esteem**	**evoke**	**legacy**
mediate	**muted**	**nurture**	**pacify**	**transient**

1. You must ____________________ a child with love and respect as well as with food and shelter.
2. The photos in my album ____________________ many fond memories of my high school friends.
3. If you study too long at one sitting, your concentration will eventually begin to ____________________.
4. To me, a ____________________ trumpet has a much more pleasant sound than one blowing at full volume.
5. When my newborn nephew starts to scream, we ____________________ him by rocking him and singing softly.
6. Part of spring's charm is that it's ____________________. It comes and goes so quickly that I can't wait for its return.
7. To show his ____________________ for her singing, the talent agent sent Mary daisies after she performed in a local theatre.
8. My cousin Bobby is the most ____________________ collector I know. He collects almost anything, from baseball cards to beer cans.
9. Shakespeare's work, a priceless ____________________ from the 16th and 17th centuries, has been enjoyed by generation after generation.
10. Rather than go to court, Mr. Hillman and the owner of the gas station agreed to have a lawyer ____________________ their disagreement.

Now check your answers to these questions by turning to page 166. Going over the answers carefully will help you prepare for the next two checks, for which answers are not given.

➢Sentence Check 2

Complete each sentence below with two words from the box. Use each word once.

avid	**dwindle**	**esteem**	**evoke**	**legacy**
mediate	**muted**	**nurture**	**pacify**	**transient**

1-2. Loud music upsets our canary, but ________________ tones ________________ her.

3-4. Della's ________________ for Rick turned out to be ________________. She lost respect for him when she saw him buy drugs.

5-6. Leo is such a(n) ________________ chef that his enthusiasm for cooking never ________________s. He's been known to cook happily for ten straight hours.

7-8. It is necessary to ________________ a human infant since it is the biological ________________ of newborn mammals to be unable to survive on their own.

9-10. In the Bible, King Solomon ________________s when two women each claim a single child as her own. Pretending that the child will be cut in two, he sees the horror this thought ________________s in one of the women. He then knows she is the true mother.

➢*Final Check:* Getting Scared

Here is a final opportunity for you to strengthen your knowledge of the ten words. First read the following passage carefully. Then fill in each blank with a word from the box at the top of this page. (Context clues will help you figure out which word goes in which blank.) Use each word once.

Remember trying to scare yourself and everybody else when you were a kid? For instance, maybe you were a(n) (1)________________ roller-coaster rider, closing your eyes and screaming and loving it all. Afterwards, you would (2)________________ your still nervous stomach by sipping quietly away at an ice-cold Coke. If a short roller-coaster ride gave you too (3)________________ a thrill, there was always the long-term fear of a horror movie. If the movie was a good one, you might be scared about going to bed for the next three months.

And remember popping out from behind corners yelling "Boo!" at your brother? The fight that followed ("You didn't scare me one bit." "Did too." "Did not." "Did too.") would go on until a grown-up (4)________________(e)d the conflict. (Parents always seemed to be there to settle disputes or to (5)________________ and reassure you at times when you needed support.)

At other times, you and your friends probably sat around a campfire late at night, telling ghost stories. Thrilled with the horror of it all, you spoke in voices so (6)________________ they were almost whispers. The storyteller who gained the most (7)________________ was the one who could (8)________________ the greatest terror in others. If anybody's fear started to (9)________________, this expert would build it up again with the story of the ghost of the outhouse, a (10)________________ handed down from older brothers and sisters to younger ones. The story always made you so scared that you needed to go to the outhouse. But fearing the ghost there, how could you?

SCORES: Sentence Check 2 ________%	Final Check ________%

Enter your scores above and in the vocabulary performance chart on the inside back cover of the book.

CHAPTER

30

Previewing the Words

Find out how many of the ten words in this chapter you already know. Try to complete each sentence with the most suitable word from the list below. Use each word once.

Leave a sentence blank rather than guessing at an answer. Your purpose here is just to get a sense of the ten words and what you may know about them.

aloof	**ambivalent**	**augment**	**dispel**	**explicit**
longevity	**magnitude**	**mundane**	**obscure**	**render**

1. Giant redwood trees have great ____________________, sometimes surviving for thousands of years.
2. When the bank teller realized the ____________________ of his error, he panicked at the thought of being held responsible for the loss of so large a sum of money.
3. Because Usha teaches belly dancing every day, it is simply one more ____________________ activity to her.
4. Anita said, "I'm ____________________ about the dress. I like the style but not that green-yellow color."
5. Because of her ____________________ personality, Wendy is not as popular as Lynn, who is much less cool and reserved.
6. The choir director said, "Let's ____________________ the sound by adding more singers instead of increasing microphone volume."
7. Mr. Stein explained the solution to the math problem, but the logic behind it remained ____________________ to most of the students.
8. The doctor's explanation was ____________________. He explained Bonnie's surgery to her in detail, using illustrations for even greater clarity.
9. A grade of A on the final exam would ____________________ any doubts Sheila may still have about her ability to succeed in computer science.
10. Staring at the sun for even a short time can ____________________ a person blind.

Now check your answers by turning to page 166. Fix any mistakes and fill in any blank spaces by writing in the correct answers. By doing so, you will complete this introduction to the ten words.

You're now ready to strengthen your knowledge of the words you already know and to master the words you're only half sure of, or don't know at all. Turn to the next page.

Ten Words in Context

Figure out the meanings of the following ten words by looking *closely and carefully* at the context in which the words appear. Doing so will prepare you for the matching test and practices on the two pages that follow.

1 **aloof**
(ə-lo͞of')
-adjective

a. Some people say that the English are **aloof,** but the ones I've met seem warm and open.

b. I knew that Taylor was upset with me about something because he was cool and **aloof** even when I tried to be friendly.

2 **ambivalent**
(am-biv'-ə-lənt)
-adjective

a. "Because I'm **ambivalent** about marriage," Earl said, "I keep swinging back and forth between wanting to set the date and wanting to break off my engagement."

b. I'm **ambivalent** about my mother-in-law. I appreciate her desire to be helpful, but I dislike her efforts to run our lives.

3 **augment**
(ôg-ment')
-verb

a. Why do women **augment** their height with high heels?

b. Because Jenna needed additional money, she **augmented** her salary by typing term papers for college students.

4 **dispel**
(di-spel')
-verb

a. Vickie's note of apology was enough to **dispel** the slight anger Rex still felt toward her.

b. I tried to **dispel** my friend's fears about her blind date that evening by telling her that my parents met on a blind date.

5 **explicit**
(eks-plis'-it)
-adjective

a. The novel's sex scene was **explicit,** leaving nothing to the imagination.

b. My parents were very **explicit** about what I could and could not do during their three-day absence. They presented me with a detailed list!

6 **longevity**
(lon-jev'-i-tē)
-noun

a. Volvos and Hondas are known for their **longevity,** outlasting more expensive cars.

b. The animal with the greatest **longevity** is the giant land tortoise, which can live several hundred years.

7 **magnitude**
(mag'-nə-to͞od')
-noun

a. Numbers in the millions and billions are of too great a **magnitude** for most people to grasp.

b. The murder case took on added **magnitude** when it was learned that the dead woman had been the mayor's mistress.

8 **mundane**
(mun-dān')
-adjective

a. Agnes reads romance novels to escape from her **mundane** routine.

b. The most **mundane** activities can turn into extraordinary events. For instance, I met my best friend while washing my clothes at the laundromat.

9 **obscure**
(ob-skyo͞or')
-adjective

a. The chemist didn't express his theory clearly, so it remained **obscure** to all but a few scientists.

b. The police easily discovered who committed the murder, but even to the best psychiatrists, the murderer's motives remained **obscure**.

10 **render**
(ren'-dər)
-verb

a. Don't let the baby near your term paper with that crayon, or she will **render** it unreadable.

b. Phyllis added so much red pepper to the chili that she **rendered** it too hot to eat.

Matching Words and Definitions

Check your understanding of the ten words by matching each word with its definition. Look back at the sentences in "Ten Words in Context" as needed to decide on the meaning of each word.

_____ 1. **aloof** a. to drive away as if by scattering; cause to vanish
_____ 2. **ambivalent** b. size; importance
_____ 3. **augment** c. ordinary; everyday
_____ 4. **dispel** d. stated or shown clearly and exactly
_____ 5. **explicit** e. having conflicting feelings about someone or something
_____ 6. **longevity** f. to cause (something) to become; make
_____ 7. **magnitude** g. not easily understood or clearly expressed
_____ 8. **mundane** h. cool and reserved; distant in personal relations
_____ 9. **obscure** i. to increase; make greater, as in strength or quantity
_____ 10. **render** j. a long span of life; length of life

CAUTION: Do not go any further until you are sure the above answers are correct. If you have studied the "Ten Words in Context," you will know how to match each word. Then you can use the matches to help you in the following practices. Your goal is to reach a point where you don't need to check definitions at all.

➢*Sentence Check 1*

Complete each sentence below with the most suitable word from the box. Use each word once.

aloof	**ambivalent**	**augment**	**dispel**	**explicit**
longevity	**magnitude**	**mundane**	**obscure**	**render**

1. The best writers can describe something ____________________ so that it doesn't seem ordinary at all.
2. The architect decided to add another pillar to the huge building to ____________________ its support.
3. "Russell seems ____________________ toward me," Janice said, "as if he both likes and dislikes me."
4. Recent research suggests that our parents' ____________________ doesn't necessarily affect how long we will live.
5. When I'm frightened, I try to appear ____________________, since looking cool and distant helps me feel in control.
6. The essence of my science teacher's genius is that he is able to make complicated, ____________________ ideas clear to students.
7. "If you keep walking on the backs of your shoes like that, you will ____________________ them as flat as the floor," Annie's mother said.
8. If Claude proposes marriage to Jean, he will ____________________ any doubts she may still have as to whether or not he really loves her.
9. "I try to make my test questions as ____________________ as possible," said Mr. Baines, "so that my students will know exactly what answers I'm looking for."
10. I began to realize the ____________________ of the insect population when I read that there are more kinds of insects living today than all other kinds of animals in the world.

Now check your answers to these questions by turning to page 166. Going over the answers carefully will help you prepare for the next two checks, for which answers are not given.

➢Sentence Check 2

Complete each sentence below with two words from the box. Use each word once.

aloof	ambivalent	augment	dispel	explicit
longevity	magnitude	mundane	obscure	render

1-2. "Drop dead" seems a pretty __________ way to wish someone reduced __________, but theater people use the expression to mean "Good luck."

3-4. Eye strain from staring at a computer screen __________(e)d the __________ of Harriet's already severe headache.

5-6. I'm __________ about playing with our rock band. I love the music we play, but I'm afraid it will __________ me deaf one of these days.

7-8. Gail is __________ only toward people whom she strongly dislikes. With all others, she soon __________s any feelings of shyness or distrust with her naturally warm and open manner.

9-10. "Does the idea that we don't always see things as they really are seem __________ to you?" the teacher asked. "If so, it will become clearer if you relate it to the __________ experience of looking down a road. Doesn't it look narrower in the distance than it really is?"

➢*Final Check:* My Sister's Date

Here is a final opportunity for you to strengthen your knowledge of the ten words. First read the following passage carefully. Then fill in each blank with a word from the box at the top of this page. (Context clues will help you figure out which word goes in which blank.) Use each word once.

I watched as my older sister, Ruth, removed the last spiked curler from her hair. We stared at the result. She somehow had (1)__________(e)d her hair limp as spaghetti. When Ruth started to cry, I comforted her with my usual gentleness: "Why are you such a crybaby about some stupid guy?"

The guy was Steven Meyer. He and Ruth were going to a high school dance. She'd had a crush on him for years, for reasons that were (2)__________ to me. (I never had figured out what she saw in him.)

When Ruth began to apply her makeup, she gave a terrifying scream that probably reduced my (3)__________ by at least a year. She informed me between sobs that a pimple had just appeared on her nose, a pimple that made her "look like a witch." I studied her face, expecting a pimple of truly amazing (4)__________. Instead, I spotted a tiny speck. Again I tried to (5)__________ Ruth's worries. "So, it makes you look like a witch. Don't you want to look bewitching?" But this only seemed to (6)__________ her grief, and she wept again. I took this opportunity to go downstairs and wait for Steven Meyer.

He arrived a half hour before Ruth was ready. Observing him through my thick glasses, I tried to figure out exactly what Ruth saw in him. We talked until she appeared at the top of the stairs. Trying to look (7)__________, she came down very slowly, wearing a cool, distant expression.

When Ruth returned home later that night, her comment about the kind of time she'd had was (8)__________: "Totally rotten." She said that Steven, far from being extraordinary, had turned out to be "the most (9)__________ sort of person in the world." It seemed Ruth had bypassed feeling (10)__________ about Steven and gone straight from love to hate.

It's just as well, since I've been married to Steven for ten years now.

SCORES: Sentence Check 2 ________% Final Check ________%

Enter your scores above and in the vocabulary performance chart on the inside back cover of the book.

UNIT FIVE: Test 1

PART A

Choose the word that best completes each sentence and write it in the space provided.

1. **feasible** **transient** **pretentious** **muted** — Dean is so __________________ that he refers to his position as fast-food preparer as "chef."

2. **inhibitions** **habitats** **precedents** **siblings** — Endangered species won't survive unless their __________________ are preserved.

3. **explicit** **avid** **fallible** **punitive** — Peter hasn't been __________________ about quitting his job, but he's hinted at it.

4. **depicted** **implored** **intimidated** **saturated** — In talking with the social worker, the abused child __________________ a life of horror.

5. **longevity** **sibling** **inhibition** **precedent** — I didn't let the kids stay up late last night because I didn't want to set a(n) __________________ for future nights.

6. **smug** **avid** **implicit** **vivacious** — When my brother complained of a shortage of cash, his __________________ message was, "Can you lend me some money?"

7. **infuriated** **jeopardized** **dwindled** **condoned** — Sandy has __________________ her son's temper tantrums for so long that he thinks they're acceptable behavior.

8. **esteem** **longevity** **legacy** **magnitude** — The poker gang laughed when Mom asked to join their game, but their __________________ rose as she won the first four hands.

9. **formulated** **gaped** **ruptured** **intimidated** — While driving home three hours after her curfew, Lucille __________________ an excuse she hoped her parents would believe.

10. **exhaustive** **fiscal** **pretentious** **vindictive** — After a(n) __________________ search during which I crawled around my entire apartment, my "missing" contact lens fell out of my eye.

11. **obscure** **deficient** **smug** **muted** — Jerome deserves his excellent grades, but he doesn't have to be so ________________ and say, "Naturally, I got straight A's again."

12. **exhaustive** **ironic** **furtive** **pragmatic** — When Cindy saw Grant's crumpled fender, she made the ________________ comment, "I really like how you've customized your car, Grant."

13. **implore** **feign** **mediate** **pacify** — Having accidentally learned about my surprise party, I had to ________________ surprise when my friends jumped out yelling, "Happy birthday!"

PART B

Circle **C** if the italicized word is used **correctly**. Circle **I** if the word is used **incorrectly.**

C I 14. *Saturate* the washcloth by wringing it out.

C I 15. I don't consider cooking an entire meal a *mundane* task because I do it so rarely.

C I 16. The poem is *obscure* because it jumps from one complicated image to another.

C I 17. Joel is such an *introvert* that he often strikes up conversations with total strangers.

C I 18. The suspect had such a *furtive* expression that he appeared to be hiding something.

C I 19. Mort's back talk *pacified* his father, who then denied him the use of the car for a month.

C I 20. After running over a sharp rock, our tire *ruptured.* Luckily, we had a spare in the trunk.

C I 21. I think I'm coming down with the flu. I've been feeling weak and *vivacious* all morning.

C I 22. Liz has a great sense of humor. Her jokes can *infuriate* me when nothing else can make me smile.

C I 23. My Great Dane *intimidates* visitors with her loud bark and large size, but she's really very friendly.

C I 24. I have to ignore Jesse completely now to *dispel* any idea he may have that I'm romantically interested in him.

C I 25. In the package, panty hose look so small that it's hard to believe they'll *constrict* enough to fit over a woman's legs and hips.

SCORE: (Number correct) ________ x 4 = ________ %

Enter your scores above and in the vocabulary performance chart on the inside back cover of the book.

UNIT FIVE: Test 2

PART A

Complete each sentence with a word from the box. Use each word once.

ambivalent	**contemplate**	**detrimental**	**evoke**
feasible	**fiscal**	**inhibition**	**jeopardize**
legacy	**magnitude**	**muted**	**reconcile**
sibling			

1. To make the bright green a more ____________________ shade, the painter added gray.
2. Music in a minor key often ____________________s sad feelings in the listener.
3. Eating dried fruits can be as ____________________ to your teeth as eating candy.
4. No one realized the ____________________ of Nora's depression until she tried to kill herself.
5. Isabel has ____________________ feelings about her job. She loves the work but hates her boss.
6. Why ____________________ dropping out of school when you've got only two semesters to go?
7. It isn't ____________________ to grow roses in our back yard. There's too much shade back there for roses.
8. My love of the outdoors is a ____________________ from my grandfather, who often hiked in the mountains.
9. The company is in such bad ____________________ shape that over half the employees will soon be laid off.
10. Dick ____________________d his chances of getting the job when he addressed the interviewer by the wrong name.
11. My ______________________s will be coming from California and Arkansas to celebrate our parents' 30th anniversary.
12. At first, Tiffany was reluctant to sit in Santa Claus' lap, but she overcame her ____________________ when she saw that he was handing out candy canes.
13. As the wedding drew near, Brenda had to ____________________ herself to the fact that her son would marry a woman she disliked.

PART B

Circle **C** if the italicized word is used **correctly**. Circle **I** if the word is used **incorrectly**.

C I 14. Karen found the chicken salad *vile*. One small taste made her gag.

C I 15. I asked Sal to *augment* the stereo because it was giving me a headache.

C I 16. Some spiders have surprising *longevity*, living as long as 20 years.

C I 17. The Daniels' *transient* marriage has already lasted over 50 years.

C I 18. When the *vindictive* tenant was evicted, he broke all the windows in his apartment.

C I 19. I admire Woody Allen because he is always so *devoid* of imagination and wit.

C I 20. Paul *sneered* at his rock star idol and asked if she would autograph his record album.

C I 21. Being a *pragmatic* person, my brother values music and poetry more than practical things.

C I 22. An *avid* reader, Judy spends much of her time enjoying newspapers, magazines and books.

C I 23. My liking for my supervisor *dwindled* as his temper grew shorter and his list of "don'ts" grew longer.

C I 24. Interested in the cartoon on TV, the little boy just *gaped* casually at his mother as she left for work.

C I 25. When a friend broke her expensive china bowl, Harriet remained *genial*, saying, "Don't worry about it. I almost dropped it once myself."

SCORE: (Number correct) ________ x 4 = ________ %

Enter your scores above and in the vocabulary performance chart on the inside back cover of the book.

UNIT FIVE: Test 3

PART A

Complete each sentence in a way that clearly shows you understand the meaning of the boldfaced word. Take a minute to plan your answer before you write.

Example: To increase your **longevity**, *exercise frequently and avoid tobacco, alcohol, and high-fat foods.*

1. One thing the nursery-school teacher did to **nurture** each child each day was ______________________
____

2. Ramona, who is **pragmatic**, spends her money on such things as ______________________
____

3. The critic summed up how **pathetic** the actor's performance was with this comment: ______________
____

4. Lionel **implored** his parents to ______________________
____

5. The **magnitude** of Carol's musical talent became clear when ______________________
____

6. A student **deficient** in study skills might ______________________
____

7. Just how **fallible** the house builder was could be seen by ______________________
____

8. To **mediate** the argument between my sister and me, ______________________
____

9. The car accident **rendered** Philip ______________________
____

10. When Mary Lou asked the fortune teller, "What will my career be?" the **cryptic** reply was: " __________
____

PART B

After each boldfaced word are a *synonym* (a word that means the same as the boldfaced word), an *antonym* (a word that means the opposite of the boldfaced word), and a word that is neither. Mark the antonym with an *A*.

Example:	**dwindle**	_____ lessen	_A_ increase	_____ turn
11.	**aloof**	_____ angry	_____ friendly	_____ reserved
12.	**detrimental**	_____ harmful	_____ orderly	_____ beneficial
13.	**intimidate**	_____ delay	_____ frighten	_____ encourage
14.	**genial**	_____ unpleasant	_____ kindly	_____ inborn
15.	**punitive**	_____ rewarding	_____ requiring	_____ punishing

PART C

Use five of the following ten words in sentences. Make it clear that you know the meaning of the word you use. Feel free to use the past tense or plural form of a word.

condone	**feign**	**implore**	**pacify**	**smug**
esteem	**habitat**	**inhibition**	**sibling**	**vindictive**

16. ______________________________

____

17. ______________________________

____

18. ______________________________

____

19. ______________________________

____

20. ______________________________

SCORE: (Number correct) ________ x 5 = ________ %

Enter your scores above and in the vocabulary performance chart on the inside back cover of the book.

Limited Answer Key

An Important Note: Be sure to use this answer key as a learning tool only. You should not turn to this key until you have considered carefully the sentence in which a given word appears.

Used properly, the key will help you to learn words and to prepare for the activities and tests for which answers are not given. For ease of reference, the title of the "Final Check" passage in each chapter appears in parentheses.

Chapter 1 (Joseph Palmer)

Previewing the Words

1. antagonist
2. epitome
3. amoral
4. amiable
5. malign
6. encounter
7. absolve
8. adamant
9. animosity
10. eccentric

Sentence Check 1

1. adamant
2. encounter
3. malign
4. amiable
5. amoral
6. epitome
7. absolve
8. antagonist
9. animosity
10. eccentric

Chapter 2 (Telephone Salespeople)

Previewing the Words

1. inclination
2. sabotage
3. wary
4. subsequent
5. curt
6. irate
7. dilemma
8. sabotage
9. zeal
10. retort

Sentence Check 1

1. dilemma
2. wary
3. inclination
4. curt
5. sabotage
6. demoralize
7. subsequent
8. irate
9. zeal
10. retort

Chapter 3 (A Cruel Sport)

Previewing the Words

1. methodical
2. obsolete
3. tangible
4. engross
5. elicit
6. adjacent
7. escalate
8. acclaim
9. terminate
10. exploit

Sentence Check 1

1. tangible
2. obsolete
3. acclaim
4. adjacent
5. escalate
6. engross
7. exploit
8. methodical
9. terminate
10. elicit

Chapter 4 (Bald Is Beautiful)

Previewing the Words

1. deter
2. revitalize
3. infringe
4. implication
5. succinct
6. inequity
7. infirmity
8. sparse
9. subjective
10. innovation

Sentence Check 1

1. infirmity
2. implication
3. succinct
4. infringe
5. sparse
6. innovation
7. revitalize
8. subjective
9. inequity
10. deter

Chapter 5 (No Luck with Women)

Previewing the Words

1. assail
2. syndrome
3. allusion
4. taint
5. euphemism
6. altruistic
7. arbitrary
8. banal
9. mercenary
10. appease

Sentence Check 1

1. mercenary
2. allusion
3. altruistic
4. assail
5. euphemism
6. taint
7. appease
8. syndrome
9. arbitrary
10. banal

Chapter 6 (A Taste of Parenthood)

Sentence Check 1

1. audience
2. sympathetic
3. childhood
4. pendant
5. quartet
6. nonessential
7. happily
8. cyclorama
9. annually
10. hypervitaminosis

Chapter 7 (Accident and Recovery)

Previewing the Words

1. flagrant
2. persevere
3. venture
4. fluctuate
5. conventional
6. rehabilitate
7. calamity
8. comprehensive
9. turmoil
10. ponder

Sentence Check 1

1. calamity
2. ponder
3. flagrant
4. comprehensive
5. conventional
6. persevere
7. rehabilitate
8. turmoil
9. fluctuate
10. venture

Chapter 8 (Animal Senses)

Previewing the Words

1. mobile
2. discern
3. orient
4. attribute
5. exemplify
6. enigma
7. enhance
8. nocturnal
9. dispatch
10. attest

Sentence Check 1

1. enhance
2. attest
3. dispatch
4. exemplify
5. enigma
6. nocturnal
7. discern
8. orient
9. mobile
10. attribute

Chapter 9 (Money Problems)

Previewing the Words

1. constitute
2. nominal
3. prerequisite
4. decipher
5. recession
6. default
7. hypothetical
8. predominant
9. concurrent
10. confiscate

Sentence Check 1

1. predominant
2. concurrent
3. constitute
4. prerequisite
5. nominal
6. decipher
7. recession
8. default
9. confiscate
10. hypothetical

Chapter 10 (The New French Employee)

Previewing the Words

1. degenerate
2. vulnerable
3. implausible
4. sinister
5. suffice
6. incoherent
7. scrutiny
8. sanctuary
9. intricate
10. intercede

Sentence Check 1

1. suffice
2. sinister
3. vulnerable
4. intricate
5. implausible
6. sanctuary
7. incoherent
8. scrutiny
9. degenerate
10. intercede

Chapter 11 (A Cruel Teacher)

Previewing the Words

1. contrive
2. gaunt
3. blight
4. immaculate
5. qualms
6. garble
7. blatant
8. retaliate
9. gloat
10. plagiarism

Sentence Check 1

1. immaculate
2. blight
3. gloat
4. blatant
5. contrive
6. garble
7. retaliate
8. gaunt
9. qualm
10. plagiarism

Chapter 12 (It's Never Too Late)

Sentence Check 1

1. exclaimed
2. biorhythm
3. patricide
4. homeward
5. inflexible
6. forceful
7. semiprivate
8. infinity
9. humanitarian
10. humiliated

Chapter 13 (Learning to Study)

Previewing the Words

1. intermittent
2. curtail
3. squander
4. incentive
5. devastate
6. indispensable
7. rigor
8. succumb
9. incorporate
10. digress

Sentence Check 1

1. intermittent
2. devastate
3. incorporate
4. indispensable
5. incentive
6. rigor
7. squander
8. curtail
9. digress
10. succumb

Chapter 14 (The Mad Monk)

Previewing the Words

1. alleviate
2. demise
3. intrinsic
4. benefactor
5. revulsion
6. infamous
7. speculate
8. virile
9. covert
10. cynic

Sentence Check 1

1. intrinsic
2. alleviate
3. virile
4. cynic
5. infamous
6. covert
7. revulsion
8. speculate
9. benefactor
10. demise

Chapter 15 (Conflict over Holidays)

Previewing the Words

1. agnostic
2. lucrative
3. abstain
4. aspire
5. affiliate
6. mandatory
7. dissent
8. deficit
9. diversion
10. benevolent

Sentence Check 1

1. aspire
2. benevolent
3. diversion
4. mandatory
5. abstain
6. deficit
7. affiliate
8. dissent
9. agnostic
10. lucrative

Chapter 16 (Dr. Martin Luther King, Jr.)

Previewing the Words

1. prevalent
2. contemporary
3. quest
4. contend
5. poignant
6. conversely
7. charisma
8. traumatic
9. proponent
10. extrovert

Sentence Check 1

1. conversely
2. extrovert
3. poignant
4. prevalent
5. contend
6. proponent
7. charisma
8. contemporary
9. traumatic
10. quest

Chapter 17 (Relating to Parents)

Previewing the Words

1. prone
2. congenial
3. relentless
4. impasse
5. rationale
6. reprisal
7. perception
8. prompt
9. flippant
10. rapport

Sentence Check 1

1. prone
2. congenial
3. flippant
4. prompt
5. rapport
6. impasse
7. relentless
8. perception
9. reprisal
10. rationale

Chapter 18 (Held Back by Fears)

Sentence Check 1

1. boyish
2. wisdom
3. discouraged
4. immobile
5. produced
6. magnified
7. duplicate
8. psychoanalyst
9. intensify
10. claustrophobia

Chapter 19 (Interview with a Rude Star)

Previewing the Words

1. facade
2. benign
3. comprise
4. redundant
5. condescend
6. haughty
7. glib
8. pseudonym
9. blase
10. libel

Sentence Check 1

1. comprise
2. redundant
3. haughty
4. libel
5. glib
6. benign
7. blase
8. facade
9. condescend
10. pseudonym

Chapter 20 (The Nightmare of Gym)

Previewing the Words

1. divulge
2. detract
3. elation
4. expulsion
5. averse
6. nullify
7. endow
8. disdain
9. ominous
10. mortify

Sentence Check 1

1. detract
2. ominous
3. averse
4. elation
5. nullified
6. endow
7. expulsion
8. disdain
9. divulge
10. mortified

Chapter 21 (Skipping Church)

Previewing the Words

1. shun
2. secular
3. designate
4. simulate
5. interim
6. latent
7. cursory
8. credible
9. deviate
10. improvise

Sentence Check 1

1. latent
2. designate
3. deviate
4. credible
5. interim
6. cursory
7. secular
8. improvise
9. shun
10. simulate

Chapter 22 (A Model Teacher)

Previewing the Words

1. diligent
2. commemorate
3. transcend
4. consensus
5. niche
6. deplete
7. empathy
8. menial
9. waive
10. complacent

Sentence Check 1

1. waive
2. commemorate
3. deplete
4. transcend
5. complacent
6. niche
7. menial
8. diligent
9. consensus
10. empathy

Chapter 23 (My Talented Roommate)

Previewing the Words

1. gist
2. conducive
3. flaunt
4. frenzy
5. viable
6. falter
7. hamper
8. repertoire
9. bizarre
10. paradox

Sentence Check 1

1. bizarre
2. repertoire
3. falter
4. conducive
5. gist
6. hamper
7. viable
8. paradox
9. frenzy
10. flaunt

Chapter 24 (Fascinating Courses)

Sentence Check 1

1. actor
2. geochemistry
3. omnipresent
4. asterisk
5. director
6. theologian
7. misplace
8. contradicts
9. Monogamy
10. populated

Chapter 25 (Cal and His Sisters)

Previewing the Words

1. intimidate
2. introvert
3. sibling
4. infuriate
5. vivacious
6. implore
7. devoid
8. smug
9. sneer
10. jeopardize

Sentence Check 1

1. vivacious
2. implore
3. devoid
4. introvert
5. jeopardize
6. sibling
7. infuriate
8. sneer
9. intimidate
10. smug

Chapter 26 (Shoplifter)

Previewing the Words

1. gape
2. furtive
3. punitive
4. feasible
5. fiscal
6. contemplate
7. feign
8. condone
9. pathetic
10. precedent

Sentence Check 1

1. gape
2. contemplate
3. precedent
4. feasible
5. condone
6. fiscal
7. furtive
8. pathetic
9. feign
10. punitive

Chapter 27 (A Nutty Newspaper Office)

Previewing the Words

1. implicit
2. depict
3. saturate
4. ironic
5. inhibition
6. detrimental
7. deficient
8. rupture
9. vindictive
10. cryptic

Sentence Check 1

1. deficient
2. rupture
3. ironic
4. detrimental
5. inhibition
6. depict
7. vindictive
8. cryptic
9. saturate
10. implicit

Chapter 28 (Roughing It)

Previewing the Words

1. constrict
2. formulate
3. fallible
4. habitat
5. reconcile
6. vile
7. exhaustive
8. genial
9. pretentious
10. pragmatic

Sentence Check 1

1. vile
2. genial
3. reconcile
4. constrict
5. formulate
6. exhaustive
7. pretentious
8. habitat
9. pragmatic
10. fallible

Chapter 29 (Getting Scared)

Previewing the Words

1. evoke
2. transient
3. dwindle
4. esteem
5. muted
6. pacify
7. avid
8. mediate
9. nurture
10. legacy

Sentence Check 1

1. nurture
2. evoke
3. dwindle
4. muted
5. pacify
6. transient
7. esteem
8. avid
9. legacy
10. mediate

Chapter 30 (My Sister's Date)

Previewing the Words

1. longevity
2. magnitude
3. mundane
4. ambivalent
5. aloof
6. augment
7. obscure
8. explicit
9. dispel
10. render

Sentence Check 1

1. mundane
2. augment
3. ambivalent
4. longevity
5. aloof
6. obscure
7. render
8. dispel
9. explicit
10. magnitude

Dictionary Use

It isn't always possible to figure out the meaning of a word from its context, and that's where a dictionary comes in. Following is some basic information to help you use a dictionary.

HOW TO FIND A WORD

A dictionary contains so many words that it can take a while to find the one you're looking for. But if you know how to use guide words, you can find a word rather quickly. *Guide words* are the two words at the top of each dictionary page. The first guide word tells what the first word is on the page. The second guide word tells what the last word is on that page. The other words on a page fall alphabetically between the two guide words. So when you look up a word, find the two guide words that alphabetically surround the word you're looking for.

- Which of the following pair of guide words would be on a page with the word *skirmish*?

skimp / skyscraper **skyward / slave** **sixty / skimming**

The answer to this question and the ones that follow are given on the next page.

HOW TO USE A DICTIONARY LISTING

A dictionary listing includes many pieces of information. For example, here is a listing from the *Random House College Dictionary*, Paperback Edition. Note that it includes much more than just a definition.

driz·zle (driz'əl), *v.*, **-zled, -zling,** *n.* —*v.* **1.** to rain gently and steadily in fine drops.
— *n.* **2.** a very light rain. —**driz'zly,** *adj.*

Key parts of a dictionary entry are listed and explained below.

Syllables. Dots separate dictionary entry words into syllables. Note that *drizzle* has one dot, which breaks the word into two syllables.

- To practice seeing the syllable breakdown in a dictionary entry, write the number of syllables in each word below.

gla·mour _____ **mic·ro·wave** _____ **in·de·scrib·a·ble** _____

Pronunciation guide. The information within parentheses after the entry word shows how to pronounce the entry word. This pronunciation guide includes two types of symbols: pronunciation symbols and accent marks.

Pronunciation symbols represent the consonant and vowel sounds in a word. The consonant sounds are probably very familiar to you, but you may find it helpful to review some of the sounds of the vowels—*a, e, i, o,* and *u.* Every dictionary has a key explaining the sounds of its pronunciation symbols, including the long and short sounds of vowels.

Long vowels have the sound of their own names. For example, the *a* in *pay* and the *o* in *no* both have long vowel sounds. Long vowel sounds are shown by a line above the vowel.

In the *Random House College Dictionary*, the *short vowels* are shown by the use of the vowel itself, with no other markings. Thus the *i* in the first syllable of *drizzle* is a short *i.* What do the short vowels sound like? Below are words from the *RHCD* pronunciation key which illustrate the *short vowel* sounds.

a bat **e** set **i** big **o** box **u** up

This key means, for example, that the *a* in *bat* has the short-*a* sound.

- Which of the words below has a short vowel sound? Which has a long vowel sound?

drug _______ **night** _______ **sand** ________

Another pronunciation symbol is the *schwa*, which looks like an upside-down *e*. It stands for certain rapidly spoken, unaccented vowel sounds, such as the *a* in *above*, the *e* in *item*, the *i* in *easily*, the *o* in *gallop*, and the *u* in *circus*. More generally, it has an "uh" sound, like the "uh" a speaker makes when hesitating in speech. Here are three words that include the schwa sound:

in·fant (in'fənt) **bum·ble** (bum'bəl) **de·liv·er** (di-liv'ər)

- Which syllable in *drizzle* contains the schwa sound, the first or the second? ______

Accent marks are small black marks that tell you which syllable to emphasize, or stress, as you say a word. An accent mark follows *driz* in the pronunciation guide for *drizzle,* which tells you to stress the first syllable of *drizzle*. Syllables with no accent mark are not stressed. Some syllables are in between, and they are marked with a lighter accent mark.

- Which syllable has the stronger accent in *sentimental*? _________

sen·ti·men·tal (sen'tə-men'tl)

Parts of Speech. After the pronunciation key and before each set of definitions, the entry word's parts of speech are given. The parts of speech are abbreviated as follows:

noun—*n.* pronoun—*pron.* adjective—*adj.* adverb—*adv.* verb—*v.*

- The listing for *drizzle* shows it has two parts of speech. Write them below:

_____________ _____________

Definitions. Words often have more than one meaning. When they do, each meaning is usually numbered in the dictionary. You can tell which definition of a word fits a given sentence by the meaning of the sentence. For example, the word *charge* has several definitions, including these two: **1.** to ask as a price. **2.** to accuse or blame.

- Show with a check which definition applies in each sentence below:

The store charged me less for the blouse because it was missing a button. 1 ___ 2 ___

My neighbor has been charged with shoplifting. 1 ___ 2 ___

Other Information. After the definitions in a listing in a hardbound dictionary, you may get information about the *origin* of a word. Such information about origins, also known as *etymology,* is usually given in brackets. And you may sometimes be given one or more synonyms or antonyms for the entry word. *Synonyms* are words that are similar in meaning to the entry word; *antonyms* are words that are opposite in meaning.

WHICH DICTIONARIES TO OWN

You will find it useful to own two recent dictionaries: a small paperback dictionary to carry to class and a hardbound dictionary, which contains more information than a small paperback one. Among the good dictionaries strongly recommended are both the paperback and hardcover editions of the following:

The Random House College Dictionary
The American Heritage Dictionary
Webster's New World Dictionary

ANSWERS TO THE DICTIONARY QUESTIONS

Guide words: *skimp/skyscraper*
Number of syllables: 2, 3, 5
Vowels: *drug, sand* (short); *night* (long)
Schwa: second syllable of *drizzle*
Accent: stronger accent on third syllable
Parts of speech: noun and verb
Definitions: 1; 2

List of Words and Word Parts